Get
Started!

Stephen
Kathy

PRAISE FOR
PERSEVERANCE

"Insightful and inspiring, *Perseverance* is a field manual for navigating past physical and mental boundaries. Kesting's rigor in drawing insights from adversity is as impressive as the miles he paddled."

—Mike McCastle, extreme endurance athlete and performance coach, creator of the 12 Labours Project

"*Perseverance* is an intimate look into the resilience one needs to complete such an ambitious adventure. By sharing heartfelt experiences throughout the course of his life, the reader is keenly immersed in Stephan's treacherous journey and pursuit of a lifelong dream. It is one man's beautiful tribute to the history and landscape of the North."

—Emily Kwok, performance coach and two-time jiu-jitsu world champion

"Like a whitewater canoe trip, *Perseverance* describes physical action so vividly you will feel the urge to itch the mosquito bites. The moments of introspection provide a welcome salve to the physical hardship described."

—Paul Mason, Canadian canoeing royalty, son of Bill Mason, world whitewater freestyle medalist, wilderness guide, author of *Thrill of the Paddle*

"In a world of overstimulation and high-tech gadgetry, *Perseverance* is a hypnotic escape into a simpler time and wilder universe. Full of grit and wit, poetry and practicality, you will not find a more insightful or trustworthy travel companion than Stephan Kesting. 'Make no mistake' and strap yourself in for this riveting and uniquely rewarding adventure."

—Ando Mierzwa, 8th degree black belt and YouTuber

"Kesting crafts an immersive dive into the wonder and challenge of solo wilderness travel."

—Frank Wolf, author of *Two Springs, One Summer* and *Lines on a Map*

"A phenomenal read. Stephan immerses us in a unique world, (one that I will never experience myself) that is both intriguing and inspiring. So many adventures, life lessons, and so much pure entertainment. And the writing itself is stellar. Thank you, Stephan, for taking us along. Your readers are better off for it."

—Burton Richardson, author of five martial arts books, full instructor in Bruce Lee's Jun Fan JKD Method

"Stephan's gripping account of his wilderness solo journey is a profound testament to resilience and determination. Meeting him whilst on my journey, I witnessed firsthand his unwavering spirit, which shines through every page of this incredible book."

—James Benson-King, extreme endurance cyclist, including a 32,000 km trip from Alaska to Argentina

"*Perseverance* is an essential trait for longevity in the martial arts along with attraction to risk, embracing discomfort, and enjoying undertakings that provide neither financial gain nor fame. Kesting has provided an evocative and engrossing account of an epic odyssey in an environment few of us will ever get to experience. I was impressed by how he was able to seamlessly share vulnerability, interweave philosophical insights and convey moment-to-moment urgency in a manner that made this a unique page-turner. A must-read."

—Alexander D. C. Kask, Takenouchi-ryu Jiu-Jutsu instructor, former executive editor Charles E. Tuttle Publishing

"I had the pleasure to read an advanced copy of *Perseverance* and I'd highly recommend ordering it. An amazing tale of nature and hardship, with a very cerebral and skilled narration. Stephan is quite a man."

—James Pieratt, bestselling author, strength athlete, ultramarathon runner

"*Perseverance* is an amazing book. It is an incredible adventure, but beyond that, it's deep and wise, comic and tragic, with unexpected turns and twists. Eminently worth the read!"

—Mordecai Finley, former marine, rabbi at Ohr HaTorah

"When Stephan writes about the challenges of 'navigating between the extreme of hypochondria and stoicism' three days into his six-week solo canoe journey, you quickly realize such contrast can be applied not only to every phase of his momentous trip, but to life itself. And this is a life well-earned."

—Derek Beres, author and co-host of the *Conspirituality* podcast

"*Perseverance* has the breakneck pacing of a thriller but in real life. Evocative and beautifully written, this book will satisfy both armchair adventurers and people who are moved to push themselves to superhuman feats."

—April Henry, *New York Times* bestselling author of *Girl, Stolen*

"A fascinating, eloquent account full of wisdom and insight on wilderness travel and life. Kesting's positive, resolute mindset in facing adversity and tackling daunting challenges is a welcome life lesson."

—Adam Shoalts, PhD, bestselling author of *Where the Falcon Flies* and *Beyond the Trees*

"Stephan's incredible account of his journey into Canada's rugged North embodies the many martial arts principles that lead to success. Train hard, train smart and aspire for perfection through repetition, repetition, repetition but most of all, never give up."

—Roman Hatashita, judo Olympian

PERSEVERANCE

LIFE AND DEATH IN THE SUBARCTIC

STEPHAN KESTING

PEGASUS BOOKS

NEW YORK LONDON

PERSEVERANCE

Pegasus Books, Ltd.
148 West 37th Street, 13th Floor
New York, NY 10018

First Pegasus Books cloth edition March 2025

Interior design by Maria Fernandez

Map designed by Gene Thorp

Library of Congress Cataloging-in-Publication Data is available.

ISBN: 978-1-63936-861-7

10 9 8 7 6 5 4 3 2 1

Printed in the United States of America
Distributed by Simon & Schuster
www.pegasusbooks.com

Dedicated to my wife, Eva Schubert,
who married me on June 29, 2019,
and then let me depart on this lunatic
voyage the very next day.

And to my brother Christoph for his gift
of a kidney that kept me alive and allowed
me to traverse this land of little sticks.

CONTENTS

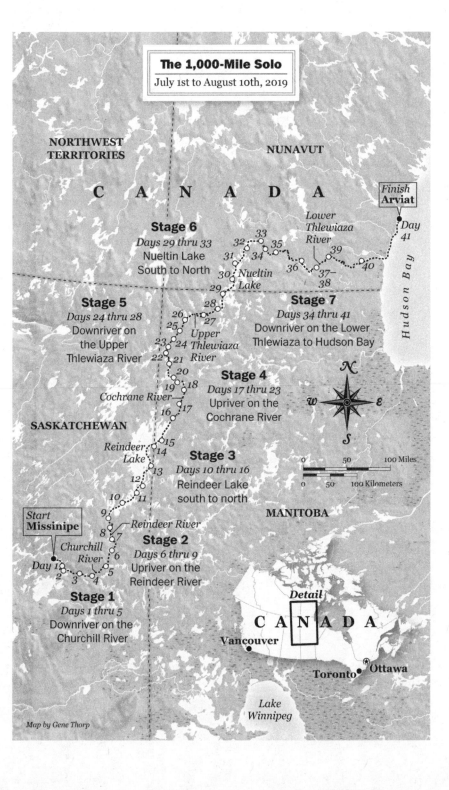

The 1,000-Mile Solo
July 1st to August 10th, 2019

NORTHWEST
TERRITORIES

NUNAVUT

C A N A D A

Finish
Arviat

Stage 6
Days 29 thru 33
Nueltin Lake
South to North

Lower
Thlewiaza
River

Day
41

Hudson Bay

Stage 5
Days 24 thru 28
Downriver on
the Upper
Thlewiaza River

Upper
Thlewiaza
River

Stage 7
Days 34 thru 41
Downriver on the Lower
Thlewiaza to Hudson Bay

Cochrane River

Stage 4
Days 17 thru 23
Upriver on the
Cochrane River

N
W   E
S

SASKATCHEWAN

*Reindeer
Lake*

Stage 3
Days 10 thru 16
Reindeer Lake
south to north

0   50   100 Miles
0   50   100 Kilometers

MANITOBA

Start
Missinipe

Reindeer River

Day 1

*Churchill
River*

Stage 2
Days 6 thru 9
Upriver on the
Reindeer River

Stage 1
Days 1 thru 5
Downriver on the
Churchill River

Detail

C A N A D A

Vancouver

Toronto **Ottawa**

*Lake
Winnipeg*

Map by Gene Thorp

TRANSPLANTATION DAY

June 8, 2015

Location: Vancouver General Hospital, British

Columbia, (49°15'41" N 123°7'20" W)

*I don't consider myself a pessimist. A pessimist is waiting for it to rain.
And I already feel soaked to the skin.*

—Leonard Cohen

The gurney rumbled through the holding area on its way to the operating theatre. The IV bag swayed above me, and all around, other patients prepared for their own imminent surgeries. Two large doors swung open, and we wheeled into the surgery. Masked doctors and nurses prepared their trays of scalpels as I was transferred to the operating slab.

I shivered, partially from anticipation but also from the cold air that kept the surgeons comfortable under the hot operating lights. I would be unconscious soon, and the air temperature would be a moot point.

A red nylon bag containing my brother's kidney was on a small metal table off to the side of the room. It had been cut from his body just minutes ago, leaving his orbit to enter mine. Never in a thousand years could I have imagined our journeys would intersect like this. That red bag filled me with both guilt and gratitude. Would he be okay? How could I repay this priceless gift?

Polycystic kidney disease had been killing me for years, inexorably eroding my kidney function down toward zero. The drop from 50 percent to 25 percent function hadn't been so bad; that drop had been gradual, and my body had had time to adapt. But the descent from 25 percent down to my current 12 percent function had been rough; short walks now left me winded, the sledgehammer fatigue was relentless, muscle cramps came out of nowhere, and mental fog made it harder and harder to think straight.

The walls were closing in. Losing my ability to do normal physical things was panic-inducing, and my quality of life fell off a cliff. I didn't know the way forward, but it gave me hope that I wasn't the first to go through this; if others had survived and overcome this, so could I.

The phone call came a hair's breadth before end-stage kidney failure and mandatory dialysis; my brother's tests had come in, we were a match, and it was time for a transplant.

The odds said I would probably survive the surgery, but the real question was how much normalcy would be regained afterward. I didn't know if I could ever return to my job as a firefighter, play with my kids, or do jiu-jitsu. And I was worried I'd be housebound and that my days of roaming far and free might be over for good.

On the brink of the knife, I felt strangely detached from the outcome. I had done everything possible to prepare, and the end of the story was now outside my control. Call it fatalism, resignation, or predestination, but at that moment, it helped to think of the dice as having already been cast. There was nothing left to do, and the outcome was now in the hands of the surgeons and the Fates. If I awoke, then I would learn the results. And if I died on the slab, then the blackness of general anesthetic would merge seamlessly into the oblivion of death. Que será, será.

In the final minutes before the operation, my mind wandered unbidden to the lakes and woods of the remote Canadian North. I had had some of my most formative experiences in that landscape, but it had retreated beyond my grasp these last few years as my life had become a blur of doctor's appointments and medical interventions. *Maybe a successful surgery would allow me to get back up there*, I thought. At the edge of a procedure that I might not resurface from, the North had emerged as a mirage I was reaching toward.

Then the anesthesiologist put a smooth silicone mask on my face and told me to count down backward from one hundred. I didn't make it very far before the world went dark.

> *When my time to go comes*
> *I'll miss the rain*
> *That falls fragrant on the earth*
> *And greens it again*
> *I'll miss the way spring*
> *Makes everything new*
> *But I don't know how to say*
> *Goodbye to you.*

> —Eva Schubert, "Saying Goodbye"

A VERY POOR START

July 1, 2019
Start: The hamlet of Missinipe, Saskatchewan (55°36'12" N 104°46'24" W)
Finish: A rocky island on Mountain Lake (55°29'51.8" N 104°29'57.4" W)
Distance covered: 25 kilometers

I must down to the seas again, to the lonely sea and the sky,
And all I ask is a tall ship and a star to steer her by;
And the wheel's kick and the wind's song and the white sail's shaking,
And a gray mist on the sea's face, and a gray dawn breaking.

I must down to the seas again, for the call of the running tide
Is a wild call and a clear call that may not be denied;
And all I ask is a windy day with the white clouds flying,
And the flung spray and the blown spume, and the sea-gulls crying.

I must down to the seas again, to the vagrant gypsy life,
To the gull's way and the whale's way where the wind's like a whetted
knife;
And all I ask is a merry yarn from a laughing fellow-rover,
And quiet sleep and a sweet dream when the long trick's over.
                                        —John Masefield

I t was 6:30 A.M., and I was ready to begin my 1,000-mile exploration of an ancient trade and migration route from the boreal forest into the Barren Lands of Nunavut and then down to Hudson Bay.

A torpedo-shaped boat sat on the shore. This 17'9" canoe-kayak hybrid was just wide enough for a single occupant and could be paddled with both single-bladed or double-bladed paddles. A folding sail was lashed to the shiny red Kevlar deck just ahead of the large open cockpit. This boat was optimized for speed and performance in waves, not cargo space, so fifty days of supplies barely fit inside. Waterproof bags lay one atop the other, held down with straps. Smaller sacks were jammed under the seat, and loose items were stuffed under elastic cords.

After shimmying into the boat, I wedged the final bag containing the medical and repair supplies between my knees, locking my legs into place against the hard hull.

Damn, I'm going to have to reorganize this stuff in the next few days, I thought. *That'll be easier once I've eaten through some of the food supplies.*

The rain started falling, the skies turned grey, and a bitterly cold wind blew from the North. I pushed off from the dock and felt the canoe bob on the waves of Otter Lake. I had been waiting for this moment for twenty-five years.

I pushed the heavy, sluggish boat out into the main section of the lake; if things went according to plan, I'd follow an ancient route known as the Old Route North and eventually get into the deep wilderness with no people for hundreds of miles in all directions.

This was the North and I was an hour beyond where the paved roads end, but the houses and docks of the tiny hamlet were a reminder that I was still in civilization. A floatplane churned across the lake bound for points unknown, and the motorboat of a native fisherman droned in the distance.

Since there was a tailwind, I hoisted a small sail to augment my paddling and felt the boat surge forward. The canoe sliced through the waves and made good time.

The water lapped against the boulder shore, creating the *splash, splash* music of the North. The forest was healthy here, dominated by spruce and aspen trees locked together to create an impenetrable wall of branches along the water's edge. This was the land of the canoe because traveling on foot through the dense vegetation would have been nigh impossible.

Rocky ledges and granite knolls dotted the shoreline, promising spectacular if rugged campsites. The incessant rain continued, and the only animals visibly active were loons and pelicans, two bird species very well adapted to the aquatic life. Seeing the pelicans amused me. Most people think of pelicans as warm-water birds you'd see scooping up fish with their giant beaks off a beach in Mexico. And while it's true that pelicans overwinter in the South, in the summer, they migrate northward, from lake to lake, until they reach some surprisingly high latitudes. In the North, they mate, lay eggs, and raise their young before returning to warmer climes.

This was the classic northern Canadian boreal forest, reminiscent of the terrain I had canoed, camped, and come of age on as a young man. Being out here again, a few days shy of my fiftieth birthday, and having the waves swell beneath me felt like a homecoming.

Otter Lake is part of the Churchill River system, which is mostly a series of large, irregularly shaped lakes connected to the next lake by short rapids. In theory, I was going downstream, but at this moment there was no discernible current beneath the boat.

The Churchill is an ancient artery that cuts west to east through the endless forest. It was an important route for the natives, the Northern fur trade, and early arctic exploration by Europeans. Ominously, just a few kilometers away, in 1820, at Otter Rapids, the first Arctic expedition of Sir John Franklin suffered its first casualty. Franklin's voyageurs were tracking their canoes up this long stretch of whitewater using ropes when one of their boats overturned. A man was swept away, and his body was never found. This was a bad omen to start that long trip; in the next three years, eleven of the nineteen men would die, some resorting to cannibalism before they starved.

The tippy boat rolled beneath my hips. In my hasty departure, I had not arranged the massive quantity of gear particularly well; bags of equipment were balanced on the rear deck of the canoe, and a giant waterproof backpack with more than a hundred pounds of food sat upright in the boat. This raised the boat's center of gravity and made it top-heavy.

Nevertheless, the combination of paddling and sailing spurred the boat on to about eight kilometers per hour, a good speed given how heavy the damn thing was. All was well, or so I thought.

Two hours into the trip, I tucked my paddle under a strap and studied the map, hoping to find the best route through an upcoming group of islands. The wind was primarily coming from behind me, but then it shifted and plowed into the sail from the side while I was distracted. The sail mast acted as a force multiplier and levered the whole boat precariously to the left.

My paddle was out of reach, making a timely bracing stroke impossible. I tried to counter the boat's rotation using my hips alone, craning my upper body toward the sky, but this wasn't enough, and the boat continued its inexorable roll toward the water. I was going in!

There was one crazy, last-ditch trick up my sleeve: I jumped free of the boat in the direction of the tip and landed in the water—*SPLASH*—while keeping my hand on the boat's gunwale.

I did this to remove my weight from the boat, push it back toward vertical with my feet, and give the tipping vessel a chance to right itself.

Jumping out of your canoe is a desperate move at the best of times. This move becomes even riskier when your boat has a sail, because if it stays upright it can blow away very quickly, leaving you stranded in the middle of the lake. Still, if you can keep a grip on the boat, it's probably better than *both* you *and* your vessel being in the water simultaneously.

The boat teetered indecisively for a second, but the force of the wind in the sail and the top-heavy load had brought it past the point of no return. It flipped, and suddenly, I floated in the lake, cold water pouring into my rain gear and chilling my skin.

Fuck!

I was flooded with embarrassment and anger. Only two hours into a 1,000-mile journey, my inattention had caused an entirely preventable catastrophe.

When I'm not in the wilderness, I work as a firefighter. In mass casualty situations with more patients than you can handle, we use a concept called triage, wherein you prioritize the patients and only treat the most urgent but "saveable" people first. This is difficult because it takes a certain detachment to walk past a critically injured patient who probably won't survive to treat another patient whose life may actually be saveable.

Bobbing up and down beside an overturned boat in a cold lake on a rainy day presented many problems. There had to be a way to fix the situation, so despite the cold waves splashing in my face I tried to stay calm, take stock of the situation, count the issues, and start triaging them.

First, my Personal Flotation Device (PFD) kept me afloat, the boat wasn't sinking any further, and I wasn't entangled in anything. These were good things.

The water was cold, but fortunately, I was wearing full-body rain gear, which functioned as an ersatz wetsuit; the water seeped in slowly, was warmed up by my body, and created a slightly warmer layer of water against my skin. Also, adrenaline and embarrassment kept me warm, at least for now.

Next on the triage list was keeping track of all my gear. The larger bags were tightly tied into the boat, but loose items like paddles, bailer, and maps were floating away, so I retrieved them and tied everything to the boat. My gear and I were now a single heavy, waterlogged bundle moving up and down in the waves, but at least things weren't strewn across the windy lake in a giant yard sale.

The situation had been stabilized for now, and I ran through the options for fixing the problem.

First, I tried to use a method of deepwater self-rescue where you turn a swamped boat on its side to drain it partially, turn it upright, grab the far gunwale, give a huge kick, and launch yourself out of the water to end up lying sideways across the boat. Then you twist, get your butt down to the bottom of the boat, and bail out the remaining water.

This flopping and twisting isn't as complicated as it sounds, especially when working with an empty boat on a flat lake. I had often taught this technique as a canoe guide, but today, conditions were far from ideal.

The waves kept jostling the boat, and the heavy bags above deck level made everything unstable. My thick whitewater lifejacket, festooned with survival gear, kept getting caught on the cockpit rim at the worst times. I tried this maneuver four times, launching myself across the cockpit, but each time, the boat rolled over and dumped me back into the water.

Next, I considered removing all the bags and tying them to one end of the boat so that they could float freely and not interfere with the self-rescue operation. I also thought about temporarily removing my lifejacket to prevent the snagging points and allow more effective slithering across the boat's gunwales.

These didn't seem like the best ideas, so I kept a firm grip on the boat and evaluated other options while bobbing in the water under a gray sky . . .

Another possibility was to climb onto the overturned boat and hope for a fisherman to come by. Earlier, a few boats from Grandmother's Bay, a small Cree village about ten kilometers away, had *put-putted* across the lake, but in this rain, most people would be staying off the water.

"Wish in one hand, shit in the other, see which fills up first," I muttered. Pinning my hopes on rescue seemed like a bad idea, and besides, I was sufficiently mortified that I didn't want anybody to witness this debacle. Deep down, I wanted to sort the problem out by myself.

I looked around. The nearest shore was about two hundred meters away, but the boat was slowly getting blown in a different direction toward a peninsula about a thousand meters downwind. One option was to abandon my gear and swim for that spit of land, hoping the wind would push my boat to the same shore afterward. But if the wind shifted again, my equipment might get blown somewhere else. My gear wasn't worth my life, but I also didn't want to lose it all just two hours into a fifty-day trip.

Then I had a revelation. The sail that had created the problem might be able to solve it, too. Maybe the sail could still pull everything—the boat, the gear, and me—to safety.

It took some underwater gymnastics and creative knot-tying, but eventually, I managed to rig the sail so it pointed straight into the air despite the boat floundering sideways in the water. Once out of the water, the sail filled with wind, and I felt the tug as the heavy boat began to move. This was no streamlined vessel—it resembled a prison escape raft with the hydrodynamics of a bag of coconuts—but nevertheless, it slowly churned through the waves.

Twenty minutes of crude and artless sailing brought me to land. This was not a friendly shore; the waves bashed the boat and my body against the fringe of half-submerged boulders and spindly shrubs at the base of a vertical cliff. But these were not normal circumstances, and this seemed like a five-star beach.

I unpacked the boat, dragged everything onto the rocks, and repacked it. Then, the shivering started, partly from the prolonged immersion in cold water and partly from the adrenaline wearing off. The way to get warm was to get moving, so I hustled back into the boat and resumed paddling across the lake, the sail safely stowed flat on the deck this time.

My mood was grim. Having something go this poorly so soon after starting was not a good sign. It shook my faith in my abilities and judgment to the core. I was supposed to be an expert paddler. . . . I knew the dangers of lake travel. . . . I had taught canoeing professionally, for God's sake, but despite my supposed expertise, I had negligently ended up in a terrible situation.

How could this have happened? And, more important, how could I stop it from happening again?

The conclusion was very simple: This trip could have no more mistakes. On that wavy afternoon, the trip's mantra became, *No more mistakes*. I must have repeated this to myself ten thousand more times in the coming days.

As the morning wore into the afternoon, there was no break in the weather. I was soaked to the skin from the incident, and the continuous rain ensured I stayed that way. Although cold and wet, I was not freezing—a testament to the Merino wool and bombproof rain gear I wore, which helped prevent catastrophic heat loss.

The trip continued downriver through a maze of islands, channels, and bays. Then the gathering swirl of the current and a droning roar from downstream announced the presence of Robertson Falls, where the Churchill River pours over a series of steep ledges, widens into a small lake, and then pours down a second cascade. Two back-to-back portages are required to get past this double obstacle.

Portaging is the art of carrying your gear and canoe around impassable obstacles. This portage was mercifully short, only a few hundred feet along an easy-to-follow trail. On the first two trips across, I carried multiple backpacks at a time, all balanced on top of each other, with hands full of paddles and other gear. The final trip involved lifting the canoe, feeling its wobbling weight on my shoulders, and teetering to the far end of the trail. The packing and unpacking at both ends of the portage took forever; so much gear needed to fit into the boat.

A few minutes of paddling brought me to the top of the second cascade and Twin Falls Lodge, a lovely fishing camp with many small cabins and buildings nestled into the lake's shoreline.

As I untied my gear with numb fingers, the Twin Falls Lodge groundskeeper came down to find out what was going on and, after a short conversation, suggested a cup of tea. Something hot seemed like a good idea, so I followed him inside.

There were no guests at the lodge at that moment—a large batch of American tourists had just flown out that morning, and another group was due the next day. Wonderful smells started permeating the large dining room, and then the groundskeeper's wife emerged with warm cookies and leftovers for everyone. This break from the cold, wet day perfectly illustrated Northern hospitality.

After an hour of socializing, the same intrinsic desire that makes animals migrate vast distances pulled me back outdoors and downriver, where the weather swung between a drizzle and sheets of rain. It was a cold afternoon; by early evening, I was shivering again, dancing on the edge of mild hypothermia. It was time to rest and regroup, so I camped on a spine of rock that emerged from the water like the hump of a prehistoric beast. It was just wide enough for a cooking area and a tent. I put up the tarp to dry out all the wet gear, then lit a small smoky fire to keep the bugs away.

The first day had not gone well, which did not bode well for the rest of the journey. I tried to tell myself that it was better for things to go wrong here, in the relatively civilized part of the North, than up in the Barren Lands of Nunavut. Still, the spectacular level of screwup while doing something I was supposedly good at scared the shit out of me.

In my sleeping bag, I lay awake late into the night, trying to devise plans to make tomorrow better than today. The *No more mistakes* mantra was just the beginning. As I processed the incident, I realized it wasn't caused by just one thing. A cascade of mistakes, omissions, errors, and breakdowns had preceded the final catastrophic outcome, and I wrote down every mistake I could think of in my tiny notebook.

"Error 1, Bad packing."

My canoe was fast, sexy, and modern, but with 250 pounds of gear and 215 pounds of paddler, it was definitely over its carrying capacity. Also, the way I had packed it meant that the boat only had to tip a little before the high center of gravity guaranteed reaching the point of no return.

I made a list of inessential items to get rid of in the first village I passed. I didn't really need a camera tripod, a folding chair, an extra tarp, the rescue leash on my PFD, a pair of fire irons, or the paperback book in my bag. Purging these items would reduce the total load by seven or eight pounds.

I also vowed to repack the heavy food bags so that they'd lie flat on the boat's belly. Everything else would have to fit around those bags like a three-dimensional puzzle.

Finally, I decided to lower the seat in the canoe by about an inch. I knew from experience that this tiny adjustment would make sitting less comfortable but would also improve the boat's stability.

"Error 2, Out in the middle of the lake."

The boat had tipped in an exposed part of the lake, where the wind had been able to blow over a long, uninterrupted distance. This meant the wind had been gusting harder, and the waves were larger than on a route along the more sheltered shoreline.

Starting immediately, I vowed to stick to less exposed routes in windy weather, hug the shoreline, and stay close to islands, peninsulas, and headlands.

"ERROR 3, MISREADING THE WEATHER."

I knew the wind was strong just before I flipped. What I missed was the extent to which it had been shifting directions; one moment it blew at my back, but the next it came at me broadside, and ultimately, one of those sideways blasts had tipped the boat over.

This meant I had to watch the wind conditions constantly. I needed to monitor its strength, feel the shifts and surges on my skin, listen to its moans, and watch it caress the waves, bushes, and treetops. Everything I noticed might be important and might predict what the wind would do in the future.

"ERROR 4, SAILING IN A STRONG WIND."

The sail had carried me along nicely for a while. It was a helpful tool, the same way that a chainsaw or a stick of dynamite is a helpful tool, but if you use it incorrectly it'll kill you.

Proper sailboats have keels that help prevent them from flipping. As a sailboat heels to one side, the righting force exerted by the weighted keel increases until an equilibrium is reached. A canoe, by contrast, lacks a weighted keel and thus is significantly more vulnerable to tipping.

I could never again drop my guard while sailing. Using the sail in strong or gusty winds was out. I decided to use it only when the wind was blowing toward the shore; if I flipped, the onshore wind would eventually blow everything back to the beach instead of carrying it out into the watery expanse.

"ERROR 5, COMPLACENCY."

Complacency was the mother of all the other errors. My comeuppance came after I had dropped my guard. A couple of easy hours had me thinking I had mastered this sailing business. I had been looking down at my maps when the fateful gust hit, which was no more forgivable than texting in a car in heavy traffic. My awareness had been split, my reaction time slowed, and my paddle was not in my hands when things went wrong.

I might be willing to take risks with my own life, but I also owed it to my children at home not to get complacent again. There are no routine lake crossings, routine rapids, or routine portages when you're by yourself in the wilderness. Travel in a place where most people will never go requires continual vigilance and controlling as many variables as possible to stack the deck in my favor.

Flipping the boat had been entirely my fault, but every sin I had committed pointed to measures I could take to prevent similar accidents in the future.

THE MAPS ARE DESTROYED

July 2, 2019

Start: A rocky ridge of an island, Mountain Lake
(55°29'51.8" N 104°29'57.4" W)
Finish: An island campsite on Drope Lake (55°25'31.5" N 104°27'01.0" W)
Distance covered: 20 kilometers

I may say that this is the greatest factor: the way in which the expedition is equipped, the way in which every difficulty is foreseen, and precautions taken for meeting or avoiding it. Victory awaits him who has everything in order, luck, people call it. Defeat is certain for him who has neglected to take the necessary precautions in time, this is called bad luck.

—Roald Amundsen, *The South Pole*

You can tell a lot about what the day has in store for you before you leave your tent in the morning. The clues at 6:00 A.M. on this particular morning weren't promising: the wind's ululation was accompanied by the rhythmic pounding of waves and shuddering nylon tent fabric. There would be no paddling until things died down.

A nagging thought percolated as I lay nestled in my sleeping bag, slipping between sleep and wakefulness. I had a sense memory from the day before of carrying my gear up to the tent site. Specifically, the two cylindrical plastic cylinders holding my maps had felt slightly heavier than they should have been. At the time, I had been too tired to give the weight difference much thought, but my subconscious had been churning away all night and had identified the cylinders as a potential problem.

What on earth had made those map containers heavy? Oh no—could it be water?! Still in my sleeping bag I unscrewed the lid of the first cylinder, and—*WHOOSH*—copious lake water poured onto the tent floor.

I swore and opened the second cylinder. *DOUBLE WHOOSH*, even more water than the first. The maps had been soaking in this water for about twenty hours.

How had this happened? It turned out that the tube itself was water-proof, but not the small holes for the swivels in the carrying sling. Even a tiny hole can let in a lot of water if submerged for thirty minutes.

In theory, the maps were waterproof. Months previously, I had spread the maps out on the truck bay floor of the fire hall and diligently applied Mapseal, a waterproofing compound, to both sides of all fifty sheets. Unfortunately, this product is designed to make paper shed a few raindrops, not make it waterproof. The maps were now completely soaked and stuck together into a soggy mass.

I gingerly peeled the paper rolls apart; every sheet was waterlogged and so fragile that they fell apart under their own weight as I held them aloft. I felt like an archaeologist handling the Dead Sea Scrolls, brittle fragments of vellum glued together by rot and time.

I felt like vomiting. This was a disaster. How was I supposed to navigate 1,600 kilometers of some of the most confusing terrain on the planet using tiny paper fragments? Ahead lay dangerous rapids, difficult portages, and routes rarely traveled. To navigate the twisting river and giant lakes with countless islands, peninsulas, and bays, I needed to know where I was at all times.

My Garmin InReach GPS unit had maps on it, but that device's screen was tiny, making it much harder to decipher the intricate landscape. Relying only on electronic navigation would also be dangerous; what if the battery ran dry? Keeping it charged would require frequent solar panel use, but regular sunshine can be scarce way up North.

My best option was to dry out the maps as best as possible and then try to reassemble the jigsaw fragments into something usable.

First, I ran parachute cord along the tent's interior to turn it into a drying rack and hung maps on it. Other wet maps were spread on the tent floor. More paper was laid on nearby rock outcrops and weighed down with branches and rocks to prevent it from flying away. Of course, as soon as this was set up, the rain started, and it became a race to gather the map scatterlings and get them under cover before they got even wetter. This pattern repeated itself for much of the morning.

In the afternoon, the wind dropped just enough to make the water navigable again. Intense squalls occasionally pockmarked the lake surface, but the dangerous breaking whitecaps were mostly gone. It was time to get moving and do at least a few hours of paddling. I carefully rolled up the wet maps as best I could.

I laboriously arranged my gear in the boat to get the heavy stuff—food mostly—as close to the bottom of the boat as possible. Then, I continued the downstream battle with wet fleece and rain gear clammy against my skin.

I slowly picked my way along the lake, using islands and peninsulas for cover from the never-ending wind. Raindrops peppered the water's surface like birdshot. Sometimes, I had to bob in the waves, waiting for a particularly fierce cloudburst to pass before venturing across larger channels. The land was soaked, too; water dripped from the trees, and the flat areas near shore were swamps dotted with spindly black spruce where any tent would slowly sink into the muck.

In the modern world, most of our time is spent indoors. We live in houses, commute in cars, and work in offices. We're almost constantly separated from the elements. Consequently, we tend to use only a few broad categories for weather: we say it's "raining," it's "windy," it's "snowing," and leave it at that.

Contrast the paucity of our weather language to that of the Inuit living in the High Arctic, who have an extensive and detailed vocabulary for the different varieties of ice and snow. Their language describes the shape, texture, and depth of snow. Recognizing and communicating these nuances is a genuine survival advantage in that environment. Over the millennia, their language has been forced toward precision on this topic.

I don't know if a person raised in a city can ever approach the Inuit level of awareness of the natural world, but spending time in a canoe is a good start. Fight your way along the shore of a windy lake, feel the spray of the breaking waves on your face, and you'll quickly become attuned to the wind's speed, direction, steadiness, and periodicity. You'll learn how it swirls over the land and the water. You start paying attention because it really matters. This awareness isn't mystical or metaphysical; it's merely your long-buried survival instinct kicking in. You wouldn't be here if countless generations of your ancestors hadn't been able to pay attention to their surroundings.

Making my way along a reed-choked section of shore, I spotted the native settlement of Stanley Mission, with low houses, rumbling pickup trucks, and motorboats pulled up on the beach.

This was the first of four small native indigenous communities I'd pass on the trip. Ordinarily, a village like this was a chance to buy some snacks and fresh food, but the boat was already so heavy that the last thing I wanted was additional weight. I didn't stop at the village except to donate excess camping gear to a somewhat confused fisherman on the dock.

On the shore opposite the town was a shockingly white church. The silhouette of its spire was visible for miles against the cold gray sky. This was the Holy Trinity Church, the oldest standing church in the province. It looked like it had been teleported here from rural England. From my research, I knew it had been built in the 1850s by Anglican missionaries and is still used for special occasions.

The church was unlocked. Light from the stained glass windows set high in the blue arched ceiling illuminated the interior. I tried to imagine what a service would have looked like one hundred years ago, a lone white priest in his robes facing a congregation of weathered brown faces sitting in the red pews.

The church would have been a beautiful place to spend some time in, but it was unheated, and I was starting to get cold. The best way to warm up was to return to the boat and paddle again.

The river takes a hard left turn at Stanley Mission, shifting its direction from south to east. Yet despite the 90° turn, the wind still blew directly in my face. It was like the weather gods were aligning the wind to oppose me no matter how the river turned. The paddle began to feel much heavier in my hands, but there was also a certain joy in being out there alone.

My first solo trip happened by accident. I was twenty-one years old, and it was just before Christmas. Usually, Ontario is frozen solid in December, a black-and-white landscape where skeletal trees wait for spring. This winter was different; an unexpected warm spell shot the temperatures up and melted enough snow to fill the local rivers flush to the banks.

I proposed a midwinter canoe trip to my nineteen-year-old brother Peter. Soon, he and I were hauling a canoe down to the Grand River, where open water coursed between snowy banks. At first, our trip went well. We floated downriver on the strong current, avoiding the dangerous piles of driftwood and bouncing through minor riffles.

By late afternoon, something had shifted in Peter's demeanor. He started complaining continuously and had random aggressive outbursts toward me.

After four hours on the river, we pulled over to the riverbank to prepare a meal. Peter was now yelling at me to instigate a fight; talking to him was impossible. Peter had his demons, including a significant drug addiction. On a typical day, he'd get high multiple times, but being unable to scratch that itch on the river was beginning to drive him crazy. He escalated quickly until he screamed, "Fuck this, I'm outta here! I can't take it anymore!" Then he stomped off to find a country road and hitchhike back to his dealer.

The snowy meadow was now silent. The drama had made me angry, but I was also determined not to let his addiction-induced histrionics ruin the trip. I made camp as soft snowflakes melted on my skin and settled in for the night. When the sun rose the following day, I continued down the river alone.

The next thirty-six hours on the Grand River ended up being one of my life's most magical and formative experiences. The river flowed through a grayscale world with winter skies and snow-covered willows along the bank. Water dripping down the paddle shaft formed icicles on my woolen mittens. Flocks of Canada geese erupted from cattail swamps growing in blind river channels. Kilometer by kilometer, the black river revealed itself.

It's not the best idea to do your first solo canoe trip on an unfamiliar river in the middle of winter; ice, snow, and freezing water hugely amplify the usual hazards of canoeing. Fortunately, I had enough previous experience canoeing to make it home safely by Christmas Eve.

That Grand River trip was a success mostly because of a book called *Path of the Paddle: An Illustrated Guide to the Art of Canoeing* by Bill Mason. Nominally a book about flatwater and whitewater paddling, it taught me the difference between the J-stroke and the Canadian stroke, onside and offside eddy turns, and low and high braces. I thumbed through the pages at the brink of the first rapid I ever attempted, studying the river features and the whitewater techniques I needed to get to the bottom safely.

Path of the Paddle is more than just a how-to manual; Mason's evangelical love of the wilderness comes through on every page of his work. I've gifted his books to friends and family; if I had the money, I'd leave a copy in every hotel room I stay in.

This was a time when the prevailing wisdom was never to do canoe trips alone. Conversely, Bill Mason was an outdoor authority who gave his blessing to those who wanted to travel solo. He advocated caution but also waxed lyrical about the adventure and joy of traveling alone.

> If you do decide to go solo, go prepared. Think of everything you do. Think about the possibility of injury even from routine actions, such as picking up and carrying the canoe over a muddy trail, chopping wood, or running rock-studded rapids. Close your eyes and imagine yourself pinned helplessly between your

canoe and a rock in the middle of a rapid. You might decide to portage the rapids. When you are chopping or splitting your firewood, imagine sinking the axe into your foot and then notice how carefully you position the safety log.

—Bill Mason, *Song of the Paddle:*
An Illustrated Guide to Wilderness Camping

Had I not memorized every page of *Path of the Paddle*, I might not have had the notion to continue alone when Peter left me at the riverside. I'm forever grateful to the mentor I never met, who taught me through his books and films.

This unexpected sojourn on the Grand River kindled an interest in solo trips that has smoldered and flared for the rest of my life. As soon as I graduated from university, I headed out alone on my next trip.

On that five-week trip, I paddled down the Missinaibi River to James Bay, then turned around and headed upriver on the Albany and Kenogami rivers, struggled over the height of land—the high ground that divided one drainage from the next—and continued down to Lake Superior.

The second half of that trip was gut-wrenchingly difficult. My previous upriver experience on shorter trips had been relatively easy, but the Kenogami was in flood and determined to wash me back down to the sea. Life became simple: get up, fight to overcome the day's adversities, and sleep. As I struggled upstream against a relentless river, I developed trench foot, covered my hands with blisters, and discovered new levels of perseverance I hadn't known existed. In every way, it was a journey of self-discovery.

Most people don't want to go to the movies alone, let alone want to do an extended solo trip in the wilderness. So, where does this unquenchable desire for canoeing alone come from?

Solo travel gives you an unprecedented amount of autonomy. You travel at your own pace, paddle for as long as you want, and camp wherever you like. There are no negotiations, no arguments, and no compromises. Everything is your choice, and everything is your fault.

Being alone in the wilderness sharpens your awareness of nature because you have to pay uninterrupted attention to your surroundings with all five senses. A breeze, a splash, a shift of your boat, and a breaking twig could all mean something, so you had better listen. Having more skin in the game focuses the mind wonderfully.

Ultimately, paddling solo is an opportunity to turn inward, creating time for reflection and focus that is hard to achieve in day-to-day life. Some monks achieve enlightenment by cutting bamboo, others by raking gravel; if a monk ever reaches Nirvana in a canoe, then I'm pretty sure he'll be paddling solo.

In the late afternoon, I reached Little Stanley Rapids, easy Class II white-water, which was nothing more than a set of large waves and a few rocks. Ordinarily, running these rapids would have been a walk in the park, but it was late in the day, I was cold, and the boat was still top-heavy. I opted to portage.

Traversing around these rapids was made immeasurably easier by a hundred-foot-long boat ramp that went around them. Built of wood, it came out of the water, ran through the forest, and then went back into the water downstream of the rapids.

I paddled toward the upstream end of the ramp as fast as possible and drove the boat over the lip. It lurched out of the water with a thump, then slid up the slanting surface like a seal exiting the sea. I dragged the loaded boat along the ramp where raised PVC pipe sliders at regular intervals made for a very easy slide. Two minutes later, I was done and grinning ear to ear; this had been the easiest portage ever.

By 6:30 P.M. my back was a twisted knot, my arms were about to fall off, and an old injury in my shoulder was throbbing with a vengeance. I unfolded myself out of the boat at a small island campsite on Drope Lake and gradually ratcheted my body upright. After two days of paddling, it felt like I'd been worked over with a baseball bat, and I didn't know how long I could continue at this pace. The route ahead contained many unknowns, and I guessed my odds of completing it were 50/50 at best. I would roll the dice again tomorrow and see how far I got.

AMPUTATION MINDGAMES

July 3, 2019
Start: An island campsite on Drope Lake (55°25'31.5" N 104°27'01.0" W)
Finish: A tiny rock Island on Keg Lake (55°24'17.8" N 103°58'20.1" W)
Distance covered: 34 kilometers

Down to Gehenna or up to the Throne,
He travels the fastest who travels alone.

—Rudyard Kipling,
"The Story of the Gadsbys"

I awoke early after a night of fragmentary sleep, having been kept awake by pain in my left shoulder, lumbar spine, and right hip. My body was a mess, but the dawn also revealed a new problem: my left hand was swollen like a grapefruit, with the pasty-white knuckles forming negative divots in the puffy flesh. The fingers ached, even at rest. This was problematic; paddling without hands is hard.

I tried to figure out the cause of the swelling, straining to remember every first aid book and every bit of medical training I had ever been exposed to. After some contemplation, it seemed likely that the balloon hand was likely caused by one of three things . . .

The first hypothesis was that the hand was swollen because the hand was taking 30,000 paddle strokes a day. If the problem was indeed overuse, then limiting the strain on the hand would probably allow it to gradually heal and return to normal.

The second possibility was that this was gout, a form of reactive arthritis caused by uric acid crystals accumulating in joints. Typically, gout happens to older people with terrible diets, but the lifesaving kidney transplant in 2015 left me much more susceptible to gout attacks. I thought I had been drinking enough water on this trip to prevent it, but if it ended up being gout, then I had the medications to deal with it; I'd be out of action for three to five days, but eventually, my hand would heal.

The third and scariest possibility was that this inflammation came from an infection deep in the hand. This seemed unlikely because the hand wasn't reddish or hot to the touch, but the consequences of an uncontrolled infection deep in the bush were so high that I decided to dip into my medical supply. I broke out a powerful antibiotic, Cephalexin, which the label said to take four times a day. The response to the antibiotic would then guide my next steps.

So now there were two overlapping crises: the crisis with the wet maps, which I needed to figure out where to go, and the crisis of the hand, which I needed to get there.

With antibiotics in my veins and using my throbbing left hand as a fingerless hook on the paddle, I headed out, trying to cover as much distance as possible before the wind came up.

The morning sky was blue and dotted with puffy white clouds, a vast improvement over the previous two days of torrential rain. Then, I had another gift from nature; all across the landscape, brown dragonfly nymphs were emerging from the water. Coordinated by some inaudible music, millions upon millions of these cricket-like insect larvae had chosen today to crawl out of the water and onto every shore. Once on land, the larval nymphs gripped twigs, logs, or blades of grass and split down the middle of their backs. A shriveled, wormlike creature pushed its way out of the discarded exoskeleton, then steadily and miraculously pumped blood into its wings, extending until it became a fully formed emerald dragonfly.

A single dragonfly can eat hundreds of mosquitos daily, so I joyfully welcomed them into the world. "I hope you're hungry," I called out as they launched into the sky on their buzzing maiden flights. They had completed their journey from aquatic crickets on the bottom of the lake to consummate hunters of the air before my eyes.

Soon came another boat ramp around Potter Rapids between Nistowiak Lake and Drinking Lake. I knew there would be lots of portaging in my future, so I was happy to cheat by dragging my boat around rapids whenever possible.

A curious yearling bear ambled along the grassy shore in the swifts below Potter Rapids, looking for food and other adventures. He looked up briefly, saw me floating by, and completely ignored me. He was more interested in his own business than he was in mine. We were each perfectly happy to take delight in our own company.

Many people wonder if I've ever felt lonely on solo trips. That's a valid question and certainly something I used to be afraid of. Before my first solo trip in my early twenties, my biggest fear wasn't encountering bears, drowning in rapids, or getting lost. Instead, I worried I'd feel lonely in the wilderness. *Big tough guy goes canoeing, only to feel lonely and pitiful.* That would have been embarrassing.

I was greatly relieved, therefore, when I finally went on that trip and didn't feel lonely for a single moment. Being constantly surrounded by nature filled my days, and I enjoyed my own company for weeks.

I've never been lonely in the woods. I used to wonder if this was normal or if something was wrong with me, but now I don't care. It's just how I'm wired, and I'm okay with that; it may be strange, but as the old saying goes, "Those that mind don't matter, and those that matter don't mind."

It's not that I dislike spending time outdoors with people—far from it. I've worked as a raft and canoe guide and have taken friends and family on many wilderness adventures. It's just that going into the wilderness alone falls into a different category and satisfies a different need than going with others.

Now, it's true that many experiences on a solo trip would be wonderful to share with other people. For example, I remember how a newborn moose struggled to its feet and stumbled into the forest on a certain bend of the Kenogami River. It was a wonderful moment, but it was mine alone. Had that been a shared experience, not only would I have felt my own delight but also someone else's. And then, in the future, two people could have breathed life into those memory embers, sustaining their glow into the future instead of that being entrusted only to me.

I have often felt lonely in the city. It's easy to feel the pain of solitude when people surround you. Those crowds make loneliness more acute, mock your isolation, and suggest that you might be fundamentally unlovable. But when you're alone in the wilderness, there's a good reason why nobody is talking to you. You're not actually unlovable; it's just that there's nobody around. The context of your isolation makes a big difference, and it's much more bearable if you *choose* to be alone and have a purpose behind it. There is a vast difference between being alone and being lonely.

Toward the end of the day, I reached Keg Lake, a large expanse with many sizeable islands and potential navigation options. I chose the Inman Channel, a sheltered and intimate route along the north shore of the lake.

A drama unfurled in the skies above the channel. First, dark clouds appeared on the distant horizon, starkly contrasting the blue skies overhead. Then sun-showers speckled the channel's still water; high-altitude winds were carrying rain many miles from their origin clouds toward me. Those clouds eventually thickened and obscured most of the sky, pierced occasionally by shafts of sunlight that contrasted with the dark gray columns of rain sweeping over the water.

The heavy boat crawled through the riverlike narrows. It was only midafternoon, but my body buzzed with pain. The voice of weakness whispered that it was time to pitch the tent, eat dinner, and hurl my aching body to the ground. I might have even stopped, but campsites here were nonexistent; the swampy forest on both shores went on for miles. It was now the height of summer, and at this northern latitude, the sunlight continued late into the evening. I kept looking for a flat, dry spot, paddling for twenty minutes, then slumping near-comatose in the seat to recover.

I constantly adjusted my paddling technique to take the load off irritated body parts and transfer it onto new body parts. To lessen my shoulder pain, I tried using more forward lean on the paddle strokes and less body rotation. To avoid further straining my hand, I continually shifted the paddle grips. I experimented with different leg positions and adjusted the height of the canoe seat, hoping to find a configuration that lessened the omnipresent back pain.

As I shifted in my seat, I thought about a conversation I'd once had with the elite powerlifter Chris Duffin about preventing little injuries from turning into big injuries. Chris is a beast of a human, and in 2018, he squatted 800 pounds every day for an entire month to raise money for charity.

It's hard to overstate how insane this is: squatting 800 pounds once is an incredible achievement, rare even at elite powerlifting competitions where competitors live for heavy iron. Normally, if a competitor manages to do this once, they feel depleted for weeks, but Chris repeated this herculean task for thirty days in a row, placing an enormous strain on his musculature, and nervous and endocrine systems. Furthermore, he only used a weightlifting belt and knee wraps, eschewing a squat suit, which could have increased his functional strength by up to 30 percent. This makes his damn near mythic achievement even more impressive.

Chris told me that he learned a tremendous amount about recovery from doing this challenge. He couldn't ignore small niggling pains because the next day, they could become full-on strains and derail his entire project. Addressing the little problems early with every tool he had prevented big problems later. There's a saying in the railroad industry that goes, "No piece of machinery ever rattles itself tighter," and the same is true of the human body.

The fact that one of the world's strongest men took his aches seriously made me better about trying to minimize my own pain. The trick seemed to be navigating between the extremes of hypochondria and stoicism; there was going to be pain, but the goal was to make it a sustainable, manageable pain rather than the precursor to a catastrophic injury.

In the late evening, I finally approached a tiny rock island topped with a few scraggly trees that had barely room for a tent. Given the alternative of sleeping in a swamp, however, it seemed like the Hilton.

Blood dripped from my neck, the work of black flies that were worse now than at any previous time on the trip. The little bastards relentlessly gnawed on any exposed piece of flesh they could find. I hurriedly built a small smudge fire with wet wood to keep the bugs at bay, then pitched the tent and wolfed down a hurried dinner.

The pain coursing through my body dropped my confidence to a new low. In a sudden moment of gloom, I wondered how to best amputate my hand if it turned gangrenous deep in the bush. After careful consideration, I decided that chopping it off with a hatchet might be faster, but using a saw would likely be tidier. It's amazing the dark corners that an unattended mind will go to . . .

THE THREE BEARS

July 4, 2019
Start: A tiny rock island on Keg Lake (55°24'17.8" N 103°58'20.1" W)
Finish: A moss- and lichen-covered campsite on Archibald Island,
Trade Lake (55°23'09.0" N 103°36'00.6" W)
Distance covered: 31 kilometers

Little by little, one travels far.

—Spanish saying

I awoke feeling utterly thrashed. It had taken hours to drift off, and after that, I slept very poorly. It seemed likely that working to absolute exhaustion and then hurtling into the tent was probably not the ideal pre-bedtime transition. Sleep is the foundation of both athletic performance and recovery. In retrospect, I wonder if reading a book beside a crackling campfire for an hour each evening would have increased the distance I could cover each day.

In the faint morning light, I once again examined my left hand. It was still swollen and tender but looked just a little better. I would continue the antibiotics for another day and then reevaluate the situation.

I ate muesli soaked in cold lake water a few spoonfuls at a time while packing up camp; lots of fuel would be required to push across the several long portages and large lake ahead.

I cast off and began moving across the still waters of early morning. The only sound was that of Canada geese flapping their wings and running across the water to take off from the lake. The boat zigzagged across the glassy surface, responding to my high-cadence marathon-style stroke.

In traditional canoeing, you use a J-stroke, where the paddle stroke is followed by a short corrective pry that keeps the boat moving in a straight line. In the more modern marathon style, however, you use only the forward component of the stroke and omit the pry; ordinarily, paddling like this would cause your boat to go in circles, so the key is to switch sides every five to ten strokes to counter the turning effect.

This zigzag paddling style, tossing the paddle from hand to hand, is ubiquitous among modern long-distance canoe racers because it allows you to maintain a high stroke rate, kilometer after kilometer, without slowing down. It's similar to the high-cadence stroke used by professional cyclists in the twenty-three-day Tour de France.

This was the first major trip where I had extensively used marathon-style paddling. Not only did it make the boat go faster, but the rapid, light strokes also didn't seem to irritate my shoulders as much as the heavier, slower traditional strokes. The continuous movement seemed to be helping; the shoulder injuries hurt just a little less than yesterday. Could it be that, against all odds, 20,000 to 30,000 paddle strokes per day were acting as a form of physiotherapy?

The smooth water and the lack of a headwind made for fast travel. Miles of lake disappeared under the keel of the boat. The ripples emanating from the boat were the only sign that someone had passed through this country.

An hour later, I came to Keg Falls. Here, the river thundered over a giant ledge stretching across the river with trip-ending (and quite possibly life-ending) consequences for any canoeist who blundered over it.

There's a clearly defined portage around Keg Falls, but to get to that trail, you first need to navigate the Class I rapids just upstream of them. This was very easy whitewater, but the roar of the falls and the dire consequences of getting washed over them made it uniquely interesting. The focus and intensity I felt navigating these swifts were entirely disproportionate to the difficulty of the water.

After Keg Falls came a stretch of Class II whitewater, which could have been fun under other circumstances, but the boat was still too heavily loaded and tippy, so I uncoiled the stern line and lined the rapids instead.

To line a boat, you attach a rope to the end of a boat and walk along the shore, guiding it down the rapids like a large and overenthusiastic puppy pulling on a leash. You judge the waves, rocks, and chutes below, and then you push your boat into the water, adjust its course with little tugs on the rope, reel it back into shore, and repeat.

This art of descending a river requires spinning a lot of plates at the same time. You must watch your boat, evaluate the whitewater below, manipulate the ropes, dance downriver on slippery rocks, and dodge tree branches on the shoreline. Lining is usually safer than running rapids, but it comes with risks. Your boat can swamp in the waves, flip upside down, or turn broadside and get fortune-cookied around a rock by the force of the water.

Lining isn't just dangerous for your boat; it can also damage you. I have a friend who lost a finger lining a raft on a remote Alaska river. His foot got stuck between two rocks, and while trying to free his foot, the rope got looped around his left index finger. The force of the water carried the raft downstream, and—*POP*—off came the finger. I think about this story every time there are ropes near whitewater, and I always carry a knife on my lifejacket to quickly cut the rope if there's an entanglement. Breaking an ankle or inadvertently looping a noose around your neck are also possibilities.

Hazards notwithstanding, lining is an essential skill for wilderness canoe travel. It allows you to navigate otherwise impassable rapids, especially in areas without well-developed portage trails.

Soon, I came to Grand Rapids. As the name suggests, these rapids were really big. The 600-meter slog around these rapids was the longest portage of the trip so far; it was steep, muddy, and blocked with deadfall. It was slow going on this poorly maintained trail, and soon, I felt needle-like stings on my neck, arms, and shoulders as the mosquitoes hunted for blood vessels in my skin with their elongated tubular mouthparts. It's not the bite that itches like crazy later; that is your body's irritated response to the anticoagulant saliva that the mosquitoes inject to keep your blood flowing down their tiny straws.

At the base of the rapids, the sun broke through the clouds to illuminate the rocky Precambrian Shield landscape. Swirling water lapped against the granitic outcrops topped with spruce and birch. The breeze carried white-water mist, which settled cool against my face. Brilliantly white pelicans soared over the rapids in search of fish. I was still bug-bitten, sweaty, and sore, but suffering had now alchemized into wonder.

Ahead lay Trade Lake. As the name implies, this sprawling lake was once part of the Canadian fur trade. Fur collected in distant watersheds needed to be transported to Montreal, many thousands of kilometers away. The canoe was the only logical way to move heavy loads across the rugged landscape, so in early summer, hundreds of voyageurs in their *canots du nord* speeded east along the Churchill River laden with furs. At Trade Lake, these men turned south, crossed the Frog Portage, and entered the Saskatchewan River system on their way to the Great Lakes.

After offloading the furs, these *hommes du nord* would turn around and make their way upstream, their boats now stuffed with trade goods. This annual cycle went on for hundreds of years, then faded into the history books as changing fashions eliminated the need for beaver fur and the railroad displaced previous modes of transport.

On the lake, the strong headwind made the water feel like molasses. The boat crawled toward the distant horizon, an elusive thin line of green forest with blue sky above and blue water below that refused to come any closer. The last thing I wanted to do was paddle, but it was only midafternoon and too early to stop. Every twenty minutes, I laid down my paddle and—overcome by weariness—stared into space. Then after a short rest, I'd slowly, creakily, pick the paddle up again and put another kilometer under the boat's keel.

The longer I paddled, the slower I went, and by evening, the boat was going so slowly that there was no sense in pushing anymore. More distance would be covered by camping now and rejuvenating for tomorrow's battle.

I arced the boat toward the only suitable beach in the area, but then two dark shapes appeared on the sand; it was a black bear mother and her cub, snuffling their way through the sand in a perpetual quest for food. I love bears, but camping here would have been stupid. A defeated sigh burst from my lips, and I picked up the paddle again.

The boreal forest here was so dense that pitching a tent between the trees was impossible. Out on the lake, I had lots of time to think about my wrecked body and swollen hand. Failure seemed imminent, and I thought I'd be lucky if I got home without losing a limb. Then I remembered Mark Twain's saying, "I've had a lot of worries in my life, most of which never happened," which put things into perspective. I might fail and I might not, but it was too soon to tell.

The intrusion of self-doubt is normal when trying to do something difficult, especially if it's a long-term project with lots of time for second thoughts.

Self-doubt is a sly, relentless animal lurking in the back of your mind, patiently waiting for a setback. In that moment of weakness, it creeps out to whisper tales of helplessness, despair, and futility into your ear. Self-doubt aims to undermine your confidence and freeze you into inaction.

You can't banish self-doubt entirely unless you're a psychopath, but the trick is to recognize it early before it gets too much momentum. Therefore, whenever you're in the middle of a challenging project, be on the lookout for the arrival of uncertainty. Expect it to come slinking into your brain and be ready so you don't get blindsided.

Eventually, you'll get good at recognizing those intrusive nagging thoughts. Greet them with, "Oh, hello again. I had been wondering when you would show up. Now excuse me while I keep trying to accomplish my goals anyhow." Meeting self-doubt with chuckling recognition will steal a lot of its power.

Of course, the opposite of self-doubt is hubris, a dangerous blend of overconfidence and ignorance. Hubris isn't good either; it has killed many young men by urging them to take foolish chances in the heat of the moment.

It's fair to say that overconfidence is more of an issue for short-term challenges and that self-doubt is more common when facing long stretches of hardship, suffering, and adversity. Ultimately the trick is to walk the narrow middle path with foolish overconfidence on one side and crippling self-doubt on the other.

Finding another open spot, a beach fringe around a small island took another hour. My body was cramping now, and I wanted nothing more than to get out of the damned boat. I approached the campsite, then shook my head in disbelief. There was yet *another* bear poking around on it.

This third bear of the day strolled along the beach, then waded into the water and swam toward a neighboring pile of rocks only a hundred meters away. His head and ears bobbed in the water, and he looked like a floating teddy bear. He was a strong swimmer, though; he covered the distance quickly, climbed onto shore, and gave a mighty shake that sent water flying in all directions.

He wasn't a large bear, maybe only 150 pounds, but even small bears have big teeth and can create a lot of chaos if they find your food or try to come into your tent. This one was problematic because he would likely return to my island after exploring his pile of rubble. To avoid a potential nocturnal bear encounter, I needed to keep going.

Limping onward into the stiffening headwind, my standards dropped rapidly. All I needed to pitch the tent was an open patch six feet long and five feet wide, but the densely packed trees just kept going and going.

It was close to 9:00 P.M. now, the sun was setting, and my arms were about to fall off when I came upon a postcard-perfect site perched on a rocky ledge and covered with moss and lichen. I knew the recent rains would make the puffy reindeer lichen extra soft, and the breeze blowing across the elevated location would keep the bugs down. It was perfect.

I extricated myself from the boat and lay on a flat rock; it felt so good not to paddle anymore. My back was a knot of agony, but this was a good thing. The pain proved I was still alive, and the exhaustion I felt was a badge of honor.

On that flat rock, I thought back to a much less happy time four years ago when I had been on death's door, crippled with end-stage polycystic kidney disease, going into surgery without assurance of survival. When my consciousness clawed its way to the surface postoperatively, I was relieved that I was still alive but unsure if I would ever become genuinely functional again. Would this new life be worth living, or would it simply qualify as not being quite dead yet? Would I ever be able to wander the wilderness again?

The answer came reasonably quickly. After a few problematic months, improvements started to come rapidly. Three months after the surgery, I was lifting weights, doing jiu-jitsu, and hiking; at the six-month mark, I completed a fifty-kilometer midwinter endurance trudge through the snowy mountains. Thanks to the miracle of modern medicine (and a healthy dose of stubbornness), I was back.

Bathed in equal parts lactic acid and gratitude, I could've stayed on my rock for hours. However, it was late, so I cooked a quick dinner over a small fire, then hunkered down and watched the skies darken over the water.

I typed out a short message to my wife to let her know I was still alive. Normally, my wife and I exchange long emails when we find ourselves in different places, but now we were limited to 160 characters typed on the tiny, unwieldy screen of a Garmin Inreach GPS device. It took a full five minutes for the tiny orange device to chirp a confirmation that the message had been sent through the trees and up to the satellite. This GPS was a very useful device, providing location data, satellite texts functionality, and very basic weather forecasts.

A rented Iridium satellite phone was the next tool to talk to the world. I didn't use this often because it dropped calls in mid-conversation and was very expensive to operate. Still, a satellite phone is mandatory in the North because getting medical advice or arranging an emergency extraction without one would be tricky.

The third device was also the largest: an Explorer 510 BGAN satellite dish. About the size of a very thick laptop, it connected to a satellite that hovered just over the southern horizon. To find that satellite, I'd turn the finicky dish from side to side, guided by a series of faster and slower beeps until it was precisely the correct pitch and angle to transmit data into space. The data transmission was glacially slow and monstrously expensive: $3,000 a gigabyte. The BGAN unit was generally reserved for uploading a few highly compressed photos to my Instagram and blog, but it could also send emails, texts, or voice calls in an emergency. Each communication option provided an extra layer of safety.

I was physically destroyed, but it had been a good day for wildlife. Encountering even a single bear is a big deal, and I had already been lucky enough to see three of them. There had also been pelicans, loons, mergansers, mallards, red squirrels, bald eagles, osprey, and frogs. *Not a bad way to spend your fiftieth birthday, I wonder what other adventures lie ahead,* I thought.

ROCK PAINTINGS AND WATERFALLS

July 5, 2019
Start: A moss- and lichen-covered campsite on Archibald Island,
Trade Lake (55°23'09.0" N 103°36'00.6" W)
Finish: A recently burned and overgrown area on
Ourom Lake (55°33'20.0" N 103°13'05.7" W)
Distance covered: 34 kilometers

We have learned nothing in twelve thousand years.
—Pablo Picasso, after viewing the
cave paintings in Lascaux, France

The morning water was a perfect mirror reflecting the sky in every direction, and despite the sun barely being above the horizon, the air was already getting hot. I took my first stroke; water dripped from the paddle, and the boat knifed eastward, sending the first ripples of the day across the lake.

My swollen hand finally seemed to be improving. It was slowly losing its grapefruit shape, and holding the paddle hurt a little less. This improved my state of mind, and emergency field amputation now seemed a little less necessary.

The river's shore was a mosaic of scars from massive forest fires of years past. The recently burned areas were covered by bright purple fireweed that filled the spaces between the bones of tilting blackened trees. On other slopes, burned long ago, deciduous willows, aspen, and birch trees had mainly replaced the fireweed. In areas burned even further back in time, spruce had reasserted its dominance as the main tree of the forest.

Fire in the boreal forest is a natural part of the landscape. There is a sense in which this entire landscape is a giant burn since the average forest here burns every fifty to one hundred years, and the plant species that grow here are adapted to the fire cycle. The dance of species as the forest burns, recovers, and matures is an ancient and predictable succession. However, with climate change the fires in these forests are increasing both in size and frequency, causing the boreal zone to contract and the species assemblages to change. I fervently hope that future generations will have access to this landscape in the same way we do today.

The first gust of wind was visible before it could be felt. It darted across the water, brushing the sky's reflection into a darker, slightly rough surface. Then, the moving air swirled around my head and was gone. This gust was a harbinger of a steady headwind that would arrive soon and make life much harder.

The distinction between river and lake here was hazy. The Churchill was up to a kilometer wide, and whenever the river ran deep, the current wholly disappeared. Eventually, the river widened out further to form Uksik Lake.

I found the rock paintings on the eastern shore. A red ochre bison, many hundreds of years old, peered out at my bobbing boat from its vertical rock face protected by a slight overhang. Other images and symbols were on nearby rocks, faded by the sun but still unmistakable.

The Churchill River system has more than a hundred rock paintings on its shores, reflecting how central this river was to the ancestors of the Cree people who still live here today. Alexander MacKenzie, the Scottish explorer who crossed North America twelve years before Lewis and Clark, wrote about natives making offerings at a site not far from where I was.

At some distance from the silent rapid is a narrow strait, where the Indians have painted red figures on the face of a rock, and

where it was their custom formerly to make an offering of some
of the articles which they had with them, in their way to and
from Churchill.

—Alexander MacKenzie, *Voyages from Montreal on
the River St. Laurence Through the Continent of
North America to the Frozen and Pacific Oceans
in the Years 1789 and 1793*

We don't know the exact meaning of these petroglyphs, but we can be
sure they were holy sites. Now they are reminders of a previous way of
life, mostly gone, where the fate of the people depended entirely on
the land. The people here hunted, lived, loved, and died on the shore
of this river for thousands of years. It had been a highway through the
primordial landscape, used for trade, hunting, and migration long before
contact with Europeans. Being here made me feel a little bit closer to
those ancient people.

I wasn't lonely, but I felt a pang for a moment. I wanted to share these
pictographs with someone, particularly with Eva, the beautiful redhead
with a confident stride I had married just seven days earlier.

Originally, Eva and I decided to tie the knot in September, after I got
back from the trip. We wanted to have the wedding in a forest grove in
the University of British Columbia botanical gardens, a setting worthy of the
play, *A Midsummer Night's Dream*.

But man makes plans, and God laughs. The university double-booked
that grove, and we lost the venue. They offered us the only other date they
had left: June 30, the day before I was supposed to leave for the North.

"Should I change the dates of my trip?" I asked Eva. "No, stick with
the plan," she said. This might have been a trap with other women, but it
wasn't here. She knew how long I had been dreaming about and planning
this trip and that the departure date had already basically been set in stone
before she proposed. There was no weeping and no crying on her part, just
pragmatically dealing with problems as they came up. It was also one more
reason I knew I had made the right choice.

So I kissed her goodbye the morning after our wedding and took a cab to the airport. Our honeymoon would have to wait; my solo-moon would come first.

I forced the heavy boat back into motion, and soon a rumble started asserting itself through the splash of the waves, indicating heavy water ahead. That deeper undertone kept getting louder until I approached a steep river-wide ledge called Kettle Falls. The river thundered over the lip ahead of me and was gone.

An ancient boat ramp ran through the forest around the falls. Built of logs harvested from the forest, this feat of bush engineering must have once been very impressive. However, the ramp was now in disrepair; many of the logs were loose and rotten, and the entire structure tilted alarmingly to one side.

A sketchy traverse on a decrepit ramp high above the ground still seemed better than carrying everything over uneven footing through the dense forest. I heaved the boat onto the first rotten log, then sledged it across the ramp to the far end of the portage. It was difficult work, but not having to unpack the boat saved at least an hour.

The base of the falls was spectacular. Water poured over the ledge, thrashed itself into a white froth, and slowly resolved into a dark blue current that swirled downstream. Dense green forest grew at the edge of the rocky shore. Fifty white pelicans floated at the base of the falls, occasionally taking to the air to find the perfect fishing spot.

It was time to release my tiny 250-gram drone from its waterproof case. This toy was an indulgence, but I had convinced myself it might be helpful to scout rapids, look for bears, and get some fantastic landscape shots.

I piloted the drone over the falls, filming the water's fury, the bobbing pelicans, and the landscape's beauty. Then I hit the return to home function on the drone's controller, and then things went seriously off the rails.

The drone disobeyed orders. It changed course and whirred toward the boiling rapids below the falls. I pulled on the controls, but it still behaved as if possessed. It veered wildly up and down and ricocheted into a dense stand of trees. I heard the rotors cutting through the leaves before it slammed into a poplar and spiraled into the undergrowth. Then, the screen of the controller went black. What the hell had happened?

Then I realized I hadn't calibrated the drone's internal compass since I had left home thousands of miles away. It had woken up at a new longitude, latitude, altitude, and declination. Of course, it was confused: none of the satellite signals it was getting made sense. Five minutes spent calibrating the drone for its first Saskatchewan flight would have prevented this.

I set off through the forest, digging through the bushes at the base of the poplar tree. It took an hour, but I finally found the mangled device dangling from a shrub and damaged beyond repair by a hard crash landing. My mistake meant no aerial footage of whitewater and landscapes for the rest of the trip. More important, this misadventure had wasted an hour of perfectly good paddling weather.

It was 6:00 P.M., and I couldn't shake the anxiety about falling behind schedule. This would have been a stunning location to camp, but Hudson Bay was still so far away. Every kilometer covered now added to the margin of safety at the end of the journey, so I decided to push on to the next large lake.

I dug my beloved carbon fiber paddle into the current below Keg Falls, and the shaft snapped in half with a loud *crack* without warning. I was lucky I hadn't been leaning out into a brace at the time, or the boat might have flipped. Cursing like a sailor, I grabbed a backup paddle and regained control of the spinning boat.

It had been a great paddle; using it felt like moving two handfuls of air and made it possible to maintain a high cadence. Unfortunately, its light construction had come at the cost of durability. Smashing the drone had been frustrating, but fracturing this paddle was serious; it had been the main engine of the entire trip until now.

There's a saying that goes, "Two is one, and one is none," meaning that every mission-critical item will inevitably malfunction, get misplaced, or get smashed into a million pieces.

This is a result of Murphy's Law: "Whatever can go wrong will go wrong." With Murphy around, you can't have a single point of failure, and the show must go on whatever happens, breaks, or goes wrong.

To prevent one tumbling domino from sabotaging your entire plan you need backups, which is why I took three paddles on this trip. First, the single-bladed lightweight ZRE carbon-fiber bent-shaft canoe paddle for flatwater that had just snapped. Second, a heavy-duty single-bladed straight-shaft canoe paddle for whitewater. The third paddle was a lightweight folding carbon-fiber double-bladed kayak paddle.

The built-in redundancy meant that if I lost one paddle and broke the other, I'd still have a way to get across lakes or down a river. This quiver of paddles also gave me options to adapt to changing conditions. Straight-shaft paddles are better in whitewater because you can easily use both sides of the blade, whereas bent-shaft paddles give you a substantial biomechanical advantage on flat water. Having different paddles also gave me options to work around injuries because each required different body mechanics.

You can't take multiples of everything because that becomes unwieldy. Instead, I tried to have redundant function, meaning there was more than one way to accomplish the same goal.

I had different scale maps and a GPS unit for navigation. I carried matches and a ferrocerium fire starter, and had a lighter buried in every waterproof bag for making fires. The belt knife on my hip, the river knife attached to my life jacket, and another blade on a multitool ensured I could cut stuff.

My communications gear included a satellite phone, the Garmin GPS, and my phone if I connected it to a satellite dish. I had a tent, a repair kit to fix the tent, and a silicon-coated nylon tarp for shelter if the tent was lost. I had a sleeping bag and enough warm clothing to avoid hypothermia.

I stored my food in two stashes, hundreds of feet apart, to prevent a bear from stealing all my food. To defend against bears, I practiced impeccable camp hygiene, had a bear perimeter alarm, and carried a 12-gauge shotgun.

That night at camp, I tried to repair the broken bent-shaft paddle, but no amount of duct tape and wooden splints fixed the blade enough to transmit force into the water efficiently. If I lost or broke one of the remaining paddles, I'd have to carve a new spare out of a log.

The good news was that all the paper map shards were finally dry, and now I could start slowly reassembling them. Small pieces of paper had to be matched up and then held together with tiny bits of tape. It was a tedious, high-stakes jigsaw puzzle that would go on for days.

As the sun set and the bugs rose, I zipped myself into the tent pitched in the shrubs between charcoal logs, the last remnants of the forest that had stood here before the fire. It had been a long day, and tomorrow I would stop traveling with the current and start clawing my way upstream against a river in flood.

UPSTREAM ON THE REINDEER RIVER

July 6, 2019
Start: A recently burned and overgrown area on
Ourom Lake (55°33'20.0" N 103°13'05.7" W)
Finish: A rocky island in the Reindeer River
(55°48'54.4" N 103°04'28.8" W)
Distance covered: 32 kilometers

Inducing flow is about the balance between the level of skill and the size of the challenge at hand.
—Jeanne Nakamura and Mihály Csikszentmihalyi,
Handbook of Positive Psychology

Today's plan was to leave the Churchill River and start stage 2 of the trip, which involved traveling upstream on the Reindeer River all the way to Reindeer Lake. This river collects water from a vast area extending almost to the Nunavut border and brings it southward. Compared to the Churchill, the Reindeer River had fewer large lakes, which meant I'd frequently be fighting strong currents. A whole new bag of wilderness travel tricks would be required.

I loaded the boat, scuffing my fingers against the rough inner hull as I maneuvered the two heavy bags holding 44 days and 150 pounds of food into place. It would be weeks until I devoured enough calories to make this load less daunting.

Within an hour, I came to the base of some wavy rapids. This was the last hurrah of the Reindeer River, where it jumped and surged one final time before mixing with the still waters of Ourom Lake and adding its flow to the volume of the Churchill River.

Had I been traveling *down* the Reindeer River, these rapids would have been easily navigated and required only a few bracing strokes. But going *up* this whitewater was another story—there was no way to paddle or wade the boat upstream against the current, which meant it was time to portage.

I disgorged the boat's contents onto the rocks beside the rapids, undoing the morning's elaborate packing ritual. The thought of constantly packing and unpacking my gear at every portage ahead filled me with as much trepidation as the portages themselves.

In the old days, the Reindeer River had been a major route into the north country, and the portages would have been well maintained. Nowadays, however, this river is rarely traveled. Canoeists here are infrequent and usually go downriver, running most of the rapids. Native hunters and fishermen are also rare in this part of the river, and when they come through on occasion, they typically blast up the smaller rapids in their motorboats.

Disuse made the portage hard to find. Willows, red osier dogwood, fireweed, and trembling aspen trees had turned the trail back into a forest. I crashed through the bushes to create a new path, stumbling under the heavy loads, wiping away sweat, and swatting at mosquitoes. I considered wearing a bug net to keep the biting insects off my face, but the undergrowth was too dense, and the fragile netting would have been shredded by the branches protruding everywhere.

Finally, I carried all the gear above the worst part of the rapid. The current was still too swift to paddle against, but the shore was a mix of boulders and bedrock, which made for relatively easy walking. It was time to use another time-honored method for ascending rivers called "tracking."

Tracking is using two ropes to pull your boat *upriver* against the current. First, you attach ropes to the front and back of your boat. Then, you shove the boat into the current, giving the front rope a little more slack to angle the boat outward at a 20° to 30° angle so the current can catch it and pull it sideways into the river. With the angle set and the sideways pressure of the water keeping your boat from bouncing along the shoreline rocks, you haul your load upstream while walking along the bank.

Tracking is an elegant way to go upstream and is usually much easier than portaging. It's a complicated procedure, though, and requires continuous adjustments to keep your boat at the correct angle, stop it from swamping, and prevent it from getting pinned on a rock.

While tracking, you're typically walking on an unstable shoreline, jumping from boulder to boulder, and wading through shallow sections of water. If you get distracted, it's not only your boat at risk but your body, too. You could easily be pulled into the river, get entangled in the ropes, or turn an ankle.

I enjoyed the tracking. Feeling the resistance from the wet rope in my hands was important. Barely submerged rocks in the path of the boat were important. Shrubs blocking the path along the waterline were important. Integrating all the information coming into my brain and making consequential decisions created an intense immersion in the moment where nothing else mattered. It was a pleasurable flow state where, for a brief time, it felt like I was doing what I was meant to do.

I recalled a conversation with a helicopter pilot years ago as he dropped me off on a survey project. I had asked him what the colors on his oil pressure gauge meant. He pointed to the green area on the dial and said, "This zone is for my clients."

Then he pointed to the yellow, "This zone is for if I get into trouble."

Finally pointing at the red, he said, "And this is for the wife and kids."

His job didn't pay him enough to operate in the red zone, and he always wanted to leave a little in reserve just in case things went wrong. Given the extreme consequences of crashing a helicopter, he didn't want to push the edge of the envelope daily.

Staying out of the red zone also applies to canoeing. When I was eighteen I befriended Gino Bergeron, an outdoorsman based in Quebec City who would go on long solo canoe and ski expeditions after every breakup in his tumultuous love life. Our meeting was inspiring because it opened my eyes to the possibility that real people could do things like this on their own. If he could do it, then I could do it, too.

Gino gave me some of the best advice I ever received for solo traveling . . .

"You can go out into the bush by yourself, you can run whitewater by yourself, you can do hard things by yourself. But when you're by yourself, the trick is always to stay a full level below what you know you can do. That way, you leave something in reserve for those life-and-death situations."

His admonition sounds a bit like the helicopter pilot who wanted to keep the needle in the green, doesn't it?

The time to push your limits is when you're in fairly safe, controlled conditions where the challenge is high and the consequences of failure are low. Don't go to your paddling limits in remote northern whitewater; instead, practice difficult maneuvers in easy whitewater on warm southern rivers with friends standing by to rescue you.

Pushing yourself to the edge of breaking is often considered brave, but the bravest guide who ever worked on Everest is dead. Similarly, the second bravest guide and the third bravest Everest guides are also dead. Bravery and the ability to push past your limits are valuable when something has gone wrong, but you shouldn't lead with it. In marginal situations, it's always better to leave something in the tank.

Upstream progress on the Reindeer River was slow. It took 2½ hours to ascend the 5 kilometers using a mix of paddling, tracking, and wading, which was less than a third of my usual speed. But it was bearable because ascending a river isn't really about the distance you cover horizontally; instead, it's about the difficulty of the terrain and the meters you gain vertically.

By early afternoon, the river widened and became a slow-moving lake with a current so lazy that it didn't hinder upriver progress. Rocky cliffs were fringed with giant blocks of stone, lying where they had spalled off from the main face long ago. The bare granite shoreline was topped with black spruce and jack pine, with trembling aspen and birch scattered along the water's edge. This was classic Canadian Shield country, the same land-scape that had sung to the Group of Seven, a group of painters operating in the 1920s and '30s who redefined how Canadians see the wilderness. This iconic wilderness first grabbed me by the throat as a little boy camping in the forests of Ontario and has been calling to me ever since.

I paddled for hours. Finally, at 6:00 P.M., I climbed a rocky ridge con-necting two islands, the dry lichen crunching beneath my feet as I set up camp. Much of that evening was spent rearranging map shards and con-necting the individually useless pieces into a usable whole using tiny strips of duct tape.

I had only covered thirty-two kilometers today, but I wasn't bothered. That was still a respectable distance, given how difficult upriver travel can be and how destroyed my body was. Would I be able to continue this pace given the obstacles ahead? I did not know.

A LEG-WOBBLING PORTAGE

July 7
Start: A rocky island in the Reindeer River
(55°48'54.4" N 103°04'28.8" W)
Finish: A tiny rocky outcrop between Steephill Lake
and Royal Lake (55°59'26.4" N 103°05'50.7" W)
Distance covered: 28 kilometers

Portaging is like hitting yourself on the head with a hammer: it feels so good when you stop.

—Bill Mason, *Path of the Paddle:*
An Illustrated Guide to the Art of Canoeing

The sun crept above the horizon at 4:30 A.M. and made a mockery of my attempts to remain asleep. Pain shot through my lower back as I sat up; my swollen hand had improved, but it seemed like that inflammation had now spread out to every other joint in my body. Or maybe the extreme soreness was because my one functioning transplant kidney just couldn't filter enough of the exercise-created waste products out of my blood; I resolved to keep hydrating, even if I didn't feel like it.

I forced myself to my feet and limped through the morning camp routine, bent over like an eighty-year-old. I had no idea where the strength to fight the current would come from today. I needed to let my aching body recover. *Maybe I'll just do a half day today. Put in a good morning, and then do nothing but recuperate in the afternoon*, I thought.

Despite feeling absolutely pummeled, it did feel normal now to wake up in a tent and prepare for a day on the water. I always find that it takes about a week for things to click into trip mode. Once in that groove, extraneous worries fade away, and you're immersed in a radical simplicity. Your whole world, labor, and all critical decisions are reduced to traveling, eating, and sleeping.

The first twenty kilometers were highly variable: slow river sections alternated with pulsing current where every foot of upstream progress had to be fought for by paddling, tracking, and wading. River levels were high, and the regular banks were underwater. Water surged through dense bushes that grew well back from the regular shoreline. It was raining, and I wondered how much that extra water would raise the river. This certainly wouldn't help my progress.

The high water, pushy current, and large waves made wading up the swifts, submerged to the hip, particularly tricky. One slip on a wet boulder could have resulted in the current surging over the gunwales and into the boat, which would probably have been the point of no return. A canoe filled with water weighs thousands of pounds, and it would have been ripped out of my fingers by the surging current.

I thought about what to do if my boat spun away in the river without me. I decided that it depended on what was downstream. If there was quiet water at the bottom of the swift, I'd run downstream along the shore and try to retrieve the canoe when it washed up on a gravel bar. But under other circumstances, the best thing to do might be to jump into the river, let the current take me downstream, swim to the boat, and try to get it to shore. And if I lost the boat entirely, at least I had enough gear in my PFD to build a shelter, light a fire, and call for rescue on my Garmin GPS unit.

When things go wrong, choosing from a small set of preselected options is much faster than coming up with new solutions out of thin air. Additionally, preplanning what to do in this situation gave me something to think about during those long hours of grinding upriver.

Shortly after noon, I reached Steephill Rapids, a constriction where the river thundered around three islands that blocked the outlet of a large lake above. There was no way I could ascend this cascade in the boat, which meant it was time to portage.

I could not find the start of the portage at the bottom of the rapids. According to the map, there was supposed to be a trail that started at the bottom of the rapids, but I couldn't find it. I guessed the old path was completely overgrown, so the only solution was to bush-crash a new route through the thick forest.

After everything was unloaded on the slick rocky shore, I climbed a seemingly vertical slope through the trees on my hands and knees while holding the end of a tracking rope in my mouth. Mossy footholds often slid out from under me without notice and left me grasping at bushes and trees to avoid sliding back into the river. Sticky spruce resin soon coated the palms of my hands. When I reached a small ledge, I braced myself and hauled the canoe up the slope behind me with the rope. Finally, I climbed back down and lugged the backpacks up one at a time. "The mystery of why they call this Steephill Portage is solved," I muttered.

It took several cycles of climbing and hauling before I got the canoe and the gear to the top of the treacherous slope.

According to the map, I was now standing on the portage trail, but the spruce forest was uniformly dense in all directions. All signs of the historical path had been reabsorbed into the forest. My maps were based on thirty-five-year-old survey data, and a lot had apparently happened in those intervening years.

It would have been easy to get lost in that forest, so I needed a compass bearing from the map to go the right way. I pulled out the map case that held today's bits of paper and identified my exact location and the nearest point of the next lake I wanted to reach. To take a bearing, I connected those two points with the straight side of the compass frame. Then, I rotated the bezel, a ring on top of the compass, until the lines within it were parallel with the north-south lines on the map.

Now, it was time to export theory into reality. I stood and rotated the compass in the real world until the magnetic needle sat inside the red arrow of the bezel. The body of the compass now pointed in the direction I needed to go. The way, however, was barricaded by a thicket of closely packed trees.

Carrying the canoe through that brush was impossible, so I dropped it onto the moss. Then I put my head down and used my hat and head as a battering ram to bulldoze through the undergrowth while dragging the boat on the forest floor behind me. I left a trail of snapped branches behind, and the forest retaliated by clawing my face, hands, and shoulders. A mixture of sweat, blood, bug spray, and sunscreen trickled into my eyes. Then it began to rain, and all the mosquitoes came out.

It took three hours of backbreaking labor to complete the relatively short 600-meter portage. When I reached the water again, I was drunk with fatigue. This had been the hardest challenge of the trip so far and the most leg-wobbling portage I had done in decades.

Wearily, I stuffed everything into the boat and continued upriver.

I came to a possible campsite location on a polished bedrock ledge. I had completed the half day of work I had promised myself, and this would have been the perfect place to lounge, rest, and recover. But in the last thirty minutes, the rain had stopped, a tailwind had sprung up, and the clouds had split to reveal the blue skies above. Traveling conditions were now perfect.

It would have been criminal to ignore such good canoeing weather. *I have to turn good weather into good miles*, I told myself, *I'll rest on a day when I have cold rain and a headwind!* So, instead of making camp early, I hoisted the sail, felt the tug of the wind, and increased my paddling cadence. Soon I was heading northward at a very respectable clip.

Eventually, the lake narrowed into a small rapid; the water flowed swiftly with patches of slower water along the shore. I accelerated in the large eddy at the bottom of the rapid, then lurched into the current and jetted across the water to the next bit of slow water. The wind in the sail and a few strategic paddle strokes kept the boat going upriver, bouncing from eddy to eddy until it arrived in the calm waters at the top of the rapid. A giant smile split my face; only a few splashes of cool water had come over the gunwales and no portaging or wading had been required. I felt like a kid after a successful cookie jar heist, and for a sweet minute my broken body didn't bother me at all.

A marathon runner once told me, "On days that I don't feel like running, I give myself permission to quit, but only after I put on my running clothes and lace up my shoes." Most of the time, the very act of getting dressed for running built enough momentum to propel her outside and into her workout.

I often used this same trick for my jiu-jitsu practice. Whenever I felt tired and uncertain about training, I told myself that I only needed to go to class and put on my gi; if, after doing that, I still didn't feel like training, then it was okay to bail and go home again. This bargain usually led to my staying and working out. Occasionally, I'd limp to class only to turn around and leave, but this was rare, usually no more than once a year. On the whole, permitting myself *not* to train led to *more* training than navigating the situation purely based on how I felt.

Similarly, this trip, too, was fueled by lies. I had often told myself, *Just get in the boat and paddle for a couple of hours—you don't need to go very far today.* Then, inevitably, that would turn into a full day, and I'd cover an additional thirty, forty, or fifty kilometers.

A body at rest tends to remain at rest, so getting started is the most crucial part of any endeavor. It's tough to crawl out of your sleeping bag in the morning when your body aches, to write the first paragraph of a chapter, or to sign up at a gym to get back in shape.

In those groan-filled moments, don't pull the metaphorical covers over your head and go back to sleep; instead, tell yourself whatever falsehoods or half-truths you need to get your ass in gear. If it still doesn't work, at least you gave it a shot. But most of the time, once the roller coaster slowly clanks over the top of the first hill, momentum takes over, and the ride continues of its own accord.

I call this the Just the Tip Principle (just the tip, just for a second, just to see how it feels . . .). To get started, give yourself permission to quit if it doesn't go well. Lie to yourself to trick you into taking that first paddle stroke, and then use that momentum to carry you through the rest of the day.

That night, I camped on a soft bed of moss high on a slightly concave rocky ledge and studied the loons on the mirror-calm water. These black and white aquatic birds are related to cormorants and are between a duck and a goose in size. Each loon pair has its own bay on a lake, which the fiercely territorial males protect with daggerlike beaks, frequently stabbing their rivals to death. Loons have even killed bald eagles hunting their babies by stabbing them in the heart with their pointed beaks.

Tonight, the three-note loon riffs mostly called out, "Where are you?," but they also sang songs indicating danger, threat, and contentment. The fierce concerto echoed across the still water as I ate dinner and reassembled the final paper fragments into usable maps. Some portions of the maps had been damaged beyond recovery, but I was pretty sure I'd be able to find my way across the landscape by compensating with my GPS and dead reckoning.

My navigational capabilities had been restored, but I was still ashamed of myself. The great map fiasco was entirely my fault. How much time had been wasted because I hadn't tested the map cases' water-tightness or the waterproofing compound's efficacy before the trip? Fifteen minutes of experimentation before the trip would have saved days of difficulty in the wilderness. I hoped there were no other overlooked vulnerabilities among my critical items.

AGAINST THE CURRENT

July 8, 2019
Start: A tiny rocky outcrop between Steephill Lake and Royal Lake
(55°59'26.4" N 103°05'50.7" W)
Finish: A rocky bluff above a small lake on the Reindeer River
(56°10'18.3" N 103°10'57.7" W)
Distance covered: 25 kilometers

Now, here, you see, it takes all the running you can do, to keep in the same place. If you want to get somewhere else, you must run at least twice as fast as that!

—The Red Queen, *Alice in Wonderland*

Conditions were difficult today right from the start. As soon as the boat slid into the water, a cold wind from the north opposed every meter of progress. For hours I slow-motion battled across three lakes, using every last landform, topographic hump, and spruce tree to reduce the force of the wind. *It has to get easier than this*, I hoped.

In the afternoon, the river narrowed into a channel that cut through a large wetland choked with willow bushes, rushes, and reeds. In calm water and with no headwinds, I usually cruised at a steady pace of five kilometers per hour. Progress here was much slower; with both the wind and the current opposing me, I had to paddle four kilometers per hour just to stay in the same place, even while hissing the boat through the shoreline reeds as close to the banks as possible.

Given the conditions, I attacked the river in a series of all-out sprints. I paddled frantically to reach six or seven kilometers per hour, then used that speed to push through the wind and current. This frantic pace could only be sustained for ten to fifteen minutes before my failing muscles refused to make further progress. There was no quiet water to rest, so when I was exhausted, I torpedoed my boat into the willow bushes and hung onto the knobby branches. There I sat stuporous until my aching arms, shoulders, and back had regained feeling, after which I'd head back into the current for another round of frantic paddling.

These work and rest periods repeated themselves over and over, creating a hypnotic rhythm for the afternoon. Hour after hour, I slowly ascended the river, watching as subtle landscape features appeared ahead of me, drew closer, and then disappeared behind me.

As I worked my way upriver, my mind slipped back to a July evening in 1992. I was twenty-two years old, had just graduated from university, and had been crisscrossing the height of land between Lake Superior and James Bay in a canoe for six weeks. After a difficult but rewarding solo trip, I was now in the tiny town of Longlac, Ontario, euphoric at having completed the trip and salivating at the idea of stuffing myself at the one local pizzeria.

While my extra-large pizza was baking I called home on a pay phone to reassure my parents that I was okay. That ended up being the worst conversation of my life.

In a shaky voice, my dad explained that my brother, Peter, had been killed in a motorcycle accident the week before when I was still deep in the bush.

Most of Peter's teenage years had been spent in a haze of drug addiction, homelessness, and collisions with the law. At age twenty-one, he had finally turned his life around, quit the drugs, and reconciled with my parents. He had been accepted into flight school to become a helicopter pilot and was selling some of his possessions to fund that dream.

Two kids arrived at our rural property late in the evening to buy his dirt bike. Peter jumped on the bike and fired up the engine to show them that the bike worked (and maybe to say goodbye to it). Then with the hubris of a young man who acts as if he will live forever, he set off into the inky night at full throttle without headlights or a helmet on his head.

Our neighbor was returning home from work and, seeing only a dark road without oncoming headlights, spun his car into his driveway without signaling. My brother and his dark bike were roaring down the road at full speed and slammed into the car that had so suddenly turned into his path.

My parents heard the booming crash, the shatter of glass, and then the screaming. "Mom. Mom. Mom!" Peter's arm and leg were broken, but those weren't the worst injuries. In his brain, the swelling that would kill him had already started.

The police showed up and mistook the aggressiveness induced by his brain injury for drunkenness. The cops arrested him, he tried to kick and bite them, and they handcuffed him. My mother was sobbing, and it took forever to get an ambulance. It was a complete shitshow. Later, at the hospital, the surgeons removed a portion of his skull in an attempt to relieve the intracranial pressure. It was to no avail; he died on the operating table.

I hung up the phone, shattered. The trip was over, and I needed to go home.

Late that night, I stumbled onto the Greyhound bus that passed through town, then transferred onto a train. The entire journey from Longlac to Toronto took twenty sleepless hours. The swing from the heights of elation to deepest depression left me dizzy.

The trip was made even stranger when a raucous cheerleading squad invaded the train. They had just won some cheerleading competition and were on top of the world. These teenagers laughed, hollered, and occasionally burst into chants—"1, 2, 3, 4. What's the team that we adore?"—as they celebrated their glorious victory. They were having a great time, but for me, it was awful. All I wanted was silence.

At home, my parents and remaining brothers—Matthias, Christoph, and Anton—were devastated. Every room was soaked in grief. The kitchen window overlooked the dirt road where Peter had had his fatal accident. My poor parents donated Peter's organs after his death and received some small solace, knowing that this saved the lives of several other young men.

The year after Peter died, I was deeply adrift, disconnected from society, and unsure of what to do next. I worked as a bike courier on Toronto's icy streets to support myself, then drifted to Montreal to work in a lab. At night, I returned to a tiny, nondescript apartment in a rooming house where other lost men limped through life.

I didn't know what I wanted and didn't know how to begin to figure it out. I mourned my brother but was also filled with anger. How could he have done something that stupid? How dare he put the rest of us through this?

One afternoon I wandered into the university map library in search of distraction. In that dangerous place, I started looking for maps of the Seal River. The remoteness and wildlife of the Seal in northern Manitoba make it one of the holy grails of canoe tripping, but honestly, the real motivation to get into the wilderness was that it seemed infinitely better than where I was.

After studying the maps, the question became how one would get to the headwaters of the Seal. I couldn't afford to charter a float plane, so I started playing connect-the-lakes on the library's 1:50,000 scale maps, the most detailed maps available for the area. Initially, I just wanted to use the intricate Canadian Shield geography to access the Seal via another river system, but one thing led to another and the project morphed into a challenge to connect as many river systems as possible.

When I emerged back into the sunlight, I had a tentative route that jumped from watershed to watershed and connected Jasper, Alberta, in the Rocky Mountains, to Churchill, Manitoba, on the coast of Hudson Bay. It was an insane plan, but in that library my pain had disappeared; the only things that had mattered for a few hours were those distant lakes and rivers.

It took eight months to prepare for that trip, and those preparations gave me purpose. It was something to focus on, look forward to, and distract me from the listlessness I was feeling in the wake of my brother's death. Maybe I was also chasing the dragon, attempting to regain the peace I had felt in the map library.

Even though the route went halfway across Canada and lay beyond the reach of roads and civilization, I knew from the beginning that this would have to be a solo trip. My previous paddling partners were firmly entrenched in their jobs or studies, making three months away impossible. But more important, I didn't want to make my plans contingent on anyone else; my world had just been rocked by the consequences of another person's decisions, and now I wanted to avoid being derailed by anyone else. The surest way to achieve this would be to try it alone.

On a cool, sunny day in mid-June, I finally pushed off into the milky waters of the Athabasca River. The fine glacial silt hissed against the hull of the boat, and clouds raced between the mountain peaks that lined the river. It felt like starting over; this was the same canoe filled with the same packs, and once again, I was heading into the unknown. The rug being pulled out from under me at the end of the previous year's solo trip had ultimately been incredibly disorienting; hopefully, this attempt would end better.

A few days in, I was gliding along the shore under the overhanging spruce trees. The repetitive paddling occupied my body, hypnotized my mind, and disabled my defenses. The grief locked deep in my chest shook itself free and rose. The plume surfaced, and I started sobbing violently. The anger, grief, and unfairness all came tumbling out for the first time. I paddled onward, a speck of despondency on a river visible from space.

That was the first time I had ever cried about Peter, but it would not be the last. The Athabasca River was my grief counselor. The solitude and time provided the space to process feelings locked away for the previous year. As the river continued north, I started feeling much lighter. The moving meditation and privacy of the deep wilderness had brought me through the worst of the sadness. I still felt flashes of sadness, but the raw grief about my brother's mortality was gone.

Peter's death was my first intensely experienced loss, but not the last. Not long after Peter's death, I sat at my grandmother's bed as she slipped away, inch by inch, until her last agonal breath. Then another brother of mine—Matthias—drowned foolishly in his early twenties, that age when young men think they are immortal and immune from consequences.

Finally, having witnessed the death of two of her sons, my mother also passed, ALS slowly paralyzing her respiratory muscles until she asphyxiated.

As a firefighter, I've worked around hundreds of dead and dying people; some went peacefully, and others went kicking and screaming. Death is never easy to watch, but it's also an honor to bear witness to someone's final moments. Each of these deaths was a tragedy, but they were also precious gifts; they were memento mori, indisputable reminders that life is short and your number of days uncertain. Everybody knows this intellectually, but it helps to be viscerally reminded occasionally.

Blink, and your childhood friends have gray hair. Blink again, and some of them are dead. Hopefully, they lived full lives before they passed and left some small mark on the universe.

My life has the most meaning at the brink of rapids, feeling storms shake my tent, and watching bears forage in the bushes. Your definition of living life to the fullest may be different, and that's okay; just remember that our mayfly lives are all careening toward death, and there's no time to waste. Get your ass in gear so that you can say you've truly lived.

> *I think of you often*
> *When you come, I will say "Welcome*
> *See what I have done with this time."*
> —Eva Schubert, "On Death"

As evening came on, I started worrying about campsites on this section of the Reindeer River. My body desperately needed rest, but the wetland just went on and on. It had been hours since there had been any dry land suitable for pitching a tent.

Just before sunset, the river channel widened into a small lake where a single rocky knoll protruded from the water. This rock was wide enough to squeeze a tent upon, which was enough for me.

Even by the standards of a challenging trip, today had been particularly difficult. I had paddled, portaged, and waded for fourteen hours straight. I was happy with my level of effort but not my results; all that effort had been spent to cover only twenty-eight kilometers today, which probably wasn't enough.

The problem was the wind. There had been significant headwinds on five of eight days of the trip so far. I estimated that the wind had reduced the distance covered each day by ten to fifteen kilometers; compounded over fifty days, and that lost distance severely ate into my safety margin.

Self-doubt snuck into my brain for the millionth time, this time cloaked in a veneer of reasonableness.

It's not your fault there's been so much wind . . . These high water levels are beyond your control . . . Maybe it's unrealistic to push this hard at age fifty with so many surgeries and injuries . . .

Self-doubt had a point. There WERE many factors out of my control, and objectively, there was a real chance that I'd be unable to finish the trip. Everything hinged on how long it took to ascend the Reindeer River and cross Reindeer Lake.

If getting to the Thlewiaza River proved impossible, at least I had options. For example, I could divert and paddle the Seal or Fond du Lac rivers. The main problem was that I didn't have the maps for these other rivers. In the North, it's not as simple as pointing your boat downstream and following the current; these waterways follow the unpredictable gouges left in the rock by glaciers and other geological trauma over the millennia. The rivers lurch left and right, take strange turns, and split into island mazes. Even finding where a river exits a lake isn't simple; without a map you could spend days searching the irregular shoreline and still not find the current.

Thankfully, this was a problem I didn't have to solve right away. For now, the answer was simple: push on every day that it was safe to travel and trust that the right course of action would reveal itself in time.

After setting up camp, I was shattered. I slumped to the ground and just lay there. My muscles felt so weak that returning to the boat tomorrow seemed like a perverse impossibility.

I don't know how long I lay there, but when I opened my eyes, I noticed beavers swimming along the edge of the sunset-tinged lake and loon choruses echoing over the water. A difficult day had transitioned into the perfect evening, and suddenly, the aches and pains seemed far away.

This careening of emotions was not infrequent on this trip, from the lowest lows to the highest highs. Being continuously exhausted had worn down my usual inhibitions, making my responses to changing circumstances raw and unfiltered. It was the very essence of being in the moment.

God grant me the strength to change the things I can, the serenity to accept the things I cannot change, and the wisdom to know the difference, I reminded myself, then tried to sleep, but I knew that a significant obstacle lay just upstream from the campsite.

DAY 9:

DEVIL RAPIDS

July 9, 2019
Start: A rocky bluff above a small lake on the Reindeer River
(56°10'18.3" N 103°10'57.7" W)
Finish: A camp in thick forest on Big Island, 2 kilometers south of Southend,
Saskatchewan (56°19'02.0" N 103°14'59.8" W)
Distance covered: 25 kilometers

The heights by great men reached and kept were not attained by sudden flight, but they while their companions slept, were toiling upward in the night.

—Henry Wadsworth Longfellow

After paddling a few kilometers, I came to a deep canyon where whitewater surged around a collection of small rocky islands in the middle of the river. This was Devil Rapids, and ascending it would be a complex and challenging problem. The current here was too swift to ascend by paddling, and the water too deep for wading. Tracking the boat upriver with ropes was unworkable because the riverbank where I would need to walk was mostly submerged.

All rapids can be portaged, but not all portages are equally feasible. This canyon terrain was much more vertical than you would expect from northern Saskatchewan. Getting around Devil Rapids on foot would have required free-climbing to the canyon rim, hauling all my equipment up behind me with ropes, then bush crashing through dense forest before descending back to the river with more rock climbing. Doing the portage this way would take at least one or two days of brutal, punishing work.

While researching this trip, I talked to two groups who had tried to ascend the Reindeer River. They had given up at this point; unable to get past these rapids, they had used a satellite phone to charter a float plane to get them off the river.

I ferried back and forth at the bottom of the rapids, looking for an alternative route upriver. Ascending along the left shore didn't look good, and the right shore looked worse.

Before embarking on the world's most wretched portage up and over the cliffs, I exited the boat and climbed to the top of a large stone block at the bottom of the rapids. The elevated viewpoint gave me a bird's eye view of the current and rocks upstream.

After staring at the water for a long time from this new perspective, a plan slowly came together. Maybe, just maybe, there was a route through the rapids. It would require a tricky combination of paddling, clambering, and tracking, but it was better than the alternative.

The ascent would be marginal and possibly result in capsizing. To prepare for potential immersion, I zipped up my rain gear and tightened the cuffs at the ends of my pants and sleeves. Then, I double-checked my PFD to ensure that none of the straps were loose, the knife was accessible, and that essential survival gear was tucked into the zipping pockets of the life jacket. Even if I lost my boat, the survival gear in the PFD would hopefully keep me alive long enough to use the SOS function on the Garmin and receive help.

A long eddy lay tight along the shore at the bottom left of the rapid. A rocky cliff was on one side of the eddy, and a long chute of standing waves on the other. I wanted to build up speed, exit at the top of the eddy, and jet ferry across the haystacks to just below a jumbled pile of rocks at the rapids' center.

I stabbed the heavy whitewater paddle into the eddy and charged up this patch of slower water. I paddled as hard as I could, but the boat skidded sideways off a rock hidden under the water's surface. The canoe was now in the current and was carried downriver, bouncing and spinning in the turbulent water. I swore and stabilized the boat with the most decisive brace I could muster.

I regrouped and began my second attempt. Again, I dug with the paddle, and the boat went faster and faster as it climbed up the eddy. This time, I avoided the submerged rock and exited the vortex at the correct place. I felt the boat get yanked into the current and fought to maintain the correct angle as it shot across the waves. Finally, I paddled like mad to get into the calmer waters behind the mid-river boulders. I was halfway up the rapids, just beside a boulder ledge where rivulets of whitewater poured between the rocks.

I hung onto a wet boulder to keep the bouncing boat in place while pondering the next move. This middle section of the river was shallower, so I got out of the boat and felt the cold river water fill up my rain pants. Then I started wading through the hip-deep water between the boulders, dragging the boat like the world's biggest and most reluctant dog. I crept upstream, climbing over rocks and pressing up chutes of water. This was tricky work: slipping here would have resulted in being carried downstream through some big whitewater.

Eventually, I came to the downstream edge of a small bedrock island. The current on both sides of the island was much too violent to ascend with ropes and tracking, so I had to drag the boat ashore and portage everything to the upstream edge, which took an entire hour. This island was almost at the top of the rapids—only about thirty feet of seemingly moderate current separated the rock from the slower, deeper water above the whitewater. I planned to get to that calm water by paddling like a berserker, so I dug as hard as possible with the paddle. It nearly worked.

The current here was deceptive, much faster than the small ripples indicated. There was no way to climb into that quiet water, and now the boat was being pushed sideways across the river toward a large whitewater chute. I had come too far and worked too hard to get snakes-and-laddered back down to the bottom of the rapid.

I opened up the angle and paddled as hard as possible for a small eddy on the far shore. The canoe shot sideways across the top of the large chute, just a few feet above a series of swamping haystacks. The boat careened into the slower water, and I tilted it upstream like a motorcyclist leans into a turn to avoid flipping. The boat had so much speed now that it didn't stop in the eddy; instead, it lurched over some boulders and slid partially up onto shore before coming to a halt. I grabbed a tree branch to keep from slipping back into the maelstrom.

It wasn't pretty, but it had worked. I hadn't gotten washed downstream, the boat hadn't capsized, and I was 90 percent of the way up the rapids, albeit on the opposite shore from where I had started.

There was one more obstacle; a boulder the size of a dump truck blocked the route along the shore and jutted out into the swirling current.

I pulled the boat onto some low rocks and climbed over the giant boulder with the bow and stern lines clenched in my teeth. Once on the other side of the massive rock, it was time to track the boat around the rock. I yanked the boat into the water with the two lines and nudged it into the current, trying to interpret each pull and shudder of the lines in my hands.

Finally, the boat eased around the boulder and came within reach; I exhaled with relief. In yet another wild mood swing, the grimness and determination that had gripped me for the entire ascent dissolved, leaving giddiness in its place. Days of difficult and dangerous portaging had been avoided. Years of mucking around in boats had given me the skills needed to get to the top of Devil Rapids in only a few hours.

One year after struggling up Devil Rapids myself, I came across J. B. Tyrrell's description of the same whitewater back from back in 1896 . . .

At the upper end of this well defined channel the water rushes between high, almost vertical rocky walls forming what is known as Manitou Rapids, where the canoes ascending are passed with difficulty over a low, rocky island in the middle of the stream and then paddled with all possible speed across the rushing current to an eddy in a bay on the eastern bank, failing to reach with they are sometimes engulfed in the heavy waves below.

—J. B. Tyrrell, *Report on the Doobaunt, Kazan and Ferguson Rivers and the North-West Coast of Hudson Bay*

Tyrrell had called this place Manitou Rapids, and my map called it Devil Rapids, but both he and I had arrived at the same solution for the same problem. It would have been useful to have read his account before reinventing the wheel.

At first, the euphoria from ascending the rapids was enough to keep me going, but then the river widened into a series of lakes much more exposed to headwinds than the canyon around Devil Rapids. My energy plummeted; it felt like I was dragging a cinderblock behind the boat. I needed a performance-enhancing drug, so I dug out a set of earbuds and popped them into my ears. As I paddled, I listened to Mike Duncan's podcast series about the French Revolution, which I had downloaded to my phone before leaving home. This mental stimulation disengaged my brain from my aching body, allowing the muscles to chug away and propel the boat northward.

I had never listened to music or podcasts on any previous wilderness trips because of ideas about violating the purity of the whistling wind, the splashing waves, and the cry of the geese. But now I needed something to distract me from the new normal of pain and exhaustion.

I came to Fafard Lake, which had both deep water and sandy shallow sections. I wasn't sure if I could safely navigate the large waves the wind raised on the lake's deep portions, so decided it would be clever to stick to the shallows.

These shallow areas were dotted with reeds, rushes, and horsetails, and the water was only a couple of inches deep in places. Soon, the boat got stuck in the mud, and paddle power alone could not drive it forward anymore.

Seeing no other way to proceed, I stepped out of the boat into the water, wrapped the tracking line around my shoulder, and dragged the boat across the mud flats like an ox pulling a plow. The boat's keel carved a deep groove in the sediment; this was hard going, but at least it used a different set of muscles from paddling. It would have been a bizarre sight from shore: a man walking on water in the middle of a big lake, dragging a boat on a rope.

The extensive shallows held surprises. I passed a clod of horsetail stems lumped together and floating in a few inches of water. The crater of this volcano-shaped mound of plant matter contained a pair of elongate light-brown eggs. This nest and these eggs belonged to a pair of horned grebes. These fish-eating waterbirds build bizarre floating nests where they mate and lay their eggs. When the grebe chicks hatched they'd ride on their parents' backs, the waterfowl version of a baby monkey clinging to its mother.

I trudged northward on the lake, mud squelching beneath my neoprene boots, and eventually reached deeper waters where I could paddle again. Soon, I came to Whitesand Dam, a large concrete structure built eighty years ago to control water levels in the Reindeer River.

At the top of the sandy trail around the dam, five people were disembarking from a motorboat. This was a Cree fishing guide and a family of four, his clients from Alberta. They had come to shore to build a fire to warm up and cook walleye caught on the lake. These were the first people I'd talked to in eight days, so we chit-chatted a bit, but I didn't want to overstay my welcome; the family was paying for a remote wilderness experience, and it didn't seem appropriate to have a long conversation.

Before I set out, the guide warned me about the windy conditions ahead on Marchand Lake.

"I'd stick close to shore if I was you. Some big waves out there!"

I had intended to stick close to shore anyway, but it was nice to have that plan endorsed by a local. I took his advice seriously because every native person in these communities knows at least one person who drowned on a lake when the weather turned nasty.

Hugging the shore greatly increased the distance I had to go. Instead of going in a straight line, I slowly traced the indentations of three large bays. These detours, the headwind, and my diminishing strength reduced my speed to an absolutely dismal pace. My earphones were now playing old-time acoustic blues; the rhythm helped put in weary stroke after weary stroke, mile after mile.

Finally, I reached the "Big Island," the five-kilometer-long cork at the bottom of Reindeer Lake. The native village of Southend was just ahead, and I could have pushed on but the only accommodation there was at a fishing lodge six kilometers outside of town. A hot shower would have been lovely, but it wasn't worth the extra trudging on a dusty dirt road. Instead, I pitched the tent on the thick moss in a dark section of forest beside the river.

Entombed in my sleeping bag, my shoulder throbbed, my back ached, and my body twitched from exhaustion. I was no longer having fun in the way that most people conceive it, but not all fun is created equal.

It was the mountain climbing community that first started using the terms Type I, Type II, and Type III fun. These numbers describe a continuum where you've got pure hedonistic pleasure at one end and life-threatening suffering at the other.

Type I fun is fun in the moment. During a Type I activity, you don't want the experience to end, and you remember it fondly afterward.

Imagine a tailwind carrying you across a lake underneath a warm blue sky . . . A guitar playing as your campfire crackles at dusk after a long day of hiking . . . Running easy whitewater with friends ready to help you if you flip . . . These are all Type I fun.

Type II fun involves a lot of suffering and usually isn't enjoyable at the time. But if you persevere, you'll usually be glad you didn't quit. This is the embodiment of the "character-building experience." It's the ideal zone for personal growth and builds resilience, endurance, and mental toughness. It also fulfils an intense need for challenge and makes you a more capable human being.

But you can overdo it, which brings us to Type III fun, which isn't something you should try to create on purpose. By definition it involves an activity where something went very wrong and resulted in a high chance of death. Making deals with God and activating your emergency beacon during Type III fun isn't uncommon, and afterward, you swear that you'll never do anything that stupid again.

Nobody ever says, "Man, I can't wait to flip my boat in the middle of a large lake without rescue nearby again." But if you survive, and after the passage of time dulls the embarrassment, it leaves you with a great story.

Today's ascent of Devil Rapids, crossing across Fafard Lake, and fighting the wind had been challenging, but as I sat back in my tent, padded by a thick bed of moss, I felt a slight smile spread across my face. Type II fun had been achieved, and tomorrow I should reach Reindeer Lake, a legendarily large, dangerous, and beautiful lake.

OUT ONTO THE LAKE

July 10, 2019
Start: A camp in thick forest on Big Island, 2 kilometers south of Southend,
Saskatchewan. (56°19'02.0" N 103°14'59.8" W)
Finish: A cabin under construction, MacFarlane Island, Reindeer Lake
(56°34'36.9" N 102°51'49.0" W)
Distance covered: 42 kilometers

Should you be lucky enough to be moving across a calm surface
with mirrored clouds, you may have the sensation of suspension
between heaven and earth, of paddling not on the water but
through the skies.

—Sigurd Olson, *The Singing Wilderness*

I parked the canoe beside an aluminum fishing boat on a pocket beach just outside the hamlet of Southend. A strange car sat on one side of the beach; it looked like a large blue VW Beetle with flat sides, little round windows, and tracks instead of wheels. I recognized this design from a museum in Winnipeg—it was a snowcar built in the 1950s by Bombardier, the Quebecois snowmobile manufacturer. It was sitting on a trailer waiting for snow, still in service after seventy years.

This town has less than a thousand residents and sits at the southern tip of Reindeer Lake. A handful of dusty roads curve around the hills of the townsite, and small houses look out onto the southernmost bay of the lake. It's a very pretty place.

I had been here before. More than twenty years ago, the local band brought me in to teach canoeing and water safety to the village kids. I arrived at the water's edge with a carefully planned curriculum that divided kids into age groups to keep things manageable. In theory, the whole thing was going to be very organized. In reality, it was bedlam.

As soon as word spread that something fun was happening at the beach, every kid in town came down to hang out. Soon, I was teaching canoeing to a much larger group of kids than expected. A single Cree elder, two teenage helpers, and I were in charge of about forty kids, all wanting to be on the water simultaneously.

I strapped everyone into PFDs and packed them into canoes. In a sheltered bay where the water was a little warmer, we practiced super-simplified paddling techniques and the basic canoe-over-canoe rescue, where they rescued flipped boats by emptying them over another boat and then helped everyone climb back in.

The kids got carried away, flipping their boats and shrieking with laughter. I remember looking out over that small bay and realizing that every single boat, including mine, was upside down in the water.

Fortunately, if the water is calm enough, you can do a canoe-over-canoe rescue even if both boats are upside down. No kids drowned, the boats all got upright again, and everyone learned the value of PFDs. It was total chaos and a ton of fun.

Reminiscing on these very different times, I walked the nearly deserted early morning streets and headed for the town's nerve center: the Northern Store. These stores are the descendants of the original Hudson's Bay Company stores and carry everything from breakfast cereals to frozen pizza, fishing lures to boat motors, and baby diapers to winter coats.

I had three main objectives at the store. First, I wanted to mail home useless items, like the damaged drone and broken paddle. Second, I had to buy duct tape to continue repairing my map jigsaw puzzle. Third, I needed

ChapStick because my weatherbeaten lips had deep bleeding cracks that sent jabs of pain through my face every time I ate or smiled.

An hour later, I had accomplished these goals but also purchased a big bag of food and treats including Lindt chocolate, cheese, cookies, a bag of coleslaw, ice cream sandwiches, and fresh cherries. This food wasn't strictly necessary because the boat was still packed with forty days of supplies, but the opportunity to add some variety to my diet was too tempting to ignore.

I inhaled the ice cream and ate fresh cherries on the store's front steps in the warm sun. It felt like I was taking a little holiday from my trip.

I pulled out my phone and noticed that it had a signal; apparently, Southend had a cell tower. For days, I had traveled across the landscape like the silent lone survivor of some apocalypse, but now it was time to assume a different persona. I reached into the box where I had stored Stephan, the father and husband, and dialed home. Soon, my wife Eva and three kids were on the call together, talking over each other, asking questions, and telling me about their plans for the week.

It was deeply reassuring to catch up on the news from home, but so much speaking after so much stillness also felt strange. Like a sailor regaining his land legs, each sentence required extra steps to force my thoughts into audible words.

Still on the phone, I wandered back to the beach and pushed the boat back into the water. Then, as the signal faltered, I said my goodbyes and headed north. I felt grateful for their support—even on a solo trip, I wasn't doing it alone. Then, the town of Southend and easy communication with the outside world disappeared behind me.

On the first part of the trip, I had gone downriver on the Churchill; in the second part I had ascended the Reindeer River. This was the third stage of the trip, wherein I hoped to traverse the length of Reindeer Lake, starting in the south, where the Reindeer River drained the lake and ending 250 kilometers to the north, where the Cochrane River flowed into the lake.

Reindeer Lake is massive, a quarter of a thousand kilometers long and more than forty kilometers wide, making it the 24th largest lake in the world. At its widest, the earth's curvature prevents you from seeing the other shore, and the sky meets an endless freshwater ocean at the horizon.

There are 25,000,000,000 gallons of water in Reindeer Lake. The Cochrane River is its largest tributary, but more water flows in from hundreds of other rivers, creeks, and streams that descend to the lake from every direction. The average drop of water recirculates in the lake for more than eight years before it finds the exit and gets sucked down the Reindeer River.

Navigation is made difficult by more than 5,000 islands and many deep bays. Dead-end channels can look like open water, while routes you want to follow are obscured behind islands that merge in the distance.

I've heard Cree natives laugh at friends who have lived their whole lives on the lake and ended up fifty kilometers down a bay without an exit before realizing they'd taken a wrong turn. People have also starved to death less than a day's paddle from Southend because they couldn't find the route back to civilization through the island maze.

The plan was to get to the north end of Reindeer Lake in about a week, but this was entirely at the mercy of the weather. An extended period of windy conditions could trap me on shore and jeopardize the entire trip; trying to plan for all the contingencies if the weather went bad gave me a headache.

Conditions on Reindeer Lake were ideal today. The canoe sliced through the still water, momentarily disrupting the blue skies and white clouds reflected there that shimmered and reformed after the boat passed. A gentle tailwind from the South provided warm weather and a light nudge forward. I hoisted the sail, paddled the boat, and ate fresh cherries. Life was good but there was no room for complacency; many people in boats much larger than mine had drowned in the waters around me. This was undoubtedly one of the most dangerous parts of the trip.

The calm waters reminded me of a close call many years ago. In my early twenties, my girlfriend and I had been paddling the north shore of Lake Superior. It was a warm and calm day, so we took a shortcut across a large bay to shave off some distance. Then, out of nowhere, a sudden windstorm came up, and in less than twenty minutes, small and insignificant waves morphed into towering monsters.

Fortunately, we got to a small, treeless rock island halfway across that bay the size of a baseball diamond and waited for the squall to pass. Unfortunately, it grew into a titanic storm that battered our refuge with towering waves and horizontal sheets of rain. It was only a five-minute paddle to the mainland, but crossing in those conditions would have been suicide. We collected every last loose rock on that island to build a series of cairns around the tent to anchor it down and break the wind. When the wind finally died three days later, we had moved more than 1,000 pounds of rock to stop the tent from blowing away.

Big lakes often don't seem risky, but humans are terrible at evaluating risk. Our attention is so easily captured by dramatic events that we tend to ignore more mundane risks, even if they're much more deadly, statistically speaking.

For example, everyone fixates on bear attacks. Before the trip, my father-in-law told me, "You're heading into the woods? Better take a gun. Actually, take two guns!" His concern was understandable—bears are apex predators with large teeth, vicious claws, and unfathomable strength.

But the numbers put this risk into context; black bears, grizzly bears, and polar bears combined kill two to five people *annually* in North America. Now compare that to the eleven people who drown *every single day*. Two to five bear fatalities versus four thousand drownings per year; it's not even in the same neighborhood.

If statistics aren't your thing, consider this: I've paddled with at least four people who later drowned, and one of them was related to me. On the other hand, I've never met someone who knew someone who was mauled by a bear. Bears should not be your primary concern on a canoe trip. Instead, you should be worried about something as simple as big lakes.

The water stretching away in all directions reminded me of capsizing on a much smaller lake on the first day of the trip. To ward off any complacency induced by the gorgeous weather, I went over and over big lake safety precautions as if they were the beads of a rosary.

The first part of the plan was to become a fervent meteorologist. The splintered shoreline vegetation and rock scoured clean of soil testified to the power of air moving over water here. The large stretches of open water on Reindeer Lake allowed moderate winds to create ferocious waves and storms to become cataclysmic.

Hot air rising off the land in the late summer afternoons causes many of thunderstorms in this part of the North, so I especially had to watch for cumulonimbus clouds. These large, anvil-shaped clouds produce lightning and squalls, both of which could be extremely dangerous if I were out in the open water. Fortunately, the clouds in the sky were white and fluffy at the moment, lacking the dark undersides of storm clouds.

This was good news that the wind was currently gentle and from the South. In northern Saskatchewan, breezes from the North or East are indicators that bad weather might be coming. Similarly, if the wind rose, fell, or shifted direction, that also suggested changing weather was coming. Even the temperature had to be observed; a sudden drop in temperature might indicate an imminent cold front is coming with attendant gusty winds and heavy rain.

The next bead on the safety rosary was choosing the right route and adapting it to changing conditions. Navigating on a large lake may seem simple; after all, you just go from one end to the other, right? Well, it's actually much more complicated than it seems, and choosing the right route is critical because it's so damn perilous to be away from land if the weather deteriorates.

In Greek mythology, the Sirens were creatures who lured sailors ever closer to shore with their beautiful songs until they wrecked upon the rocks and drowned. In the Canadian North, the sirens work the other way; they lure you further and further out into the middle of the lake with promises of tranquil water and gentle breezes.

I generally don't go more than 250 meters from shore in good conditions. When conditions become marginal, I stay much closer to land, usually no more than 50 to 100 meters.

This idea of staying close to shore is a good rule, but you can't always follow it. Let's say there's a bay you could cross in thirty minutes by going in a straight line, but it would take four hours to hug the shore and go the long way around.

In this case, your route would depend on your experience, the estimated time at sea, your paddling skills, the strength and direction of the wind, the size and shape of the waves, your boat, the air and water temperature, the availability of rescue, and the presence of islands on your crossing. Hopping from island to island is particularly useful for significant crossings. If a storm comes up, you can take refuge on the island or hide behind it, sitting out the bad weather sheltered from the worst of the waves.

The third component of staying safe lies in paddling technique. Your paddle has three primary functions as it passes through the water: power strokes to move the boat forward or backward, steering strokes to control the boat's rotation, and bracing strokes to stop the boat from tipping. Often, these strokes are done one at a time, but in big waves, you often need all three things to happen—power, steer, and brace—with a single pass of the paddle. The angle of your paddle might adjust multiple times a second as you feel the boat shift underneath you.

Solid paddling skills allow you to go out into relatively big swell and maintain the correct angle of the boat relative to the waves.

Whitecaps slamming into you broadside will off-balance the boat, fill it with water, and capsize you, so you don't want your boat sideways to the waves. Pointing directly into the waves isn't always much better—especially if the waves are steep—because you don't want the front of the boat to dive down into the waves and turn into a submarine. Pointing your boat directly downwind with a following sea where the waves are coming from behind you can result in you surfing down the face of larger waves. This is tremendous fun until a slightly bigger wave sneaks up behind you and swamps your boat or turns it broadside.

If it's dangerous to be sideways to the waves, head directly into them and point away from them. Then what are you supposed to do? The answer is "quartering," a procedure where you zigzag across the lake at a 30° to 45° angle, allowing the bow's buoyancy to lift the boat up and over the waves without diving into the water. The problem is that once you commit to maintaining a certain angle in the waves, it can be very difficult to take a break if you get tired. Quartering in heavy conditions is a technical skill that takes time to develop, and I was glad I had practiced it in gentle winds and smaller waves before heading out onto Reindeer Lake.

I would have felt a lot better about being out on the big water had I been able to snap my spray deck across the top of the canoe. These waterproof fabric covers take time to install, and make it difficult to get at your gear, but they also add a considerable margin of safety by keeping the lake's water out of your boat. Unfortunately, the mountain of food—still forty days' worth—sat so high that I couldn't stretch the spray deck over it all, so the lifesaving fitted nylon cover was useless and stuffed deep in a gear bag for now.

If water came over the gunwales, I had a large bailer to remove it, but bailing while paddling can be tricky; the waves don't stop when it's time to empty your boat. This is why I also tightly tied all my waterproof gear bags into the boat. Even the heaviest portaging bag still weighs less than the equivalent volume of water, meaning that your bags can provide just enough flotation to keep a swamped boat upright, giving you a fighting chance of slowly paddling it to shore.

There weren't many options if my boat took on water, swamped, and flipped. There would be no other boat with which to attempt a canoe-over-canoe rescue, a technique covered in every beginner canoeing course.

There are techniques to upright, empty, and reenter a swamped boat solo, but they're only reliable in calm weather and small waves—my Day One debacle on Otter Lake proved that. If I flipped out here, there were only two choices: stay with the boat and hope to get blown to shore, or abandon ship and try to swim to land as fast as possible. The trick would be not drowning or getting hypothermia before reaching shore.

Everybody knows you should wear a life jacket when you're canoeing, and on this trip, I wore my PFD 99 percent of the time. A good PFD keeps you afloat, but it won't prevent hypothermia, which is usually the actual cause of death in such situations. On this trip, there was no room for wetsuits or drysuits, but I resolved to wear rain gear with the wrists and ankles cinched tight over synthetic insulation for all dodgy crossings. If I capsized, this ersatz arrangement would hopefully retain enough body warmth to keep me alive until I washed ashore. Still, the bottom line was that if I swamped my boat far from the shore or if the wind was blowing away from shore, I would probably die.

I snuck up side channels and hopped between Westlake Island, Birch Point, Sanford Island, Hodgson Island, and the Jones Peninsula on the western coast of Reindeer Lake. These headlands and islands would serve as refuges if a storm came up.

The blue water abutted boulder shores or splashed into cliffs formed by bedrock slanting into the water. Endless spruce and aspen forests marched away from the water and into the forever. There was an eternal feeling and a profound simplicity to this country, life clinging to thin soil over ancient rock.

I tried to picture the day, 99 million years ago, when a giant asteroid flashed through the sky just a few miles to the east. This area had been under a warm, shallow, saltwater sea teeming with plesiosaurs, mosasaurs, and fish. The unimaginably massive impact explosion left a giant circular crater, 11 kilometers across, called Deep Bay, that you can still easily see on maps. This crater—predictably—is rumored to be home to a giant, elusive reptilian monster. Alas, I did not see the beast of Deep Bay as I paddled up the lake.

Eight hours later, I was crawling across the still-sleeping lake, the paddle maintaining a mile-devouring cadence. I was tired, but in the absence of a headwind, the boat jumped forward with each stroke. Sunbeams cut through the clouds and made the lake dance with a white fire. The only noises were the splash of the waves, the cries of loons, and the occasional distant thrum of an outboard boat. A few uninhabited cabins were scattered along the shore.

Then, faint music echoed across the water. Was this a paddler with a portable speaker? Was someone playing music at their cabin? I did not know, but the music got louder as I paddled onward. Eventually, it became apparent that the music came from a low island with a verdant canopy of birch and spruce trees. It alternated between country and gospel songs. What on earth was going on?

A long beach came into view where a large celebration was in progress. Hundreds of native people circulated between cabins, and a line of motorboats was pulled up on the beach.

Kids were swimming in the water, and rowdy boys were throwing each other off a wooden dock into the water. They went silent for a few seconds as my boat pulled up, then erupted in a cacophony of questions.

"Who are you?"

"Where are you going?"

"Can I go for a ride in your canoe?"

I was explaining that my boat was too full to take any extra passengers when a Cree elder—an older man with weatherbeaten cheeks wearing a striped shirt and jeans—wandered over from the fire.

"Hello," he said, staring down into my boat. "Where are you coming from, and where are you going?"

"I started in Missinipe ten days ago, and I hope to get to Hudson Bay in another forty days."

"That's a very long way. Better come up to camp and have some dinner."

I discovered this was a yearly family camp held by the Peter Ballantyne Cree Nation. During this celebration, parents, grandparents, kids, and grandkids from nine different Cree communities spend a few days camping with music, food, and a focus on traditional culture.

The elder escorted me through the festivities. People talked in a jumble of Cree and English. Live music played in the background, and kids ran everywhere. A plate of pork, chicken, beans, rice, macaroni, and vegetables was shoved into my hands, along with a mug of dark tea.

I was introduced to the other elders sitting around the large campfire. I sat at the fire for hours, listening to the elders talk and asking the occasional question.

The man who had invited me up was Hector Morin. His father had fished commercially on the lake in the 1950s, and Hector had been raised on the water. These days, he worked as a fishing guide for southerners looking to catch that massive northern pike or lake trout. His extended family was heavily represented at the celebration that night.

Hector took the time to go over my maps. He reiterated that large lakes are the most dangerous part of any wilderness journey and pointed out protected routes, good camping sites, and exposed areas I should only attempt when the winds were low.

As the sun set, musicians packed up and celebrants headed home in their boats. I asked Hector's advice about good camping nearby; he thought for a moment, then invited me to overnight in one of his nearby cabins.

Hector's family's site was a short paddle away—a grassy area with his own tidy cabin, a historic log structure falling to pieces, and a third new cabin still under construction. Fortunately, this last building had recently been sealed against the weather, so all I had to do was spread my sleeping bag on the floor. Fastest camp setup ever!

The clouds rolled in at sunset, and soon the rain was drumming hard on the watertight roof of my personal cabin! I was profoundly grateful for the hospitality. This reflexive generosity with food and cabins is typical in the North, and it hearkens back to an earlier time when an individual's survival depended on the group's goodwill. Not sharing resources in those conditions would have been a surefire way to end up on a very short branch of your family tree.

I always feel deep gratitude for people like Hector who take the time to share their local knowledge with travelers like me. Their stories make the journey a richer, more nuanced experience, and their advice might be the difference between shipwreck to success.

CROSSING THE LAKE

July 11, 2019
**Start: A cabin under construction, MacFarlane Island, Reindeer Lake
(56°34'36.9" N 102°51'49.0" W)
Finish: North end of Upistutik Island, Reindeer Lake
(56°45'6.3" N 102°26'48.5" W)
Distance covered: 34 kilometers**

*The key is your ability to get in shape the first week or two and have
your body adapt on the trail because no matter how hard you train,
it's impossible to properly prepare your legs and your mind for a 24/7,
two-month adventure.*

—David Horton, legendary ultramarathoner

I emerged into the cool morning at 5:30 A.M., happy to see that the rain had stopped. The lake surface was calm, a good day to put kilometers under the keel.

There was already movement over at Hector's cabin as he prepared for his day. I went over to say goodbye but didn't manage a clean getaway because he immediately started cooking bacon and eggs for me. I stuffed my belly with foods I hadn't tasted in a while because refusing would have been rude, right?

Packing the boat was easy because I had only taken out the essentials the night before. By 7:00 A.M. I pushed the canoe through the shoreline reeds and started paddling north. A few minutes later, Hector's rumbling motorboat cut a wide arc around me as he headed to pick up his clients for the day, waving as he went. Once past, he opened up his fifty-horsepower outboard motor and rapidly disappeared.

The lake was about to get much, much wider, and I now had to choose between continuing northward on the eastern or the western shore of the lake. Once committed to a side, crossing back would be very difficult. I weighed the options as the boat rocked gently in the waves. The western shore would be a little more sheltered if a big weather system blew in from the West, but I knew more about the eastern shore, which was also slightly shorter and could save me about a day of paddling. So much depended on whether I had correctly assessed the dangers and calculated the probabilities. Would this be when the odds finally caught up with me?

I scanned the sky one last time for incoming bad weather, exhaled deeply, and started cutting across to the eastern shore. This was the narrowest point of the lake, but even here, it was still a twenty-kilometer crossing. That's a long time to be out at sea, even with perfect weather conditions. The only thing that made this crossing possible was a chain of islands I could follow to avoid being more than a couple of kilometers from land if the weather turned bad.

The route hopped from MacFarlane Island to Priestly Island, Mooney Island, Milton Island, Shaw Island, Upistukik Island, and the far shore in a high-stakes game of connect the dots. Each island's character reflected both its geological history and how the lake's storms had sculpted its vegetation. Some were nothing more than sandbars, barely protruding above the water. Others were jumbles of boulders topped with a dense forest. My favorites were the picturesque domes of smooth granitic rock sprinkled with tenacious clumps of mosses, lichens, and spruce trees.

The Canadian Shield here consists of some of the oldest rock on the planet. Billions of years ago, giant mountains were here, taller than the Himalayas.

The deep immensity of time had ground them down into the rolling hills that remain today.

Most recently, Reindeer Lake and all the lands around it had been locked in a vast ice sheet during the Wisconsin glaciation that ended about 10,000 years ago in North America. That ice, several kilometers thick, had exerted unimaginable pressures and had left its signatures everywhere. It carved curves into the bedrock, ground stones to powder, and pushed materials across the land like an unspeakably large bulldozer.

Imagining the landscape being rearranged by the ice occupied my thoughts and distracted my aching body for many kilometers that day. These gigantic world-shaping forces put everything into context; I was but a transient flicker on an ancient landscape that paid my passage no heed and would not mourn my absence.

My deep immersion in the landscape was facilitated by solitude. Instead of being distracted, amused, or frustrated by traveling companions, journeying alone was an invitation to study unfolding clouds on the horizon or the shape of a boulder for as long as it took. Ric Driediger, my former canoeing boss, had expressed this well when he said,

> My job as a guide is to make sure that my guests have the best possible experience. When I'm going solo, my focus obviously shifts. I experience the wilderness in a way that I can't when I'm guiding. Oh, there are certainly brief moments when I'm guiding that I feel truly connected to the wilderness. But when I'm going solo, those moments become days. It is a totally different experience.
>
> —Ric Driediger, *Stories from the Churchill*

Not everyone has ambitions to go into the bush alone, which is perfectly fine. It isn't for everyone. But if you're intrigued by the concept, here's some advice to get you started . . .

First, start small. Many people have never been in the outdoors solo, so try going for a short two-hour hike on a well-traveled trail by yourself. Or paddle to a nice campsite beside a small lake, cook a meal over a camping stove, and then spend the night in a tent alone. By starting small, you'll find out if you actually enjoy the experience of going solo. Then escalate slowly; go a two-day trip followed by a three-day trip. If you hate the experience, no problem; it wasn't for you at this time.

My solo experiences started with a two-day trip on a relatively easy river and then a few three-day hikes. Those baptisms made me curious about more extended trips, and before I knew it I was hooked and exploring obscure rivers on a six-week romp through northern Ontario!

Second, make your skills bombproof. On a solo trip, there's no one else to help out, so you have to competently do it all.

Can you pitch a tent and light a fire in any weather yourself? Can you find water, assess if it's drinkable, and treat it if not? What are your navigation skills like; can you reliably navigate both with your GPS and with a map and compass? Can you tie a bowline, clove hitch, figure-eight, trucker's hitch, square knot, and a double half hitch without referring to a book? How would you repair your stove, your canoe, and your tent? What about first aid—do you know what to do for all the most common injuries? There is no cavalry coming, so it's all on you.

Third, stay a full level below what you know you're capable of. When you're alone, you can't operate at the limits of your skills, so maintain a buffer to deal with emergencies. If nobody's around to help, then move a little slower and more carefully. For example, I've run Class IV rapids in little whitewater boats and am comfortable in Class III rapids in a tripping boat. But in the wilderness by myself, I generally stick to Class II+, just to leave a little in reserve in case something goes wrong.

Fourth, learn about the plants and animals you might encounter so that you'll be more attuned to the natural environment. This improves your ability to notice subtle environmental cues that keep you safer. You may observe the weather shifting a little earlier, you may find a better route for a portage, and you may spot wild animals faster. It'll improve your survival skills, from fire-lighting to foraging.

LEFT: I was dying from kidney failure, but there was a red bag waiting for me in the operating room. It contained my brother's kidney, freshly excised from his body and waiting to be transplanted into mine.

Kesting/Kesting
2015/6/8

HUMAN ORGAN
FOR TRANSPLANT
Handle with Care
Keep Cool - Do Not Freeze

Dr. Nguan

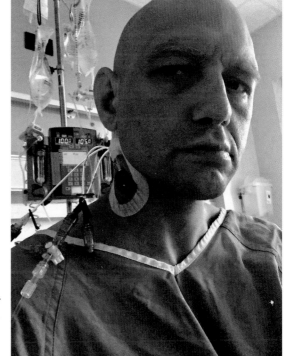

RIGHT: Infections and other setbacks were frequent after the transplant, but as I slowly got stronger, I began wondering if it would be possible to finally explore a remote region of the subarctic I had first heard about thirty years before.

On June 30th, 2019, I married Eva Schubert, and the next day, I left for the North. In my defense, this departure date was set in stone *before* she proposed, and to her credit, she told me to go ahead with the plan and then never complained.

ABOVE: In Missinipe, Saskatchewan, on the shore of the mighty Churchill River, ready to start a fifty-day unsupported journey in a Sea-1 hybrid canoe full of food and supplies. BELOW: The waterproofing I had applied to my paper maps turned out to be entirely inadequate. After capsizing in the river, the maps started shredding and falling apart. This required drying them out whenever it wasn't raining, which wasn't very often.

LEFT: High-quality rain gear and a bombproof tent are two of the most important accessories you can have in the North.

BELOW: When the clouds parted and the sun came out, the scenery on the Churchill River was spectacular.

A boat ramp beside a rapid made for an easy portage; no offloading and carrying was required. When the route turned northwards the portages would soon get much more difficult.

ABOVE: On one marvelous day, millions of dragonfly nymphs emerged from the water and crawled onto land. The adults then slowly emerged from their larval shells and took to the air. BELOW: A quick breakfast beside a campfire on a tiny island in the boreal forest on the Canadian Shield.

ABOVE: Dragging the boat through along a dense, overgrown, bug-infested portage circumventing a waterfall on the Churchill River. BELOW: After a week of rain, the weather finally broke. Paddling across this watery mirror felt like being in a dream.

ABOVE: On longer trips, I always take three paddles; what if you break one and lose the other? As luck would have it, my favorite paddle snapped in half without warning on only the fifth day of a potential fifty-day trip. BELOW: I turned north off of the Churchill to ascend the Reindeer River against the current. Here I'm enjoying the one warm meal of the day before collapsing into the tent.

A strong natural history repertoire improves your survival skills, but the benefits go deeper than the merely practical. This knowledge changes how you relate to the landscape. Instead of being surrounded by anonymous trees in the forest, knowing the names of certain species feels like recognizing old friends in the street.

So, learn some cool facts about your area's three most dominant tree species. Be able to identify the most common birds and land animals you might encounter. Study the most abundant smaller plants and memorize which berries you can eat. Read about how the native people used those plants and animals. Become versed about cloud formations and what they mean for the weather tomorrow. Understand the disturbance and regeneration cycles in the ecosystems you'll be visiting. All this will keep you safer, make you more perceptive, and significantly deepen your experience of the journey.

In the middle of the day, I took a short break on a tiny, unnamed rock atoll that looked out over the lake. This spot was so convenient that it had doubtlessly been used as a rest spot for thousands of years by natives, explorers, trappers, and traders.

I broke out the solar panel and tied it to the back of the canoe. The plan was to charge my battery pack using the strong midday light as I paddled and then use that stored energy to recharge my GPS, camera, phone, and satellite dish at night. My paddling days were getting so long that using the solar panel with a few hours of weak light in the evening wasn't working.

My numb fingers fumbled the battery pack. It fell from my hand and ker-plunked into waist-deep water. I retrieved it immediately, but the damage was done; the battery pack made an ominous noise, the tiny LED screen flickered, and then the whole thing died.

Water had entered the metal housing, and I had to get it out. I didn't have the tools to disassemble it, so I carved holes through the less essential-looking parts of the plastic housing with my multitool. Liquid dribbled out of these newly gouged holes; this was not a good sign. I filled a Ziplock bag with handfuls of dry pasta and added every water-absorbing package from the drug containers in my medical kit. Then the battery, the pasta, and the desiccant packages went into the plastic bag, where I hoped that some of the moisture would get sucked out of the wiring and circuits.

Losing that battery would be a real problem—it was my insurance policy in case cloudy weather made it impossible to charge the electronics directly from the solar panel. I didn't want an overcast week to disable my lifeline. There was nothing to do for now but paddle onward and see if the battery started working again in a few days.

Hours later, I came to the northern tip of Upistutik Island and a perfect campsite. It was a rocky peninsula fringed with jack pine and spruce with water on three sides. A gentle breeze blew through the open location, keeping the bugs at bay.

Ten hours of paddling had frozen my body into the sitting position. It took a series of slow-motion contortions to extricate myself from the boat's cockpit; my back threatened to spasm if I made the slightest wrong move. I almost fell into the water when my unresponsive legs balked at stepping up onto the shore.

The day ended as it had begun, in pain. It hurt both to stand up and to lie down. The difference was that I had been able to paddle for longer and take fewer breaks today—I hoped these were signs that my body was adapting to the stress instead of breaking. It was too soon to tell for sure, but maybe I'd be able to finish the trip after all.

THE GATHERING STORM

July 12, 2019
Start: North end of Upistutik Island, Reindeer Lake
(56°45'6.3" N 102°26'48.5" W)
Finish: North end of MacDonald Peninsula
(56°52'4.6" N 102°16'33.0" W)
Distance covered: 19 kilometers

The canoe is the simplest, most functional, yet aesthetically pleasing object ever created. In my opinion, this is not a statement that is open to debate. It's a fact! It follows that if the canoe is the most beautiful work of human beings, then the art of paddling one must rank right up there with painting, poetry, music, and ballet.
—Bill Mason, *Path of the Paddle:*
An Illustrated Guide to the Art of Canoeing

From the safety of my sleeping bag, I checked the rudimentary weather forecast on my GPS, and it wasn't good. Powerful winds were supposed to blow in soon, and there might only be a few hours of safe passage before things got ugly out on the water. I broke camp as fast as I could without eating anything; calories could be inhaled while paddling.

At first, the breeze was tentative, sneaking through the forest and only rustling the skinniest grasses. As I stuffed the boat, the wind began to build slowly and inexorably, and dark clouds shrouded the rising sun.

Putting on my gear felt like buckling on armor before a battle. First came my regular clothing covered with a fleece jacket, then a heavy Arc'teryx raincoat and rain pants to protect against the wind and inevitable rain. Finally came a hat, gloves, and a red PFD. The locals who live on Reindeer Lake like to deadpan, "It's important to wear your life jacket out on the lake . . . It makes the bodies easier to find."

Packing only took an hour, but the wind was coming in hard from the northwest by the time I pushed off. The first part of the route had many islands and narrow channels that would provide some shelter from the wind. Conditions weren't too bad so long as I could sneak along in the relatively calm fifty-foot downwind fringe of the islands to my right. Whenever there was a break in the islands, I was hit by the full force of the wind coming in from across the lake. At least the waves were still of manageable size; the going was only tricky and not yet dangerous. But no place on Reindeer Lake would be safe if the weather deteriorated much more.

Doggedly, I crawled along the sawtooth shore of MacDonald Peninsula, working twice as hard to go half as fast. The map showed that eighteen kilometers ahead, a long island lay tight against the mainland. If I could just get there and slip into those narrows where there was protection from the gale blowing in from across the giant lake, then I could keep going.

But the wind just got stronger, and the waves hammering my boat kept getting larger. Cold water sprayed my face and dumped in my lap. The only thing in my favor was that the wind was blowing *toward* the shore, so if the boat capsized, I'd probably be able to swim to land; the boat, however, would probably be smashed in the wild surf. Had the wind been blowing from shore out to sea, the risk calculus would have been completely different.

Occasionally, the canoe's bow dove down into the trough of the waves and water washed over the closed deck. It was startling to watch the front of your boat disappear underwater, but the craft's buoyancy always reasserted itself, bringing it back to the surface, shedding water left and right. These partial submersions were dangerous, so I started quartering to give the boat more time to climb up and over the waves. This made for a dryer, more stable ride but also made the going much slower since I was no longer proceeding forward in a straight line.

The wind's fury increased yet another notch. Waves started to curl and break into a white foam with increasing frequency. Breaking waves are much more hazardous than regular waves because their steep angles give them more power to tip your boat. It was time to get off the lake, but everywhere I looked, waves exploded against the shoreline boulders—landing here was impossible, so I had to keep going. A small semicircular indentation on the map indicated a sheltered cove just one kilometer ahead.

Under normal circumstances, I could have covered this distance in ten minutes, but it became an hour-long struggle in these foul conditions. With eviscerated muscles, I braced the paddle for stability, pulled it to move the boat forward, and used almost invisible corrections to keep going in the right direction. The nerves on my face strained to feel shifts in the wind, my legs and hips responded to every tilt of the boat, and I listened for the telltale sound of a breaker bearing down upon me. Every few seconds, I reevaluated the situation and made a new plan for handling the next wave.

Sixty minutes later, I rounded a small cape and finally slipped into the cove's sanctuary. A crescent of exposed bedrock now protected me on three sides, and the canoe bobbed gently on the muted swell even though the wind still cracked overhead. I nudged the canoe into a crack in the granite, the tiny anchorage only a few inches wider than the boat itself. Snug at last, I sat in a stupefied daze, grateful for asylum from the waves and completely depleted from the intense physical and mental effort.

I crawled out of the boat on all fours and slowly pushed myself into a standing position. The wind continued to pick up, and whitecaps hurtled onto the shore before dissolving into showers of spume. I had gotten off the lake just in time, and it looked like I would be here for a while. Fortunately, there were worse places to be windbound; I set up camp on giant rock slabs scoured clean by summer storms and winter winds, then crunched over lichen to pitch the tent among the trees that grew well back from the shore.

Life was not easy, but it was simple. The goal of the trip was to arrive at the destination without dying. Having that one clearly stated aim was liberating, and everything else flowed from there.

On most days achieving this goal meant I had to push for as long as possible without taking excessive risks. On windy days, the overall goal was unchanged, but the priorities shifted to doing whatever would enable success in the future. If I couldn't paddle, then spending that time repairing gear, eating food, studying the maps, and napping would all contribute to covering more distance when the wind eventually dropped.

In regular life, your focus is often fragmented by a thousand clamoring urgencies; days and weeks can go by without you getting closer to achieving your goals. There's a reason that Prussian military genius Carl von Clausewitz advised, "Pursue one great decisive aim with force and determination," and not "Slice your attention into tiny unusable fragments."

The ability to prioritize is paramount. My trick is to ask myself, *What is the ONE thing I absolutely must get done today?* I try to do this in the morning *before* the inevitable barrage of diversions, notifications, and distractions begins. This simple statement of intent helps prevent other people's priorities from hijacking my to-do list, and clarifies my thinking. It's great when you achieve more than one thing, but it shouldn't be your intent. After all, the man who chases two rabbits catches neither.

Back on the rocky shore, I awoke from a nap. The wind was still high, but the sun had come out, and the tent was now almost uncomfortably warm. I rolled over and groaned from the pain—I'd been paddling, tracking, wading, and portaging for twelve days without a break. Surprisingly, the two injuries I had started the trip with—the rotator cuff in my shoulder and the tendinitis in my elbow—were doing better; somehow, canoeing had been excellent physiotherapy for those body parts. But the rest of my body could feel each of the quarter-million paddle strokes I'd taken so far, and my energy levels were crashing. I was just so damn tired all the time. Too much work and insufficient rest made it harder and harder to lurch into action.

Later that afternoon, I sat on the rocks eating a chili I had dehydrated months previously and stared out over the main body of the lake. The whitecaps looked a little smaller, and it felt like the wind had lost a bit of its bite. It was still too rough to paddle, but maybe conditions would continue to improve. I crawled back into the tent to take yet another nap.

The wind kept dropping, and by 7:00 P.M. it was possible to cross open water again. I broke camp and set off across the quieting waters. It was magic hour now, that time of day when the setting sun's light amplifies the full colors of every tree and rock. In the next hour, I covered six more kilometers; a much faster pace than earlier in the day. All the suffering from earlier in the day was suddenly worth it.

As I pilgrimaged north, a line of thunderclouds marched across the horizon, backlit by an orange and purple sunset. The birds stopped chirping, and an impending sense of rain lay thick and heavy on the lake. A storm was inbound, and it was time to make camp.

I found a convex slab of rock that would shed water outward and quickly pitched the Hilleberg tent on it, stringing extra lines out to trees, logs, and rocks for added stability in the wind. I dragged the canoe onto shore, tied it down, and filled it with boulders to stop it from blowing away. Dinner was a hasty protein shake and an energy bar.

Equipment secured, I dove into the dry tent as raindrops the size of grapes exploded on the waterproof fabric while thunder rolled in the sky.

IN THE WET

July 13, 2019

Start: On the north end of MacDonald Peninsula
(56°52'4.6" N 102°16'33.0" W)
Finish: A rocky headland overlooking the breadth of Reindeer Lake
(57°11'40.1" N 102°3'47.0" W)
Distance covered: 43 kilometers

If the wind isn't blowing, it's time to be going.
—One of my mantras on the 1,000-Mile Solo

The thunderstorm passed by morning, and the giant lake was smooth except for concentric ripples where cold raindrops impacted the water. I didn't feel like emerging from the warm sleeping bag, but it was time to break camp and get my ass into the boat. "If the wind isn't blowing, it's time to be going," I muttered as I donned heavy rain gear, neoprene boots, gloves, and my old but reliable canoeing hat.

The key to staying warm in the wet is to keep moving, so I ate breakfast while breaking camp. A few spoonfuls of muesli . . . carry the first food bag from the forest to the boat . . . a bit more muesli . . . retrieve the second food bag from a different spot in the forest . . . a little more food . . . pack the tent.

By 7:20 A.M. the boat was back in the water, heading toward the nearest island to the north. This crossing would have been foolhardy during yesterday's storm, but today, it was a leisurely ten-minute paddle.

The maps led me to a thirty-kilometer-long protected route that twisted around the shore and some large islands. If the weather took a turn for the worse, there would be plenty of protection here. The channel was quiet—natives traveling by powerboat between the three villages on Reindeer Lake generally prefer taking the direct route across open water rather than this more circuitous detour. I was a bit surprised, therefore, when shortly after noon, the sound of raindrops was augmented by the muffled hum of an outboard motor. I rounded a corner and came across three men in a boat fishing at a very narrow part of the channel.

During our pleasantries, I found out the trio consisted of an old Cree guide helping a father and son team from Wisconsin search for the northern pike of their dreams.

"Where did you come from?" the younger Wisconsin man asked.

"From Missinipe. I started thirteen days ago."

"You've come all that way by yourself? Aren't you lonely?"

"I've been a parent for sixteen years," I laughed, "And I've had all the talking I need for a lifetime! I'm just taking a little break from it."

The old Cree guide nodded. The rhythms of the North naturally include time being with people and time being alone. Like many locals, he worked as a guide in the summer, an inherently social activity. But then he spent the winters trapping, which involves many days of solitude.

We chatted about the route ahead and the tiny indigenous hamlet of Kinoosao in the next deep bay; I wouldn't have time to visit it, which was a real shame. Then, it was time to say goodbye and cover some distance.

As I paddled past Kinoosao Bay, my mind turned to David Thompson and J. B. Tyrrell, two of my favorite Canadian explorers who had also traveled on this lake long ago. Reindeer Lake was then and remains today a hub that connects the subarctic to the waterways of the South.

The vast distances these explorers covered are mind-boggling. Consider the introduction to *Report on the Doobaunt, Kazan and Ferguson*

Rivers and the North-West Coast of Hudson Bay written by J. B. Tyrrell in 1896 . . .

"Sir, I beg to present a report on the geology and general resources of the region explored in 1893 and 1894, embraced in an area of about 200,000 square miles lying north of the fifty-ninth parallel of latitude and west of Hudson Bay. The explorations included the examination and survey of Telzoa or Doobaunt, Kazan, Ferguson, Chipman and Cochrane Rivers, Chesterfield Inlet, and the coast of Hudson Bay from Chesterfield Inlet to Churchill, and two overland routes traveled in winter with dog teams and sledges, between Churchill and Nelson Rivers."

Did you catch that? Tyrrell covered *200,000 square miles in two years*, which is an insanely large area, especially given that it was mostly unknown to him and had to be covered by canoe and dogsled. Reading his notes while traveling through the North today is a great way to learn about this region's geology and natural history, but also links you to the past in a very tangible way.

The wind picked up as the day went on, and the rain became colder. The warmth draining from my body triggered a sense memory, and I was transported back to June 1992 on the shores of the Kenogami River in northern Ontario. After paddling upstream for twelve hours in a cold rain, my clothing was soaked, the temperature was plummeting, and I needed to warm up fast.

The good news was that dry clothing was stashed safely in a waterproof bag, but I couldn't operate the buckles and snaps that held the bags shut; my numb fingers simply refused to obey commands. The solution to my problem was inches away but quite literally out of reach. Was I going to freeze to death simply because I couldn't get through a few waterproof layers of fabric? What a ridiculous way to go!

There has to be a solution. Think, think, think! Can I slit the bags open with a blade? What about cutting the straps? I got out my knife but then had a less destructive idea; I bent over and used my teeth to bite down on the hard plastic buckle. Gnawing like a beaver, I finally got the angle right, and the first fastener popped open. I bit down again on a second buckle, and the bag's contents tumbled onto the grass. I seized a jacket and a dry shirt before the rain soaked them. It was glorious to slip into that dry clothing and feel my body regain sensation.

I had just experienced hypothermia, an abnormal drop in your body temperature that is the biggest killer in the outdoors.

As your extremities cool, your fine motor skills degrade—this was why I couldn't manipulate small objects like the clasps of the backpack. It wasn't hypothermia yet, but it's getting close.

Shivering that you can't control announces the arrival of mild hypothermia. Your core temperature is now less than 35°C (95°F), and shivering is your body's attempt to warm itself up with muscular contractions.

You should take action now before your body gets colder and the situation gets much harder to reverse. The problem is that, as your brain cools, you become irritable, confused, and prone to making bad decisions. This impairment of mental function is insidious; despite your best efforts, you become stupid and unpredictable. It might seem like a good idea to head deeper into the woods, skip that meal, and generally do the opposite of whatever might fix the situation.

If things worsen and your core temperature drops below 32.9°C (89.6°F), you enter moderate hypothermia. Shivering actually stops now because your body has given up trying to rewarm itself. Your words become slurred, and your thoughts confused. This is now a severe medical emergency; you can recover, but only if other people help rewarm you, typically by moving you to a shelter, wrapping you in blankets, and sharing their body heat.

If your core temperature drops below 28°C (82.4°F), you've reached severe hypothermia. At this point, your body completely crashes; you might hallucinate or, paradoxically, take off all your clothing. Eventually, your heart and breathing slow down, and you become unresponsive. Rough handling at this point can cause heart attacks, and if you do nothing, you'll slip into a coma and die. Rewarming someone this far gone requires advanced medical care in a hospital.

Hypothermia is the single biggest outdoor hazard, whether summer or winter, spring or fall. It kills far more people in the outdoors by far than any other hazard.

Had we lived, I should have had a tale to tell of the hardihood, endurance, and courage of my companions which would have stirred the heart of every Englishman. These rough notes and our dead bodies must tell the tale.

—Robert Falcon Scott, *Message to the Public*,
written in Antarctica before he froze to death

My previous brushes with hypothermia were never far from my mind on Reindeer Lake. I used four strategies to mitigate this threat . . .

The first was maximizing my insulation. I was already wearing fleece layers and rain gear, but now I tightened my cuffs and zipped up the jacket until just my nose and eyes protruded from the hood. The inch of foam in the life jacket provided another layer of insulation. Then, I unfurled the nylon sail and laid the material across my lap to protect my legs from the wind, which kept my thighs a little warmer.

The second was eating more. I became deliberate about stoking my body's metabolic fire, eating something every thirty minutes: energy balls, salted nuts, chocolate, anything. It didn't matter if I was hungry; food is fuel, and waiting until I was in the mood to eat would have been courting disaster. Although it was the last thing I wanted to do, I also forced myself to periodically drink the cold lake water. Dehydration decreases circulation, and that makes you more susceptible to the cold.

The third hypothermia countermeasure was to work harder so that my body generated more heat. This meant increasing the stroke cadence and stopping less often, keeping me warm and making the boat fly through the water.

The fourth preventative measure was frequent self-assessment to make sure I wasn't slipping into hypothermia. It's so easy to fool yourself when it comes to hypothermia, so I continuously checked to make sure I wasn't shivering and still had full use of my fingers. Being tough is one thing, but letting the cold addle your brain and make you do stupid things is another.

Preventing hypothermia isn't sexy, and the precautions aren't fun. Still, you have to take this issue very seriously if you want to avoid becoming another statistic.

The cold rain continued for twelve hours. In the evening, the gray clouds split apart to reveal patches of blue sky. Then the wind dropped, the lake became placid, and the sunset drenched the terrain in golden light. Another splendid Canadian Shield campsite appeared; this one on a giant slab of granite jutting from the shore into the lake, dotted by low jack pine growing in the crevices that held scraps of soil.

It was getting late, so I broke out a US Army MRE, an acronym for Meal, Ready to Eat. This heavy green brick contained plastic pouches of wet food requiring minimal preparation. The main course of cheese tortellini looked suspicious and tasted awful. The nutritional breakdown on the label was equally horrifying, so I consigned the MRE to the fire and ate trail mix and beef jerky from my snack bag instead. I don't know how soldiers can survive on these things; no wonder they're often called Meals Rejected by Everyone or Meals Refusing to Excrete.

This was my fault. I should have tested the MREs before packing them into the food bag. The bottom line is that you should test everything you can think of *before* your trip. As the old saying goes, "The more you sweat in peace, the less you bleed in war."

Find out if your phone connects to your GPS *before* you're in the forest . . .

Take your "waterproofed" maps into the shower at home to find out exactly how waterproof they are . . .

Set up your tent in your backyard because you don't want to discover that you're missing a pole *after* your floatplane drops you off on a remote lake . . .

Taste your culinary experiments at home because that nutritionally balanced glop you assembled in your kitchen might be an inedible glue when you cook it in the wild . . .

Check your firearm to make sure it's compatible with your ammunition. I once packed 3-inch ammunition for a shotgun with a 2.75-inch chamber on a northern trip, which could have had the gun blowing up in my face.

The more you test your gear and procedures *before* a trip, the less will go wrong *during* the trip.

The culinary disappointment was a small, insignificant thing in the grand scheme. My tent's door framed a spectacular view as the setting sun, calm water, blue sky, and distant low islands blended into one another. Loons warbled goodnight. I had covered some decent distance today, and life was good. I laid my head on the bundle of clothing that served as a pillow and tried to sleep despite a whirring brain, calculating routes and risks for the exposed shoreline ahead.

A DANGEROUS HEADLAND

July 14, 2019

Start: A rocky headland overlooking the breadth of Reindeer Lake
(57°11'40.1" N 102°3'47.0" W)
Finish: At the Manitoba-Saskatchewan border
(57°30'9.6" N 102°0'9.0" W)
Distance covered: 49 kilometers

Have I really done everything I safely can do today?
—Another mantra of the 1,000-Mile Solo

The deep bay ahead was forcing a decision. I could either go the long way around the bay's edge, which would take most of the morning, or I could head out far from shore and island-hop across the mouth of the gulf. Winds are usually the calmest in the early morning and late evening, making those the best times for large crossings. The lake was glassy-flat right now—perfect conditions. With a touch of fear, I set out, stroking hard for the far shore and suspiciously eyeing the heavens for any indication of a developing storm.

Fortunately, the auspicious weather soon became even better. The lake remained calm, and a light tailwind wafted from the South. I flew across the water to the far shore. I had won a victory and saved at least three hours, but I still had to be very careful. Reindeer Lake here had fewer islands, leaving me much more exposed if the weather turned. I had gotten lucky with my first capsize but had no illusions about Reindeer Lake being as forgiving if the same thing happened again here.

In regular life, we separate ourselves from nature. Houses keep us dry, air conditioning keeps us cool, furnaces keep us warm, and cars allow us to travel insulated from the weather. At worst, a windy afternoon might lead to the power going out, or a sudden snowfall might make you late for work. These inconveniences are essentially nonissues in the grand scheme of things, and in the city, we can mostly ignore the weather. However, this all changes in the outdoors; a wind you wouldn't notice in your car might kill you in a canoe, so you need to be obsessed with the weather. Everything depends on the weather in a very visceral sort of way.

The breeze was steady and angled slightly toward the shore, so I cautiously hoisted the sail to augment my paddling horsepower. The sail increased my speed when paddling, and if I rested for a few minutes, the boat still carried on slowly northward without any effort on my part. Momentum is both a physical and psychological force, and making progress at all times was very encouraging.

The downside of the sail being up was having to be on yellow alert all day, watching for shifts in the wind or errant waves. This was a worthwhile tradeoff; if there had ever been a day to chew through mileage, this was it. The perfect weather was a transient window of opportunity in a harsh landscape; a few months earlier, this lake would still have been covered in ice, and in another month, autumn storms would start ripping across the landscape. The season for canoe trips in the North is not long—mostly July and August—because it's bracketed by ice and snow on both sides.

The voyageurs carrying furs and trade goods across Canada in the 1700s and 1800s covered thousands of kilometers every season. Subsisting on pemmican, they paddled all day, resting only five minutes every hour. During these breaks, they smoked their pipes, so they measured distance in "pipes" rather than hours or miles.

At the start of the trip, I'd only been able to paddle for twenty to thirty minutes before having to take a break. But now my body had hardened, and I could paddle for an entire hour without stopping and then rest, refuel, and rehydrate in five minutes. I was slowly adopting the voyageur's pattern of paddling in pipes. There was still pain in all my waking moments, but at least I was covering more distance for the same amount of pain.

This was a remote part of Reindeer Lake. I only saw one boat today, a loaded barge in the faraway distance, likely hauling supplies for someone's cabin. But the loons were out in force, and their yodeling connected this day to every other trip I had ever done in the North.

Mile after mile of bouldery shore ticked by, interrupted only by an occasional rock outcrop or a sandy beach. Those beaches were particularly beautiful; shallow bays where gentle waves lapped on unspoiled white sand. With a few palm trees, the scene would have been tropical.

There was no time to laze on a beach; I had to push on. Ahead was a giant headland called North Porcupine Point, which protruded into the lake and was surrounded by open water on three sides. The exposure of this cape created the potential for unbroken wind and enormous waves. The aerial photos I had studied indicated that the shore here was mostly rocky bluffs, which made me nervous. I had no idea how high these cliffs might be and whether I could get off the lake if the weather turned bad.

Ric Driediger, a friend of mine who ran Churchill River Canoe Outfitters in Missinipe, had suggested traversing this crux section at night when the winds are generally at their lowest. I was fully prepared to paddle nocturnally, but as afternoon turned into early evening the wind dropped and the waves became minimal. The lake had blessed me twice in one day with perfect conditions when I needed them most.

Dramatic granite cliffs sloped into the water on my right, and the endless water stretched away to my left, with the far shore hidden behind the earth's curvature. This would have been a horrible place to get caught in a storm, but the weather held, and navigating around North Porcupine Point went smoothly.

Less than an hour later, I bobbed in the sheltered waters of a small bay on the other side of the danger zone. It was 6:20 P.M., I had been paddling a long time, and several perfect campsites beckoned me from the shore.

I crunched the boat onto the gravelly beach and was about to set up camp when the question arose unbidden, *Have I really done everything I can safely do today?* After a moment of reflection, it was clear that the answer was no, dammit, I had not done everything I could do. There was still some gas left in the tank. Squeezing every mile out of the good days was necessary because bad days were inevitable in the future. Reluctantly, I returned to the heavy boat, turned it around, and slogged out to sea again.

I finally set up camp at 8:00 P.M. on a large granite shelf overlooking the lake. I had been in the boat for twelve hours straight. I had eaten in the cockpit, peed into a bailer, and only stretched my legs briefly on land twice. The GPS said I was now 38.6 kilometers from the last campsite, but that distance was measured as the bird flew. Once the detours around islands and through crooked channels were factored in, I had paddled over forty-eight kilometers today. This wasn't bad for a fifty-year-old body in a boat heavily laden with gear.

Significantly, in the last minutes of the day, I had also crossed the line separating the provinces of Saskatchewan and Manitoba. The forest looked the same on both sides of that border, but it was an important milestone nonetheless. Hopefully, the next border would be the edge of Nunavut and the treeless tundra of the Canadian Arctic.

Today's route had included several risky open water crossings with significant exposure. If things had gone wrong during those sections, then they *really* would have gone wrong. Before heading out to sea I had weighed the risks and benefits based on years of experience and the information available to me at the time, and everything had turned out well. It's easy to be retroactively self-complimentary when a decision turns out well. *See, now that I've survived, I always knew it would be okay!* but balancing risk and reward is necessary anytime you're in the outdoors.

I am well acquainted with risk. There have been many long canoe trips in the North, Class V whitewater kayak expeditions in steep-sided canyons, training and competing in full-contact martial arts, helicopter-based survey work in remote mountains, multiple bear encounters, and decades of working as a firefighter. There have been close calls during these adrenalized activities. Rapids and waterfalls, which I was lucky to run unscathed, helicopter incidents that could have left me head-less, and a few fires where—had things gone differently—I might have received a line-of-duty funeral with full departmental honors instead of a few medals.

I've also seen the consequences of other people's misadventures many times. I've tended to hundreds of people in their last moments, lost friends and paddling partners to whitewater, and two of my four brothers died doing adrenaline sports.

The single most significant underlying factor for the accidents I've seen was inadequate risk assessment. Here are five principles I use for evaluating and mitigating risk.

First, don't take risks for other people.

There's an adage that goes, "My right to swing my fist ends where your nose begins." In other words, you can take risks for yourself, but you cannot take risks for other people.

Driving without a seatbelt might be dumb and reckless, but the risk of doing this falls primarily on your own shoulders. As a grown-ass adult, informed about the consequences, this should be your choice to make. In an accident without a seatbelt, it'll be *your* face smashing through the windshield and *you* bearing the consequences of your actions.

Contrast driving without a seatbelt to decisions where the outcome of your choices primarily affects *other* people. For example, drunk driving; if you crush a case of beer, then head out on the road, and crash into a mother hustling her kids to gymnastics, then obviously, you're not just hurting yourself. By driving drunk, you're putting people at risk who never consented to be part of your activity.

Simply put, it's okay for free-climber Alex Honnold to climb El Capitan without ropes, but it's not okay for him to climb that same cliff with his six-month-old child strapped to his back.

Things become more complicated when you consider trickle-down effects. For example, if I drunkenly wrap my car around a tree, the firefighters and paramedics answering the call aren't available to help others. Or if I drown on a river, the rescuers trying to recover my body are also at risk (roughly ⅓ of all whitewater drownings are rescuers trying to help someone else). And if I have children and get myself killed, those kids inevitably end up bearing the consequences of my actions, too.

Informed consent is necessary because you can't agree to take a risk if you don't truly understand the consequences. Let's say you're new to whitewater, and we go paddling, but I neglect to tell you the river is freezing cold and has Class IV whitewater. This trip puts you in grave danger, and if you die, then it's *my* fault, not yours. You couldn't meaningfully consent because you didn't have the information needed to make an intelligent decision; you didn't even know what questions to ask!

As a basic principle, we should try only to take risks where the consequences of that risk mostly fall on our own shoulders.

Second, you should take calculated risks. Don't take risks just for the sake of taking risks; be sure there's a good reason for incurring that danger.

Perform a risk-to-reward evaluation *before* you do something dangerous. Slow down and think for a second before you speed up.

Firefighters have to evaluate danger-to-benefit ratios for many of the decisions they'll make at an emergency scene. One of the most influential thinkers on firefighting was Chief Alan Brunacini, who led the Phoenix Fire Department for twenty-eight years. His writing and tireless work with national agencies changed how fire departments everywhere do business.

One of Brunacini's most famous sayings was, "Risk a lot to save a lot, risk a little to save a little, and risk nothing for what is already lost." That means if my crew and I arrive at a house with flames and thick black smoke pumping out of every window, then we're NOT going to grab hoses and run inside. This much heat and smoke means that any victims inside are almost certainly dead. Doing an interior attack here would risk a lot to save very little: too much risk, too little reward.

On the other hand, if we pull up and there's a fire developing in a day-care center packed with children, that changes everything. Now, there's a much bigger potential reward—living kids—and we'll take more risks to try and deal with that situation. The outcome is never guaranteed, but at least if something goes terribly wrong, it'll be easier to explain why we died to our families.

Firefighters try to assess the risk of every fire; they don't just charge blindly into every burning building. Similarly, you should do a risk-to-reward analysis for every dangerous activity and only proceed where you have something to gain.

The third principle is having a risk budget.

A financial budget constrains how much money you can spend in a given time. If you buy one thing, it means you don't buy another.

A risk budget is the same; it specifies a certain amount of danger you're willing to put yourself in, which you can take piecemeal or all at once. Take a risk if it achieves something vital to you, but then dial it down in another aspect of your life. You don't need to reflexively accept every risk that comes your way.

Mark Foo was a brash big-wave surfer who once said, "It is not tragic to die doing something you love." And when he actually did die in the giant waves over the treacherous shoals at Mavericks in California, it wasn't a tragedy. Surfing gave his life meaning.

It might be worth it to pay the ultimate price for doing something you love, but it makes much less sense to die doing something mundane. Incur necessary risks to do something you love, but don't take unnecessary risks.

Or, put another way, if you love skiing, take risks on the slopes but don't die in a car accident on the way to the mountain.

Fourth, acknowledge the worst-case scenario.

For every action, you must consider both what you might gain and what you might lose. Be clear about the upside and the downside. This means you need to acknowledge the credible worst-case scenario.

Ask yourself, *What's the worst outcome that could reasonably happen if I pursue this course of action?*

Wilderness expeditions require you to think like this all the time. A fun rapid becomes a very different animal if there's a waterfall just below it; if you screw up and go over the waterfall, you'll probably die. If you're free-climbing a cliff, it matters if the drop below you is ten feet or one thousand feet.

You can't take calculated risks or live within your risk budgets if you don't consider the most likely worst-case scenarios.

The fifth principle I use for taking risks is always having a backup plan.

Even the best-laid plans often go sideways. Hope is not a strategy, so you need contingency plans for these bad things.

Many people take crazy risks with no backup plans and still survive. "See?" they'll say, "I didn't take any precautions, and everything turned out okay. That proves taking precautions is silly."

Hang on just a second . . . You only hear stories like this from people who survived; anyone who died doing some crazy thing isn't boasting about it at the bar. Also, even unlikely events become certainties if you take enough risks on a long enough timeline. Let's say you're doing something with a 99 percent chance of success. You'll probably be alright if you only do that thing once or twice. But if you do the risky thing 1,000 times, then failure becomes inevitable.

We often practice mayday procedures in the fire department for scenarios where a firefighter is trapped or disoriented. The truth is that mayday situations don't happen very often, but when they do, the consequences are very high. They are incredibly stressful events for both the trapped firefighter and the rescuers, which means the steps to follow must be so ingrained through training that they become automatic.

Whenever you do something risky, think about all the credible worst-case scenarios and have a contingency plan for that event. That way, if something terrible happens, you'll already have a plan ready, which will hugely speed up your response and make it much more effective at a time when you'll doubtless be under a ton of pressure.

DAY 15

WINDBOUND BY DAY, PADDLING BY NIGHT

July 15, 2009
Start: At the Manitoba-Saskatchewan border
(57°30'9.6" N 102°0'9.0" W)
Finish: In the bushes beside a tiny, bear-infested beach
(57°36'10.4" N 101°46'39.3" W)
Distance covered: 24 kilometers

Climbing and meditation are the same. When the pain is really forcing you to go down you keep going up, you are really on the edge of possibilities, on the edge of life and death.

—Reinhold Messner

The thin nylon tent walls shivered violently from the wind. I unzipped the door and saw rows of whitecaps sliding toward the shore from my elevated perch on a granite ledge. It was only 6:00 A.M., and rough weather this early in the day was a really bad sign.

So much for covering the last thirty kilometers to the end of the lake today, I thought. Then, like a groundhog that didn't see its shadow in early February, I burrowed into the sleeping bag and returned to sleep.

A few hours later, I reemerged and took stock of the situation again. It was a warm day, and dramatic white clouds raced across the blue sky, but it was still much too windy to travel. I was stuck here, at least for now.

Survive first, win later, I reminded myself. This idea comes from jiu-jitsu: avoid catastrophic defeats while using technique, patience, endurance, and mental toughness to work methodically toward victory in the long run.

Let's say you have to fight a very angry and much larger aggressor. Covered in tattoos, he towers above you and looks like he could bench press your body weight all day. What you don't want to do here is turn the fight into a tit-for-tat slugfest where his strength and weight advantage will likely overpower you.

Often, a bigger fighter will try to end the fight quickly by using his strength to knock you out or crush you unconscious. This initial blitz is the most dangerous time; you'll have to use all your technique, strategy, and cunning to weather the storm. However, the longer the fight goes, the more equal things become. His fury will abate, and exhaustion will begin to negate his superior attributes. When he becomes tired, he won't be nearly as strong, and at that point, you can turn the tide and start to launch your own attacks.

Surviving first and winning later works in fighting, but I've also used this concept in many other situations. For example, my divorce in 2010 was financially devastating; I went from living in a nice condo I owned to squatting in a dingy rental basement, worse than anything I lived in during my student days. Child and spousal support payments ate up most of my income.

Trying to win immediately in this situation would have involved going to the casino and putting all my remaining money on black, hoping for a big payout. Instead, I hunkered down and went to the mattresses. I cut all unnecessary expenses and kept my remaining financial powder dry. I worked side jobs wherever I could to earn extra cash. It took hundreds of late nights and very early mornings, but eventually, I ended up in a better place than before.

It helps to remind yourself that, in life, sometimes you're the hammer, and sometimes you're the nail. Some days, you'll be unstoppable, and everything will go according to plan. Congratulations, you were just the hammer. Huzzah! Now remind yourself that this too shall pass. Other days will be downright terrible; nothing will go right, and you'll tap out more times than a bongo drum player. Welcome to being the nail. Once again, remind yourself that this, too, shall pass. Pick yourself up, brush yourself off, try to figure out what went wrong, and then work on fixing it! Like Winston Churchill said, "If you're going through hell, keep going."

To win in impossible situations, you first need not to lose. You can't win if you're knocked out of the race permanently, so limit your downsides. Then use your know-how, patience, and endurance to work toward the big win relentlessly.

The morning and afternoon were spent resting in the warm sun, repairing gear, eating, and napping. I remained on standby, ready to break camp at a moment's notice if the wind dropped.

Being windbound on large lakes comes with the territory; the weather is beyond your control, so all you can do is be ready to seize opportunities when they arise. Strong winds on large lakes often diminish in the early evening. If that happened and I ended up paddling into the night, I wanted fuel in my body, so I ate a large pasta dinner at 2:00 P.M.

At 3:00 P.M. the wind waned just a little, and the whitecaps became a smidge smaller. Just to be ready, I packed everything into the canoe. *It'll really suck if the wind doesn't drop and I have to set everything up again in the exact same place*, I worried.

By 6:00 P.M. the whitecaps were gone, and there were no signs of threatening weather in the sky. I hopped into the packed boat and struck out across the bay ahead of me, aiming for an island halfway across. I paddled hard into the wind to minimize time spent on the open sea and quickly reached the island. Using it for shelter, I bobbed in the water, double-checked for any approaching thunderstorms, and then struck out again for the far shore.

I continued north, weaving through groups of small islands and channels. The northern sun approached the horizon at an angle, stretching the sunset out into a spectacle that lasted hours. I covered twenty-four kilometers in under four hours that evening, a strong pace and proof that even a half day's rest can do the body good!

By 10:00 P.M. the last brilliant colors in the sky were fading. It would soon be dark, but the entire shore was covered by a dense, hummocky forest that left almost no room for tents. The only option was a narrow strip of beach between the water and a black spruce bog, but the sand was covered with old bear prints. It looked like this was a regular haunt for at least one local bruin.

Camping here didn't seem like a good idea, but it was too late to find another site. Even though most bears want nothing to do with humans, it's still a little worrying when you're intruding so directly on their habitat. I used the dying light to squeeze the tent into a bumpy spot between two spruce trees and a large willow shrub just at the edge of the sand.

I ran the thin monofilament line of the bear alarm around the tent and through the trees; finding the nearly invisible line with my fingertips was finicky work, made more difficult still by the relentless mosquito attack that arose in the now-breezeless night. Slapping and cursing, I set the alarm up and dove into the tent, where it took ten minutes to kill the mosquitoes that had drafted in behind me.

I stacked my bags against each wall and slept between them in the middle of the tent; a few waterproof backpacks wouldn't stop a bear from ripping through the thin tent walls, but it might slow him down by a few seconds, giving me a bit more time to prepare a good response. To prepare that potential response, I parked the shotgun to the right of my body and put my headlamp, knife, and hatchet to the left.

I already knew I probably wouldn't sleep well; the presence of the bears and the abrupt transition between hard paddling and bedtime would see to that. I had rested earlier in the day, though, and another crappy night wouldn't kill me. I set the alarm for 5:00 A.M. to get on the water as early as possible the following day.

BROCHET, BROWNIES, AND BACK UPRIVER

July 16, 2019
Start: In the bushes beside a tiny, bear-infested beach
(57°36'10.4" N 101°46'39.3" W)
Finish: Kamechayt Rapids on the Cochrane River
(57°58'06.3" N 101°28'13.5" W)
Distance covered: 52 kilometers

Does anyone know where the love of God goes
When the waves turn the minutes to hours?
The searchers all say they'd have made Whitefish Bay
If they'd put fifteen more miles behind her
They might have split up or they might have capsized
They may have broke deep and took water
And all that remains is the faces and the names
Of the wives and the sons and the daughters.

—Gordon Lightfoot,
"The Wreck of the Edmund Fitzgerald"

The sun had barely crept into the sky, but my boat was already cutting through the calm water. I could feel the gentle following wind on the back of my neck, nudging me toward the native village of Brochet. Given the conditions, I decided to shave off ten kilometers by cutting across the mouth of Brochet Bay instead of going the long way around.

This was a big crossing, but it was made safer by following an island archipelago in the bay. Some islands were just a few boulders heaped together, and others were larger and adorned with forest, but I would never be more than twenty minutes from solid land if the wind came up. The abundance of islands also limited the size of waves that could build up in a given wind, further reducing the chances of broaching, swamping, and flipping. Still, to be on the safe side, the sail stayed safely furled upon the boat's deck as I paddled like a man possessed.

As I went on, signs of civilization became more common: occasional cabins appeared in the forest, boats were pulled up on beaches, and the faint sounds of outboard motors as fishermen came and went.

My boat slid between two low islands, revealing the small town. Humble houses sat on a sandy rise, and a few larger buildings—like the town store and band office—provided bright splashes of color. The spire of the church pointed to the sky. A lone pickup truck rumbled down the main road, trailing a cloud of dust.

This tiny town had been established in the 1860s as a trading post and Catholic mission. In those days, the Qamanirjuaq caribou herd overwintered in this area and gave their name to Reindeer Lake. Back then, there were both Cree and Dene residents, and there were even times when inland Inuit living at the very edge of the tree line came south to Brochet to trade. Nowadays, the population is mostly Cree, and the caribou don't tend to come this far south anymore, but the town remains.

I beached my canoe beside some aluminum boats just as wind gusts started jetting across the water behind me. I was glad I had started early in the day and was now in more sheltered waters.

I stumbled up the beach, rediscovering my land legs, and exchanged pleasantries with an old Cree man sunning himself on his porch. I passed the Catholic church, once the domain of Father Egenolf, an eccentric priest who had traveled widely in this region by canoe and dogsled. He had spoken both Cree and Dene and was a recurring character in several Farley Mowat books. Brochet seemed nice, but I didn't want to stay for long; momentum was on my side, and there was still a long way to go.

The clerks at the Northern Store kindly allowed me to charge my assortment of electronics as I wandered the aisles. At the back of the shop, past the canned food, cleaning supplies, and fishing rods, was the post office. As I had done in Southend, I mailed a box home filled with empty dry bags, maps of the country behind me, and anything else I could get rid of to lighten my load. All the remaining MREs—the heavy, disgusting, and unhealthy army rations—went in the trash. This lightened my load by about fifteen pounds, making it a bit easier to haul the boat upriver and lug the gear over portages.

Soon my basket was filled with a collection of calorically dense foods that offered a break from the routine—three ice cream sandwiches, a giant bag of brownies, several boxes of cookies, and a bagged salad. The relentless daily exertion had stoked my metabolism so high that I could now eat whatever I wanted.

I walked back to the boat, mostly ignored by the residents of this dusty town. I was, after all, just another in a long line of travelers passing through for their own reasons. I paddled through a protected channel bordered by willow-, spruce-, and birch-covered islands. Having shelter now was fortunate because the wind had really picked up while I was in town; sizeable open water crossings would have been suicide.

An hour later, I had devoured the three ice cream sandwiches and had made a good start on the bag of brownies. Then, as I passed between two small islands, the canoe felt slightly sluggish; I took another paddle stroke, but the canoe just didn't accelerate beneath me the way it should have, and I noticed that the current was gently pushing me backward. This was the point of transition, where the Cochrane River flowed into the waters of Reindeer Lake. This marked the end of the Reindeer Lake traverse and the beginning of the next stage, the ascent of the Cochrane River.

The voyageurs never traveled on the Cochrane; they stayed on the larger routes to the south. But this river was still an important route north for the early explorers and for the native peoples bringing beaver furs to the

Hudson's Bay post in Brochet to exchange for trade goods. In summer, they traveled by canoe, and in the winter, by dogsled and snowshoe. I'd be following in the footsteps of thousands of people, all long since dead.

In theory, I should have taken this moment of transition to ponder profound things and think deep thoughts. However, the impending challenge of fighting up another river pushed everything else from my head. The contemplation and search for the meaning of this moment would come later.

Against all expectations, the first part of the Cochrane River ascent was relatively easy. The current here was slow, and the same wind making Reindeer Lake so dangerous was blowing directly upriver, precisely where I needed to go. I hoisted my small sail, which shuddered as it filled with wind and pulled the canoe upstream. With the powerful tailwind and easy paddling, the first ten kilometers of upriver travel were completed in style. Only once did I have to jump into the water to pull the boat up a small set of rapids.

You don't get very many warm southern tailwinds to carry you upriver; my face erupted in a silly grin, which persisted for most of the afternoon. Great opportunities don't come along very often; when they do, you should take advantage of them by riding that horse into the ground. So I charged onward, resolving to remember this day when upriver traveling became more difficult in the future.

At 7:00 P.M. I reached Kamechayt Rapids, where a giant mass of whitewater crashed down a series of bedrock steps, wafting a mist that settled cool on my face. This was the end of easy sailing and the beginning of hard portaging. My back creaked as I hoisted the food bags, and began shuffling through the forest, sweating from the load and swatting at black flies.

There are easier ways to make it to Hudson Bay, like taking an airplane. I suppose I do it the hard way for many of the same reasons that climbers clamber up mountains, runners run ultramarathons on bleeding feet, jiu-jitsu practitioners train ten years to get a black belt, and tourists flee from stampeding bulls in Pamplona.

These painful, dangerous, time-consuming, and exhausting activities all function as rites of passage.

In ancient Greece, young Spartan boys entered the agoge, a brutal system of abuse, toughening, and physical education. At the other end of this crucible was the possibility of becoming a full Spartan citizen and permission to get married.

In many East African tribes, adolescent boys must be circumcised to be considered men and become full members of society. Their foreskins are cut off in public ceremonies without anesthetic; the participants are expected to be stoic and not flinch even as the blade cuts into their skin.

In Australian Aboriginal, culture it was common for adolescent boys to journey in the wilderness alone for months. Not all teenagers who went into the bush survived, but it was an essential ritual to enter adulthood.

By definition, these different rituals of transformation weren't easy. Success was not guaranteed; failure, injury, and even death were possible. But if these rituals were easy, then they wouldn't be meaningful.

Of course, there are both personal and societal lenses through which suffering is interpreted. Two hikers can get soaked in the same cold downpour and come away with radically different life lessons; the first hiker might interpret it as Type II fun, and the other might decide never to go hiking again.

Solo canoe trips in the Canadian North have repeatedly served as rites of passage for me, both pivotal life experiences in themselves and markers between different life stages. Wilderness canoeing is my thing, but that doesn't mean it needs to be yours. And probably you shouldn't sneak out of your house to assassinate serfs with a dagger like ancient Spartan youths, get flogged with wet ropes like a sailor crossing the equator for the first time in the Royal Navy, or have your genitalia publicly mutilated like the Maasai.

While there isn't one ordained rite of passage in our society anymore, the good news is that there are many demanding challenges you can voluntarily put yourself through. You should choose a self-improvement ritual that'll push you physically, mentally, and emotionally. It should be halfway between too easy and suicidally dangerous. If you're not at least a little bit scared by it, then it's too easy. As long as it's hard and success isn't guaranteed, then it might work for you.

There is a certain glory in voluntarily embracing suffering and risking failure to get to transformation and transcendence. Rites of passage serve as markers of psychological time, lines in the sand where you can say, "Regardless of what happens now, I'm a little different from when I began."

The portage trail was easy to find, snaking through the dry lichen-filled forest and marked by a series of old logs sinking into the ground. These logs were laid out like an upside-down railroad track; the rails running end to end were on the bottom, and the shorter railroad ties were laid on top crossways. It wasn't functional anymore, but this had once been a boat-skidding track where locals had hauled their boats around the rapids. I carried the canoe to the far end of the portage, then set up camp back at the base of the rapids. It was getting late, and the rest of the bags could be portaged tomorrow.

Clouds of black flies bedeviled the evening; they were much worse now than at any previous point of the expedition. Every few seconds while cooking or setting up the tent, I had to rub my hand over my face to kill any new attackers chomping on exposed skin.

The riffles and rapids of the Cochrane were the ideal breeding ground for black flies. They require moving water to reproduce and lay their eggs in the current. The eggs hatch into tiny aquatic larvae that attach to the rocks and feed on tiny detritus in the moving water. The larvae grow underwater, doing no harm, and can reach incredible densities; some studies have counted up to 600,000 black fly larvae per square meter of river bottom. When all those larvae finally transform into their adult form and take to the air, they become legendarily awful; during peak black fly season, a single kilometer of river can produce up to a billion black flies per day.

Once hatched, black flies search for a blood meal to get protein for the eggs they need to lay to repeat the cycle. Usually, this blood is obtained from animals, but they'll also take it from canoeists foolish enough to camp near them. It was mid-July, and they were guaranteed to make life miserable whenever the wind dropped.

I built a fire, knowing that the carbon dioxide emitted by the burning logs would confuse the bugs and make it harder for them to home in on me. But as soon as the food was put away, I retreated into the tent; outside, there was only the choice between watering eyes from sitting right in the smoke or constant attack from the bugs if I moved even one foot backward.

In the tent, I wrote some notes and stitched torn clothing. On all sides came the sound of drizzling rain, except it wasn't water falling against the tent; it was many thousands of insects hitting the nylon, looking for a way in.

I was apprehensive about this section of the trip. The water was very high, my boat very heavy, and the timeline tight. I kept thinking about the late-August storms on the tundra and being a sitting duck for hungry polar bears on the coast. The faster I ascended this river, the more safety margin I would have. On the other hand, I knew I wasn't the first person to ascend the Cochrane; this had been a route north for as long as there had been people here, and if they could do it, then so could I.

The strategy was simple: push upstream as hard as possible every day without destroying either my boat or my body. Whether this effort would be enough to complete the trip in time was out of my hands.

ARRIVAL IN ESKER COUNTRY

July 17, 2019
Start: Kamechayt Rapids on the Cochrane River
(57°58'06.3" N 101°28'13.5" W)
Finish: The base of large esker
(58°11'49.6" N 101°17'28.9" W)
Distance covered: 39 kilometers

But what a fierce joy to be riding with a thousand white-maned horses racing the wind down some wild waterway toward the blue horizons.

—Sigurd Olson, *The Singing Wilderness*

The river was swollen from all the recent rain, with water surging over the banks and into the dense willow bushes on both sides. Sometimes the current even ran into the spruce forest, cutting new channels between the densely packed trees.

The day started with a series of paddling sprints. The current was so swift that I could only maintain an all-out paddling pace for a few minutes before resting in an eddy until my heart stopped pounding. Then I would repeat the process.

Soon, I came to the bottom of a steep drop where giant waves pounded through a long cleft in the bedrock. While pondering my options, I heard the drone of a motorboat on the river behind me. A Cree man worked the tiller of the outboard motor, throttle fully open. His wife sat at the front of the boat, and several teenagers sprawled on the seats.

The boat didn't slow down; instead, it attacked the rapids and worked uphill through the waves, darting from side to side to avoid the biggest curling waves. The motor screamed against the current, but the driver calmly guided the boat upstream, briefly waving as he flashed by. Then, the boat disappeared around a bend and was gone.

This was a reminder that I was still close to the village of Brochet. The boaters might have been heading to their cabin, hunting, or meeting up with friends; this was their backyard, and their ancestors had traveled up and down this river for thousands of years. Encountering people on the river would become much less frequent in the days to come and then cease entirely during the second half of the trip.

There was no possible way my canoe could follow that boat up the middle of the rapid. That aluminum craft had a forty horsepower motor, whereas an Olympic rower in top condition produces about half of one horsepower. No paddler, no matter how strong, could ascend this whitewater.

Fortunately, an exposed bedrock ledge at the side of the rapids allowed for easy walking with no bushwhacking required. It took half an hour of unpacking, half an hour of portaging, and half an hour of repacking to get around one hundred meters of rapids, but that was still a pretty good pace.

After the bedrock rapids came hours of hard upriver slogging. The flood had buried some of the whitewater marked on the map and created new rapids where none were marked. I paddled and tracked the boat upstream using ropes. Maintaining the boat at the correct angle while walking upstream was trickier here than on the Reindeer River because there usually wasn't much of a walkable shore. Consequently, I had to manipulate ropes while sloshing through moving water that flowed over slippery rocks.

When tracking became impossible, I slipped into the waist-deep water and waded upstream, gripping gnarled roots and willow branches with one hand while pulling the boat upriver. This was a treacherous form of underwater rock climbing where my feet felt for unseen footholds amid the rocks, and the cold current threatened to rip the boat out of my hands.

When most people think of "willows," they imagine a tree, perhaps a tall weeping willow with a thick trunk, deeply furrowed bark, and long graceful twigs adorned with silver leaves blowing in the wind.

Those are NOT Cochrane River willows . . .

The willow species in the North are not trees; instead, they grow as gangly shrubs and bushes, roughly the height of a tall person. Found in dense thickets on riverbanks, they send their scratchy branches out over the water in search of light.

These horizontal branches create a dilemma for wading upstream. You can either crash through the branches close to shore where the footing is better and the water slower, or you can go farther from shore around the branches, but now the deep, swift current makes keeping your footing harder, and you risk getting washed away downriver.

In the late afternoon, I came to two significant stretches of whitewater: Kasakweeseeskak Rapids and Kamacheechawasik Rapids. Both unpronounceable names represented formidable obstacles to upstream progress.

Kasakweeseeskak Rapids was a long chute where the water pulsed between steep, muddy banks. The willow branches here formed a wall that extended far out over the river and stretched from beneath the water's surface to high overhead. I decided that Kasakweeseeskak probably meant *Willow Hell Rapids* in the Cree language.

There was no portage here, and carrying my gear through the dense forest would have taken the rest of the day. That left only the brute force option. "Heroism is endurance for one moment more," I muttered to myself, then tied the boat to a tree and climbed through the water while breaking branches off of shrubs to clear a path for wading.

Then, I pulled the boat forward a few feet and repeated the process. It took hours to reach the top; this was the hardest, slowest wading I had ever done, but also just a harbinger of other challenging ascents to follow.

I was wet, cold, and tired, but for discomfort, context is everything. The fact that slipping into that cold water served to get me closer to a goal created a psychological framing that made all the difference. Chest pain in the middle of the night is terrifying—a possible sign of a heart attack. But chest pain from shrieking muscles and burning lungs after a hard workout is experienced entirely differently. The sensations might be very similar in both cases, but in the first case, you feel fear, and in the latter, you might feel pride.

I'm used to pain and discomfort, but cold water immersion was different. Just because you're good at dealing with one kind of pain doesn't automatically mean you're great at dealing with another. I always think about Lance Armstrong's first marathon after he retired from cycling. After he crossed the finish line, the seven-time Tour de France winner described it as ". . . without a doubt the hardest physical thing I have ever done."

Really? Harder than six to seven hours a day of pedaling in the Alps? Harder than twenty-three back-to-back days of cycling in the 3,500-kilometer Tour de France? It's strange that a lifelong endurance athlete with a history of pushing his body to an unbelievable degree, even with all that doping, would consider three hours of running more difficult than the ludicrous amount of cycling he had done. But he was used to the pain of cycling and *not* used to the pain of running.

If you do something difficult repeatedly, you slowly acclimate to that activity. You still feel the pain, but it no longer bothers you as much. It's not about being born tough as nails; it's much more about your attitude adjusting over time. That's why athletes become good at dealing with their own particular brand of pain. Powerlifters get used to the pain of deadlifts. Boxers learn not to freak out when they get punched in the face. Runners get used to burning lungs and bleeding feet. Grapplers become accustomed to getting crushed on the bottom.

Adaptation takes time, and also has its limits. For example, ascending the river, I had to find the balance between pushing beyond my comfort zone and not breaking anything permanently. If I pushed too far, then hypothermia could kill me, and other cold-related injuries like trench foot and chilblains could severely impair my ability to continue upriver.

Finding this balance can be difficult, especially if you're new to an activity and don't have the base of experience to judge what's truly dangerous. With time, you'll learn to distinguish good pain from bad pain and discomfort from injury.

Getting tougher and being able to function in situations that would have been untenable previously is all about experience. Unfortunately, as Mark Twain once said, "Good decisions come from experience. And experience comes from making bad decisions." So you have to minimize the consequences of all those initial bad decisions. When I teach jiu-jitsu to beginners, I advise them to tap out early and tap out often. They lack the experience to judge the difference between discomfort and actually getting injured. I tell them, "Tap out early for now and be a hero later. With time, you'll become tougher."

At about 5:00 in the evening I came to the third and final stretch of serious whitewater of the day, Kamacheechawasik Rapids. The surging waves here were several hundred meters long. I tried not to think about how much fun it would be to ride the waves downriver, and then threw myself against the current again.

The river rebuffed my initial efforts. As I waded upstream, the water got deeper and deeper, rising from my hips to my chest to my neck. I could go no further without getting swept away, so I clambered onto the shore and into a muddy clearing full of horsetails.

Both shores were packed with trees, shrubs, and branches without any portage routes or game trails. These were thickets worthy of *Sleeping Beauty*, and it wouldn't have been surprising to find bodies of fairytale suitors tangled in the shrubbery. Getting my canoe and gear through this mess looked impossible.

I was saved from a full day of lumberjacking through the forest with my hatchet and folding saw when I spotted a small side stream that paralleled the main river. This channel was a transient feature created by high water carving a temporary path between the trees. This tiny creek was only six to twelve inches deep, and I crawled on my hands and knees, slithering under branches and hauling the loaded boat behind me. The *Sea-One* crunched over the coarse gravel. The resin rasped off the fiberglass hull is probably still on those rocks today, but it was better than cutting a new portage trail from scratch.

This tiny streamlet rejoined the river at the top of the rapids, and it was with relief that I slid the boat back into the primary current. Getting up the Cochrane River required the use of every trick in the book and the invention of some new ones.

In the evening, I arrived at Kapuskaypachik Lake. There hadn't been any decent campsites for hours, so I was thrilled to see a large sand esker on the far shore. Eskers are tall ridges of sand and gravel that snake across the landscape for kilometers. Canoeists are always looking for eskers because they usually provide well-drained open spaces with fewer bugs than in the surrounding forest.

I always feel ridiculously happy when I see an esker snaking over the landscape. It's a sign that I'm back North, the land dominated by ice in the not-so-distant past.

The eskers in northern Manitoba were formed 8,000 to 10,000 years ago at the end of the Wisconsin glaciation. As the glaciers retreated, the freshly liberated meltwater had to go somewhere, and it drained downward through the glaciers. At the bottom, it coalesced into large rivers that ran in tunnels under the ice toward the newly exposed land at the glacier's terminus. Sand and gravel were carried along in the moving water and deposited in long ribbons on the floor of the ice caves that were left behind when the glaciers were gone, making eskers the beds of ghost rivers that once ran under the ice.

There was a five-star campsite on a beach at the base of the esker. Moose, wolf, and bear prints were all over the sand; the wildlife liked it here as much as I did. I paid extra attention to setting up the bear alarm around the tent that evening.

It had been a full-body struggle all day, much of it was submerged in cold water, and my muscles vibrated with fatigue. I fell into the tent after charging through the evening tasks as fast as possible. But the transition from adrenaline mode to sleep was too abrupt, and I tossed for hours before fading to black sometime after midnight.

UPRIVER AGAINST AN UNFORGIVING CURRENT

July 18, 2019
Start: At the base of large esker (58°11'49.6" N 101°17'28.9" W)
Finish: On a sandy beach with tons of bear sign, Cann Lake
(58°25'11.8" N 101°09'47.4" W)
Distance covered: 30 kilometers

It's not the years, it's the mileage.
—Indiana Jones, *Raiders of the Lost Ark*

I woke up much sorer than when I went to bed. My body was just not recuperating from my exertions and was slipping a bit further into the hole every day. I was playing with fire, and I knew it.

Physical activity makes you stronger in the long term but weaker in the short term. For example, the total amount you can bench press goes *down* immediately after a hard bench press workout because your muscles are now tired and less able to produce force. You don't get stronger until you've had sufficient rest and nutrition to allow your body to recover and grow beyond its former limitations.

Furthermore, if you keep pushing yourself without sufficient rest and recovery, your work capacity will decrease and eventually, inevitably, inexorably, you'll get sick or injured. This is called overtraining, which happens when you break your body down faster than it can rebuild.

Overtraining breaks you down before you reach the starting line. Undertraining breaks you down before you reach the finish line.

—Bob and Shelly-Lynn Glover,
The Competitive Runner's Handbook

Athletes and coaches learned long ago that to increase athletic capacity, you must have the correct amount of time between training stimuli. If the recovery period is too short or the training sessions too severe, then the result is overtraining. On the other hand, if the time between training sessions is too long, the base capacity level never actually increases. It's easy to break an athlete down; the tricky part is building them up.

To excel at a physical craft, you need to get good at the nonglamorous aspects of the art, like mastering your sleep, dialing in your nutrition, and becoming an expert at preventing and healing from injuries. To become a black belt in execution, you must also become at least a brown belt in recovery.

Getting a respiratory tract infection like the flu, a cold, bronchitis, or sinusitis is a classic sign of overtraining. I've read that almost 15 percent of marathon runners catch a cold the week following a race, whereas only 2.2 percent of runners who trained for the same race but didn't compete became ill. In the short term, severe training hurts your immune system.

Injuries are another result of overtraining, and every athlete has his weak link, that part of his mind-body system that breaks down first when exposed to heavy stress and overtraining. For some people, overtraining often triggers lower back pain, and for others, their knees start to ache.

Other indicators that you might be overtraining include an increased morning heart rate (best monitored first thing before you get out of bed), apathy, depression, and lack of enthusiasm for training (physiological cues that your hormonal and endocrine systems are drained), and disrupted sleep patterns.

My difficulty falling asleep despite being completely exhausted was due to overtraining. Finding a sleeping position that didn't hurt was impossible, and the stress hormone cortisol coursing through my body didn't help either. Cortisol can be very disruptive to your sleep, and in a perverse double whammy, not getting enough sleep undermines your recovery and further contributes to being even more overtrained.

When you're a teenager, you can work out hard, stay up all night, and bounce right back the next day. You just can't do that when you're older, and at age fifty, I felt every hour of lost sleep.

Many athletes who still perform at an elite level into their late thirties and forties do so by becoming fanatical about sleep. LeBron James in basketball, Roger Federer in tennis, Usain Bolt in sprinting, and Tom Brady in football slept at least ten hours a night and often took extra naps during the day. You really can't overstate the importance of getting lots of high-quality sleep for recovery and performance.

Each hour that a helicopter flies in the air necessitates at least an hour of maintenance on the ground. Pilots insist on this because you don't want the Jesus nut—a large nut holding the main rotor to the mast of the helicopter—to detach and turn your bird into a plummeting rock. Sleep is the mechanic that maintains your body.

If I could have waved a magic wand and changed anything about the trip, I wouldn't have made it easier, and I wouldn't have made it shorter. I would have improved the quality of my sleep.

Dizzy from fatigue, I broke down camp and followed the Cochrane north through a large shrubby marsh in a shallow valley bounded by a distant spruce forest. Beyond the dense willow walls of the main channel were older arms of the river, now slowly being filled in by vegetation. The dance of erosion and deposition reshapes rivers all the time, but the most significant changes occur during high-water events like spring flooding. I tried to imagine the gigantic floods that had finally heaved the river out of one of those forgotten channels and into its present-day course.

The current was relentless, and padding up the middle of the river would have been impossible. I steered the boat toward the rushes at the river's edge, where the water was slower. Even in these slower waters, my usual five kilometer per hour pace was reduced to a measly two kilometers per hour by the current and a steady headwind.

For the next ten hours and twenty kilometers I thought about little else other than finding the route of least resistance up the river. I continuously zigzagged from shore to shore, searching for slightly slower current or the smallest degree of shelter from the wind. There was just endless winding water amid the wetland shrubs and submerged spruce trees, so I paddled, rested, ate, and drank without leaving the boat all day.

By evening, I started worrying about where to pitch my tent; there hadn't been any dry land for a long time. The battered topographic maps, held together by tape, indicated that Cann Lake was just ahead and lay at the convergence of several eskers. I was counting on acceptable camping sites there.

Indeed, as the current of the Cochrane transitioned into the deeper waters of Cann Lake, a fantastic array of campsites revealed themselves. I landed on a large crescent beach backed by an open forest of widely spaced birch and spruce trees. A pleasant breeze kept the bugs down to reasonable levels. It looked like an idyllic setting to call home for the night. There was just one problem: bears.

There were bear tracks on the beach. Logs had been torn apart by bears looking for grubs. Large piles of bear scat everywhere. White caribou bones poked ominously through the dense green mat of crowberry plants. The caribou had most likely been shot by native hunters in the winter, but no matter how carefully hunters clean a carcass, some meat scraps are always left on the bones, meaning that local bears probably associated this place with food.

Even with all this bear sign I was just too tired to move to another site, so I stayed and deployed full bear precautions.

The first level of bear protection is awareness. You don't want to stumble upon a bear at close range or accidentally get between a cub and its mother, which would likely trigger a reflexive self-defense attack by the bear. The open landscape made keeping an eye on things relatively easy. As I set up camp and cooked dinner, I glanced around every ten or twenty seconds to ensure no curious bruin had silently wandered onto the scene.

The second bear precaution is to be punctilious with food. In bear country, you want to cook and eat your food far from your tent to avoid smells that might lure a hungry bear into your sleeping quarters. Accordingly, I cooked my pasta after walking several minutes down the beach and carefully washed my dishes and hands. The remaining food and the cooking gear were stored in two large waterproof and smell-proof bags, which I then hid in different spruce thickets 200 feet apart. Even if a bear stumbled upon one of these stashes, it would be unlikely that he would discover the other, leaving me with some food rather than no food.

The third level of bear defense was setting up the PackAlarm around the tent and testing it several times. I would use that tripwire alarm every night for the rest of the trip.

The fourth bear precaution was having my folding stock 12-gauge Winchester Marine shotgun handy. Loaded with buckshot and slugs, it was a handy noisemaker and a self-defense tool of last resort. Many people consider guns to be the first line of defense, but usually, if you have to use one, you screwed up a long time ago. At most campsites, the gun sat just outside the tent as I did the evening chores, but tonight I carried it around like a soldier trudging through some tropical jungle.

Bears aside, this was still a beautiful place to spend the evening. I didn't have time for many campfires on this trip, but the setting demanded one. A match applied to birch bark topped with dry spruce branches instantly crackled into a fire. The smoke created an insect-free safe zone, and I plunged naked into the lake for the first deliberate bath in nineteen days. Afterward, I warmed up beside the flames, connected to the long line of people who have crouched in similar ways ever since humans have been able to control fire.

DAY 19

UNDERWATER WILLOW CLIMBING

July 19, 2019

**Start: On a sandy beach with tons of bear sign, Cann Lake
(58°25'11.8" N 101°09'47.4" W)**

**Finish: On a native camping area in an area with almost no campsites
(58°32'05.0" N 101°22'56.9" W)**

Distance covered: 28 kilometers

You've been climbing and you think, Oh God, I'm completely knackered, and I can't move up another foot. Yet if you actually stop and think about it you're not anywhere near knackered, I mean, you've got lots of strength left. What it is, is that you feel sorry for yourself. You've been going at this for 6 hours now, and it's your brain that's tired. The brain is tired underneath the mental strain of it, forcing upward and not knowing. I mean, you're just completely isolated from all the millions of people in the world. There's nothing anybody in the world can do to help you—you're completely in charge of your own world.

—Don Whillans, British mountaineer

In the morning, the good news was that no bear had rampaged through the campsite. My tent, food, and canoe were all safe. The bad news was that the wind was now raising small whitecaps on the lake and had brought a cold drizzle in from the northeast. Conditions seemed marginal, but after studying the map, I decided there might be just enough of a wind shadow to the lee of the shore to sneak onward.

I struck out, paddling as close to land as possible. To make progress, I had to dodge into every bay and hide behind every headland, using the terrain to lessen the force of the wind.

At Thuycholeeni Lake, I had to cross from the downwind to the upwind side. The wind blew unobstructed across the water, hitting the shore (and me) with vicious gusts and crashing waves.

The protected shore I wanted to reach was only 500 meters away, a trivial distance under normal circumstances. However, the wind, waves, and horizontal rain made this crossing an all-out brawl. It required all my strength to advance, and if I stopped paddling for an instant, the boat got blown backward. Unwilling to concede a single inch of progress, I pulled on the paddle again and again, and after a half-hour battle, I finally reached the protected eastern shore. I slumped into the boat; it took a long time for my heart rate to drop and feeling to return to my arms.

Eventually, I forced myself back into action, and I followed the shore northward. Gradually, the wind drove the fog and rain clouds away, revealing tall cliffs and bedrock hills around the water. The vertical scenery of Thuycholeeni Lake was very different from the flat river valley the day before.

The rolling hills also revealed the scars of a vast forest fire that had raced through the landscape sometime in the last ten years. I had seen hints of this fire on the shores of neighboring lakes, but it was on the hillsides above Thuycholeeni that the full measure of the inferno became apparent. This inferno had incinerated all the trees and most of the ground cover, leaving behind scorch marks on bare bedrock. This desolate and beautiful landscape was a harbinger of the treeless tundra to the north.

The vast scale of this conflagration was exciting to imagine, but I also felt grateful not to have witnessed it in person. Fires this big create their own weather systems; the superheated air shoots upward, sometimes into the upper atmosphere, where it can create pyrocumulonimbus clouds or fire-induced thunderstorms. These storm clouds spread the fire further, both by generating lightning and carrying burning brands for kilometers downwind.

The remaining smoking landscape after the fire must have seemed apocalyptic; how could anything ever grow here again? But the wheel of fire has rolled across the boreal forest countless times since the ice retreated; nature had always recovered before and was recovering now.

Purple streaks on the hillside indicated areas with enough soil left to allow fireweed to grow and flower. The forest was also beginning to reestablish itself; the tips of diminutive jack pine seedlings were already poking up through the fireweed flowers. This conifer emerges from tough wax-covered cones that remain dormant on the ground for decades. When a fire vaporizes the forest, it also melts the wax on these cones, opening them up and releasing millions of seedlings to reforest the devastated landscape.

Past Thuycholeeni Lake, the twisted river afforded excellent protection from the thudding wind, but the narrowness of the channel meant the current was intense. Almost every swift required waist-deep immersion, wading, and tracking to ascend. Climbing the rapids below Peacey Lake was particularly nasty. The willow boughs here jutted so far out over the water that they made wading along the shore almost impossible. The water was too deep to go far enough into the river to get around the branches, and I could not carry my equipment through the dense forest on foot.

It was time to try a new technique. I left the boat behind and slithered forty feet upriver through the dense shoreline forest with a length of floating rope. I tied one end of the rope to a solid tree and threw the rest of the coils into the current. The floating rope was carried downstream and came to rest against the outer edges of the willow branches that bobbed in the current.

Then, I retrieved the boat and waded upstream using the fixed line for stability. The rope provided just enough of an anchor to walk in the chest-deep current and pull the boat behind me without losing my footing. Like a Himalayan mountaineer following fixed ropes established by the Sherpas, I slowly climbed upstream until I reached the rope's end, dragged the boat to shore, then repeated the whole process.

Entanglement is a real danger anytime you're using ropes near moving water, especially with a lot of wood around. This threat is further amplified if one end of the rope is anchored to a solid object because if you get washed downstream with the rope wrapped around your neck, arm, or leg, you could easily drown. With this in mind, I checked the bright yellow rope's position after every step upstream. The fact it was a floating material made it easier to keep track of and less likely to entangle my body underwater. I also obsessively checked and rechecked the river knife mounted on my PFD; in an emergency, I might only have one opportunity to sever a rope holding my bobbing body underwater.

I spend a lot of time in the woods catastrophizing. What if I get wrapped in a rope in whitewater? What if a small cut gets infected? What if my boat turns sideways and broaches around a rock in a rapid? What if a critical piece of equipment breaks? What if a bear eats half my food? What if I can't keep to my timetable?

This isn't reveling in negativity; optimism and pessimism *aren't* incompatible. The poet Adrienne Rich said, "It is important to possess a short-term pessimism and a long-term optimism," which speaks to holding these two worldviews on different time scales.

Being a pessimist *in the short term* forces you to anticipate what can go wrong and how to fix it if it does. Expect everything that can go wrong to go wrong. Anticipate setbacks, and don't be attached to the outcome of any one specific effort. And, of course, have plans to minimize the fallout from the most likely failures.

At the same time as you're anticipating all the problems, it's important to keep pessimism from pervading your entire worldview. *You have to be a long-term optimist.* Believe that you'll eventually arrive at the desired outcome if you keep striving, adapting, and overcoming.

Balancing this short-term pessimism and long-term optimism is a fine art. It's okay to be discouraged by setbacks so long as you bounce back and try again the next day. Expect failure, have backup plans, keep going, and be ready to take advantage of opportunities when they appear. Put in long hours, squeeze everything you can out of the excellent weather and tailwinds that come your way, and you'll likely complete your journey.

After an hour of underwater rope climbing, I reached Peacey Lake. This lake alternated between two entirely different characters. When the sun shone, the wave crests sparkled, and the vibrant new growth glowed green on the hillsides. But the scenery seemed much less inviting when the sun was obscured behind thick clouds and dark waves lashed the jagged rocks on the shore. The highs and lows of a wilderness trip were condensed into minute-long cycles as the sunlight flared and faded.

Eventually, I came to Chipewyan Falls, where the water plunged over a ledge that ran from shore to shore. The remnants of an old wooden boat ramp around the falls made the portage easier. As I slid the boat over the rotting logs, I was encouraged by the fact it had become noticeably lighter due to my slowly eating through the food stash.

Back on the water, I limped along in autopilot mode, going slower and slower as the evening went on and my muscles weakened. I needed to rest, but there were only two types of shorelines here: fields of angular boulders the size of garbage cans and swampy muskeg forest where the ground would slowly sink beneath any tent. Neither looked like a particularly good place to spend the night.

By 7:30 P.M., I was so tired that I started thinking about harvesting a giant pile of shrubs and laying them down on the wet hummocky moss to create a platform for my tent. I was not looking forward to this; I have used these improvised campsites of last resort on other trips, and they always sucked.

Just as I was coming to terms with sleeping in a swamp, a sandy bank appeared at a river bend. I climbed the small bluff with shaky legs to find a dry terrace behind it. Other travelers had used this site—there was even a wooden tripod for smoking meat made above a fire pit. I was sure this site had been used for hundreds, if not thousands, of years; good campsites in areas with scarce options will always appeal to trippers, regardless of whether they're paddling Kevlar or bark canoes.

Soon, the tent was set up on a soft crowberry and reindeer lichen surface. Wet clothing dried in the last rays of the low-angle sun. Dinner bubbled over the fire. The wind dropped, the evening became calm, and I watched the endless surge of water passing by my camp.

I had only traveled for ten and a half hours today, but that had been unceasing labor against a relentless wind and a cold current. I was mentally and physically fried, but there had been no major disasters, so it had been a good day. One more big push tomorrow and I should reach the tiny native village of Lac Brochet. This would be my last brush with civilization for the rest of the trip.

DAY 20:

PADDLING, WADING, TRACKING, AND DRAGGING TO LAC BROCHET

July 20, 2019
Start: On a native camping area in an area with almost no campsites
(58°32'05.0" N 101°22'56.9" W)
Finish: In a clearing on a tiny island just offshore from Lac Brochet
(58°36'22.7" N 101°30'25.8" W)
Distance covered: 23 kilometers

Things have been going wrong long enough
To know when everything is just right,
I've been walking in the dark long enough
To know when I have finally seen the light,
I've been losing long enough
To know when I have finally found the one,
And even a blind man can tell
When he's walking in the sun.

—B. B. King, "Walking in the Sun"

I woke at 5:30 A.M., emerging from the tent to a cool, silent landscape. The sun rose directly over the river, slowly burning off the mist lingering on the water.

Moving in slow motion, it took way too long to break camp and get on the water. Before leaving, I put on the dry clothing that had been hanging overnight. It felt warm and luxurious against my skin. I got underway, and just around the first corner, there was yet another rapid that could only be ascended by wading. I groaned and slipped back into the cold river to drag the boat upstream. I had been in dry clothing for exactly twenty minutes.

Gripping, walking, slipping, cursing, and pulling in the waist-deep water got me about halfway up the rapid, but then the banks of the river became too steep and the water too deep to continue. Even with ropes, I could no longer wade upriver without getting swept away, so I hauled the fully loaded boat up the overhanging bank and into the swampy forest. If there had ever been a portage here, it was now wholly overgrown after decades of disuse. Nobody goes up the Cochrane River without an outboard motor anymore.

The dense riparian forest of spruce, birch, alder, and willow made portaging the boat on my shoulders almost impossible. The boat ricocheted off trees and was hooked by branches at every turn. *Screw it!* I dropped the boat to the ground and threw a few bags into it, then dragged the partially loaded boat through the forest under the branches, crawling on my hands and knees. The logs and rocks of the forest floor took little chunks out of the canoe, and the black flies took little pieces out of me. It was slow, difficult work, and the abysmal rate of progress was depressing; getting up this one kilometer rapid took more than two hours.

One of my martial arts teachers, the legendary Dan Inosanto, once told me that of all the physical attributes, it was endurance that was the most important. "If you're tired you're not strong, if you're tired you're not fast, if you're tired you won't have good technique, and if you're tired you're not even smart."

Endurance is critical for expressing all the other attributes and technical skills. Strength, stamina, knowledge, speed, balance, flexibility, judgment, coordination, agility, power, technique, strategy, and tactics go out the window if you're tired.

This ability to keep working in the face of fatigue, hardship, and suffering is a complex attribute encompassing aerobic endurance, anaerobic endurance, muscular strength, and mental strength.

Twelve months before the 1,000-mile solo, I planned to do a lot of paddling and upper body weight training to get into shape for the trip ahead. Mixing these two approaches would have given me both sports-specific and general conditioning. But everything went to hell when I injured my right shoulder doing jiu-jitsu—a lower belt caught me in a weird armlock during a sparring session. On the edge of my shoulder ripping apart, I stubbornly wriggled, squirmed, and shimmied instead of tapping. I eventually got out, but this victory came at a cost: the ligaments I strained and the tendinitis that followed made the right arm excruciatingly painful for a whole year.

Soon after that injury, I also banged up my other shoulder in a nasty fall sustained while racing on an electric skateboard. Why was I, a grown man, racing on a skateboard? That's a valid question I'm refusing to answer, but the bottom line is that *both* of my shoulders were now injured.

How the hell was I supposed to prepare for the hardest adventure of my life when almost all upper body exercise was off the table?

The answer came from talking to Mike McCastle, a US Navy sailor, endurance athlete, and pain artist. In 2014, Mike tore the anterior cruciate ligament in his knee while training at the Naval Special Warfare Preparatory School. During his recovery, he decided to try and beat the world pull-up record that SEAL David Goggins then held.

Mike McCastle's first attempt was an impressive failure; he did 3,202 pull-ups in 17 hours but had to quit 828 pull-ups short of the record when his bleeding hands refused to close around the bar. He had pushed himself so hard that he developed exertional rhabdomyolysis. In this condition, your blood is flooded with so many muscular breakdown products that it puts you at risk of kidney failure and potentially fatal cardiac arrhythmias.

Mike had been knocked down but was determined to try again. When he was released from the hospital, he returned to training, and fourteen months later, he absolutely obliterated the old record, doing an astounding

5,804 pull-ups in 24 hours. And, to make it even more mind-blowing, *he did all that while wearing a thirty-pound backpack.*

From 3,202 pull-ups to 5,804 pull-ups, now with additional weight. How did he improve so much? First, he had longer to train for the event, and second, he did more cardio. The cardio improved his endurance, accelerated his recovery, and trained his system to remove the waste products from his blood more efficiently.

That was the answer I needed. I might not be able to work on my paddling technique or the muscular endurance of my shoulder injuries, but by God, I could work on my heart and lungs. I spent nine months hiking the steep mountains above Vancouver, running stairs, and grinding on the StairMaster for countless hours. The goal was to strengthen my body's engine and increase my aerobic capacity. I watched in satisfaction as my times got faster and my resting heart rate fell.

Eventually, lifting light weights and doing shorter paddles became possible again. I still had to limit upper body training to avoid reirritating the shoulders, so most of my training was still straight cardio. At least I could train my physiology and psychology to keep going even when fatigued.

Were my preparations perfect? Not at all, but the strong aerobic base meant that one potential area of failure—my cardiovascular system—had been removed from the equation.

Endurance training causes a thousand changes in your lungs, heart, muscle fibers, and hormonal system, but it also changes you mentally. You become tougher because you become comfortable with discomfort.

Even though I had never trained by crawling on my hands and knees and pulling a hundred-pound sledge behind me, all that cardio sure came in handy now. Up, up, up the river I scrabbled. Finally, the riverbanks became less vertical. Wading and then paddling became possible again. So long as I kept going, I would get there; the important thing was just not stopping.

The final rapids before Lac Brochet were different. They were wider and shallower, finally allowing me to use the tracking ropes again. I climbed from rock to rock in the warm sun, using the lines to nudge the boat through moving water. This was a fun challenge, starkly contrasting with the suffering earlier in the day; these swings between emotional highs and lows were just part of the rhythm of the voyage.

Soon, I was at the southeast corner of Lac Brochet, a substantial body of water. I felt giddy about being done with current and willows for a while. Even so, getting to town wouldn't be easy because the gusty breeze had grown into a significant wind, and rollers were now battering the lake's southern shore.

A direct route across the lake was untenable, so I paddled in an extended counterclockwise circle along the lake's edge. This indirect route added significant distance to the journey, but the sun was out, the sky was blue, and it wasn't raining. Paddling a few extra kilometers was a price I was happy to pay.

In midafternoon, I landed on a small beach just outside the town, which—confusingly—is also named Lac Brochet. This tiny village is defined by the water, so everyone has a boat. I pulled my canoe onto shore between two motorboats and headed for the Northern Store.

I intended to collect a care package from home. Weeks ago, I had sent a satellite text to my wife asking for specific equipment to be sent north: a replacement carbon fiber bent shaft canoe paddle, two rolls of heavy-duty Gorilla Tape, and some high-end chocolate to feed the body and nourish the soul.

Sadly, my hoped-for equipment wasn't at the Northern Store's post office. It was stuck in some northern aerodrome and would only arrive in Lac Brochet months later; in the South, you can order almost anything you want and have it delivered in twenty-four hours, but there are still pockets of the world that don't work that way.

I left the store without my resupply. Not getting the replacement paddle meant that I only had two paddles for the rest of the trip, which reduced my margin of safety. Furthermore, it guaranteed more pain in my future; having that differently shaped paddle would have allowed me to alternate between different stroke mechanics and avoid exacerbating overuse injuries.

On the plus side, I did buy some cookies, a pint of ice cream, a pound of fresh cherries for a late afternoon snack, and insect repellent. Using more bug repellent was a compromise; until now, I had primarily relied on clothing and bug nets for protection, but the atrocious numbers of black flies and mosquitoes were making mealtimes miserable. Had there been more time, I would have lit smudge fires while eating, the traditional way to keep the bugs away. Recently, the days had been so long that there was no time for fire, and it was simpler to rub bug dope onto the back of my hands, neck, and cheeks before gulping down my food.

I paddled away from the beach at 4:00 in the afternoon, knowing I'd likely had my last human contact for the rest of the trip. Being alone didn't worry me—I had spent enough time in the bush alone to be okay with solitude—but from now on receiving help or getting evacuated would be much more difficult. Paying attention to every last detail while paddling, portaging, and camping to avoid preventable accidents was now a matter of life and death.

No more mistakes, I repeated for the thousandth time.

Storm clouds ambushed me just around the first headland. First came the white noise of raindrops hitting the water, and then the entire lake and everything on it was pelted by the cloudburst.

The island where I camped wasn't much more than a pile of boulders. A few trees and bushes grew in the cracks between the rocks around a flat area covered in bunchberry flowers that was just big enough for my tent. There was no need for dinner; I had eaten several thousand calories of ice cream and cookies in Lac Brochet. I collapsed into my sleeping bag listening to the wind rip through the trees. The GPS promised even worse weather tomorrow.

BRUTALLY SLOW PROGRESS

July 21, 2019

**Start: In a clearing on a tiny island just offshore from Lac Brochet
(58°36'22.7" N 101°30'25.8" W)
Finish: A rocky campsite at the south end of Misty Lake
(58°49'16.3" N 101°40'14.9" W)
Distance covered: 38 kilometers**

Oh my body has been punished.
Lord, I think I've had enough.
Oh my body has been punished
With too much and not enough.

—The Violent Femmes,
"I Know It's True but I'm Sorry to Say"

I arose at 5:30 A.M., too worried about the dire weather forecast to sleep anymore. Still sleepy, I stumbled into the nigh-invisible tripwire of the bear alarm and set off the shrieking siren. It was the world's loudest alarm clock, and now I was fully awake.

Only the gentlest breeze rustled the treetops at that moment, but that didn't mean I could relax. Lac Brochet was a very large lake, and the forecast promised lots of wind soon, so I had to push hard and get to more protected waters before conditions deteriorated.

An hour later, the wind had come up on the water. "Why is it always a headwind?" I grumbled as choppy waves struck the front of the canoe. The wind kept increasing in strength and rapidly approached the limit of navigability. I stole along the north side of the lake, staying close to shore to avoid the biggest waves.

My body mechanically went through the motions wave after wave, stroke after stroke. I desperately wanted to take a break and rest, but stopping would have resulted in getting blown backward and undoing the progress that had been won through brutal labor.

Five hours of nonstop paddling brought me to a bend where Lac Brochet twisted to the north. As long as I stayed tight to the western shore, the wind could no longer roar unimpeded across the water directly at me, which was a relief. Progress was slow now because my arms, shoulders, and back were all spasming; even my buttocks ached from sitting. I stopped every fifteen minutes to fall backward onto the bags behind the seat, lying motionless until the knots of pain relaxed enough to continue.

I limped along like this at half-speed for several hours, thinking about when Martin Luther King Jr. said, "If you can't fly then run if you can't run then walk if you can't walk then crawl, but whatever you do, you have to keep moving forward." My trip was far less noble than the struggle for civil rights, but the idea of somehow making progress despite your limitations resonated deeply with me that long afternoon.

A light haze materialized in the sky along the western horizon, and the air smelled a bit like a campfire in the evening. "Smoke from a distant fire, maybe in a different province," I told myself.

There was one more stretch of whitewater to ascend before calling it a day: White Spruce Rapids. At first, I hopped from boulder to boulder and tracked the canoe with ropes. I was still tired, but it felt great to use a different set of muscles and not sit anymore.

However, progress came to a screeching halt when I encountered the worst shoreside willow thickets of the trip. Not only did the branches stick out farther over the moving water than ever before, but now the branches were entangled with deadwood, creating a series of miniature logjams along the shore. It would require every trick I had discovered to get around these damn willows.

First, I waded upstream, ducking my head down, almost into the water, to get under the projecting branches. Then, I resorted to using a floating line as a handhold to ascend around the willow branches. I also had to dismantle the driftwood logjams by hand, throwing the wood far out into the current to clear a path for the boat.

Finally, the branches were too thick to go under or around, and I invented a new trick called "willow sledging." Here, I pulled the boughs down into the water one at a time and held them in place until there was a floating raft of live wood, still attached to the shore, bobbing in the river. Then I heaved the canoe on top of this unstable mess to pin it in place and wriggled onto the branch raft like an injured seal emerging from the ocean. Finally, I crawled ahead over the floating branches, dragged the boat behind me, and pulled down the next branches to repeat the process. It was hard work with definite disaster potential, but it was still better than portaging through the trackless forest.

Working atop this pulsating tangle of branches transported me back to a series of similar logjams that are burned into my brain forever.

In early May 1995, two years after my younger brother Peter died on his bike, I found out that my next youngest brother, Matthias, had disappeared on the Suskwa River close to the town of New Hazelton in northern British Columbia. I couldn't pack up my gear fast enough, and soon my van was hurtling through the night toward his last known location, 800 kilometers away.

I reached the river the next day and learned that Matthias and two friends had decided to tackle the dangerous Suskwa River Canyon in a cheap canoe designed for fishing on quiet ponds. They had only two lifejackets for three boys, and to make matters worse, the river was in spring flood, meaning it was now an ice-cold Class IV torrent. They had no business being on the river, and their canoe soon swamped and flipped. The other two kids had narrowly escaped with their lives, but Matthias—without a lifejacket—got swept downstream while trying to recover the canoe and disappeared. The first searchers on scene had found the canoe but not my brother.

Matthias had now been missing for two days and was most likely dead, but I hoped against hope that he was stranded on some rocky ledge in the canyon, unable to get out. The local search and rescue team had already scoured the canyon, but maybe they had missed something; I had to look for him.

With the help of a local paddler, I paddled and hiked that river for three days. I was in a daze, but I also had to control my grief and stay focused. This was an undeniably dangerous river, and it wouldn't have taken much for a potential rescuer to become another fatality. My parents had suffered enough; they didn't need to lose a third son in two years.

Knowing that drowned bodies tend to get caught up in wood, we stopped at each logjam and probed around it with a long aluminum pole. I dreaded feeling a bouncy resistance indicating a body at the end of the pole, but it never came. Part of me was secretly glad we never found him under those logs; I don't know how I could have looked into his face if we had pulled him from the water.

In three days of searching the Suskwa, all we found of Matthias was his canoe paddle. It gradually became clear that he wasn't bivouacked somewhere in the forest; he was dead. These days by the river helped with the mourning process because there's nothing like searching for someone's body to drive home the fact that they're truly gone.

Before leaving New Hazelton, I took an axe to the canoe Matthias had paddled. Nobody was ever going to use that shitty boat again. Six weeks later, some Gitxsan kids from the native village of 'Ksan came across my brother's body in an eddy at the junction of the Bulkley and Skeena Rivers. Another hundred feet and he would have been swept out to sea and never found. Even now, thirty years later, I feel terrible for what those kids had to see, but that grisly discovery allowed my poor parents to physically bury their son, albeit in a closed casket ceremony.

How did this disaster change my relationship with the outdoors? I feel guilty saying it, but it didn't change at all. I kept waiting for a shift in my connection to rivers and canoeing, but it never came. I don't claim to understand why, but maybe it's because my relationship with the outdoors began before I had those brothers and continued after I lost them. After all, one of my earliest memories is camping with my parents beside Crane Lake in Ontario. I couldn't have been more than three years old, but I can still see the water beckoning beyond the screen door of the tent.

It's also possible that I disassociated the loss of a brother from the fact it had happened on a river because I had previously used rivers to process other grief. If I had allowed the role of the wilderness in my life to change, that might have invalidated all the good it had previously done for me.

Back on the surging drift piles of the Cochrane River I mentally saluted my lost brothers, told them that I wished they were still here with me, and carried on upriver.

With great relief, I eventually eased the canoe into the calmer water above the rapid. It had been a savage thirteen-hour struggle against heavy headwinds, challenging rapids, and hostile rapids, making for the hardest and longest day of the trip so far.

My destination tonight was a very specific spit of rocky land. Unlike all the other campsites on the trip, this site was familiar because I had previously camped there. Twenty-six years earlier I had been on a different solo journey from Jasper, Alberta, to Churchill, Manitoba. That route and my current route formed a giant X on the map, the two trips overlapping in the middle by less than a hundred kilometers, and I was now in the middle of that overlap section.

On that previous trip, it had also taken one day to cover the thirty-eight kilometers between this campsite and the town of Lac Brochet, which meant that at age fifty, I was still keeping up with my twenty-three-year-old self. Arguably, I was even outperforming that younger version of me because, back then, I had been going downriver, whereas today, I had been going upriver. Of course, today's efforts had nearly killed me, whereas, in my twenties, it had probably been an easy day. I preferred not to think too hard about that.

The smoke on the western horizon had thickened, and it now tinted the sunset with wild shades of orange, purple, and violet. The smell of smoke was overpowering. I convinced myself this soot was probably blowing in from Alberta or British Columbia, provinces hundreds of miles away that often have giant forest fires in the summer. Little did I know how close the fire was and how dire it would soon make my situation.

RACING AGAINST THE FIRE

July 22, 2019
Start: A rocky campsite at south end of Misty Lake
(58°49'16.3" N 101°40'14.9" W)
Finish: On a small sandy terrace above the Cochrane River
(58°59'21.1" N 101°47'28.8" W)
Distance covered: 38 kilometers

Only through experience of trial and suffering can the soul be strengthened, ambition inspired, and success achieved.

—Helen Keller

An eye-watering, throat-choking haze of smoke blanketed the morning landscape. The sun was a dim orb behind a thick sooty film, and the gray shore merged with a gray sky and gray water to obscure the horizon line in every direction.

This smoke will make the route-finding difficult, I thought. Today's journey followed the river through a series of complex lakes, but it was impossible to see any features or landmarks farther than a kilometer away. In these conditions, it would require a map and compass, GPS, and intuition to find my way across even the smallest lakes.

Halfway across the first lake, I had a three-part realization that the problem was more serious than just impaired navigation . . .

First, the sheer amount of smoke indicated a large forest fire nearby, and . . .

The smoke was getting thicker as I went, therefore . . .

The fire was directly ahead of me, and I would likely cross its path soon. This was NOT good news. The wet bandanna tied across my mouth to keep the ash out of my lungs would offer no protection from firebrands raining down into the water.

Floating in the smoke-shrouded lake, I studied the map with more purpose than ever before. There were a few different options . . .

I could retreat to the town of Lac Brochet. That sandy town wasn't in a forest, making it an area of refuge. Furthermore, if the fire grew out of control and threatened the settlement, air evacuation options would exist. But returning to Lac Brochet might delay the trip by a week or more, and I *really* didn't like the idea of undoing all that difficult upstream grinding from yesterday.

Another possibility was hunkering down on a small island in the middle of a large lake and waiting for the fire to die down, change direction, or burn past me. This option didn't appeal either; it's challenging to predict the speed and direction of a wildfire. What if it took days or weeks to pass? Or what if the fire suddenly turned north and blocked my route to Nueltin Lake and the Thlewiaza?

I decided the best solution was to charge directly at the fire. The maps showed that twenty-five kilometers upstream, the Cochrane River turned sharply to the right. As long as I reached that hook before the fire did and the wind direction didn't change, I might be able to sidestep the blaze like a matador evading a charging bull. Once I got out of the way, it wouldn't matter if the fire burnt up this section of the Cochrane River.

Everything now depended on speed, so I paddled forward with burning eyes and a special intensity. The water was relatively calm, so I kept a high stroke cadence and pushed the boat through the bizarre gray world, stopping only to wet my bandanna and take compass bearings.

The Cochrane River here is a series of lakes connected by a thin string of river. From 30,000 feet, it would have looked like Jackson Pollock had splashed blue paint across a green background. The abundance of lakes worked in my favor because traveling on the flat water was much faster than fighting upstream on long river segments. The lakes were also dotted with rocky islands where I could ride out the firestorm if I didn't reach the hook in time.

The possibility of incineration gives you an incentive to look for information in the most subtle of details. I studied the wall of smoke that circumscribed my world and noticed that when the route zigzagged to the east, the smoke got slightly better, and when it went to the west, the smoke got somewhat worse. The density of the smoke also changed as the wind shifted. These clues allowed me to roughly triangulate the location of the fire, and it seemed that it raged somewhere just beyond the hook. I had to hurry—if I didn't get to that point today, I might not get past it at all.

Two lakes—Belfie and Misty Lakes—were separated by powerful whitewater. I could hear the roar of those rapids from more than a mile away and braced for another brutal session of underwater willow climbing against moving water.

Then I noticed an alternate route between the two lakes: a tiny creek created by the unseasonably high water levels that jumped the banks of the lake above and trickled down to the lake below. I splashed up that knee-deep creek and arrived at the upper lake in just a few minutes. The same high water engorging the rapids and making upriver travel so hard had finally helped me! This tiny sneak route saved an hour of work, and I was giddy about it. It was a small victory, but precisely what I needed on today of all days.

I raced across Belfie Lake and reentered the river. It was now only twelve kilometers of wading and paddling to the hook. This was still hard work, but luckily, the river here was lined mainly by Myrica gale, a sweet-smelling shrub that doesn't stick out nearly as far over the water as the infernal willow shrubs. Wading through the water close to shore without climbing over willow branches made progress much faster.

I climbed the river into ever thicker smoke. The sky was apocalyptic, like Sauron was turning this land of blue skies and green trees into Mordor. I continuously checked behind me to see if the fire was sneaking around and cutting me off from the downstream escape route.

At 6:00 in the evening, after twelve hours of continuous work, I reached the hook. Under normal conditions, this curve in the river would have been a perfectly ordinary and unremarkable meander, but today it held a very special significance. Ahead was the fire, billowing smoke into the sky. Behind lay the lakes and river I had just ascended. And to the right, the river headed off in its new northeasterly trajectory, away from the inferno's path of destruction.

Arriving here before the fire was a great relief, but this location would likely soon be engulfed in flames. I needed to keep going and put some miles behind me before I could rest. Now heading in a new direction, I pushed on as fast as possible with dog-tired arms. The sky behind me was black, but ahead, it was blue. Onward, onward . . .

Two hours later, I dragged the boat onto the shore below a stunning lichen-covered campsite on a terrace overlooking the inky water. This site was almost certainly safe from the blaze; it was far away, on the opposite side of the river, the temperature was dropping, and the wind was still. The odds of the fire flaring up at night and overrunning this location tonight were minimal.

I could barely move but felt just a little bit proud; this had been a real test of tenacity. That being said, any toughness I possess has been built up slowly through years of tempering.

Part of toughness is physical conditioning. After all, like Vince Lombardi said, "Fatigue makes cowards of us all," and I was now very grateful for all those breathless hours I'd spent humping up and down Vancouver's North Shore mountains. That had built a deep reservoir of cardiovascular endurance, which had paid off when I needed to push through endless upriver slogging today.

The other part of toughness is mental: a determination to keep going through pain and suffering. How does one build this stoicism? By repeatedly exposing oneself to manageable doses of suffering over time. For me, this included all the cardio, weightlifting, jiu-jitsu sparring, and every other physically tough thing I've ever pushed through, but it also contained the endless studying in university libraries, getting my degrees, recovering from surgeries, plowing through financial difficulties, and everything else long, difficult and tedious I had struggled to endure.

An overlooked aspect of toughness is the ability to contextualize and survive failure. This, too, is developed through training. If you lift weights seriously, you will inevitably fail on some lifts. If you rock climb, you will fall off of some cliff faces. If you do jiu-jitsu, you will get tapped out. In all these cases, you learn to pick yourself up, brush yourself off, figure out what went wrong, and then try to fix it!

Having your ego repeatedly crushed in training teaches you that temporary setbacks are part of life and not necessarily the end of anything. It teaches you to always come back for more, and what is toughness, if not the willingness to repeatedly bang your head against a wall until it falls over? Life is predictably full of rapid, unpredictable reversals of fortune. Part of getting through the hard times is reminding yourself that they don't last forever. Whatever the details of your misery, remember that this, too, will pass, and don't dwell too intently on your current condition.

Today I dodged a forest fire by ascending 38 kilometers of river in 13½ hours of paddling. My body and mind were now utterly thrashed. I didn't even prepare a dinner—instead, I numbly chewed some trail mix as I set up camp, then collapsed into the tent, and was done.

ACROSS THE HEIGHT OF LAND

July 23, 2019
Start: On a small sandy terrace above the Cochrane River
(58°59'21.1" N 101°47'28.8" W)
Finish: On the portage at the north end of Lowell Lake
(59°05'15.3" N 101°43'37.6" W)
Distance covered: 12.5 kilometers

*It seems like suddenly coming into some strange new world. I have
never in all my northern travels seen country just like this.*
—P. G. Downes on crossing into the Thlewiaza watershed,
Sleeping Island: A Journey to the Edge of the Barrens

The backbreaking labor of the past days caught up with me, and I
slept until the shockingly late hour of 7:15 A.M. I broke camp in slow,
hobbling motions. Dark clouds of smoke still hung low on the eastern
horizon, emphasizing the need to put more distance between the forest
fire and myself.

The next three hours consisted of relatively easy upstream work. The
wider, slower sections could be ascended by paddle so long as the boat stayed
tight against the rush-lined banks. The swifts were mainly conquered by
linking eddies with front ferries and occasional bursts of all-out paddling.

Wading was easier here because the river was shallower, and the willows were not so dense.

Somewhere on the west side of the river was the portage that connected the Cochrane River to the headwaters of the Thlewiaza River. This portage was the beginning of the Old Way North, an ancient route that had connected the Dene of the forests to their northern caribou hunting grounds and the Inuit of the Barren Lands to southern trading posts. It had been used by many explorers whose journals I had read: J. B. Tyrrell in 1892, Ernest Oberholtzer and Billy Magee in 1912, P. G. Downes in 1937, and Farley Mowat in 1947.

In olden days, this trail had been marked by a large pine tree with an axe-chopped blaze. But this area had been burned over, and the arboreal indicator was long gone. Different maps put the beginning of the portage in various locations, suggesting the trailhead had shifted over time. All travelers, whether Neolithic hunters or modern canoeists, prefer portaging across dry, elevated eskers rather than slogging through wet muskeg forest. So, when a sandy moraine started running parallel to the river's eastern shore, I knew the trailhead must be close.

A small path arose from a shallow willow-lined bay and snaked up that sandy ridge. This area had recently burned, making it hard to tell whether this path through the young trees was the portage or a heavily used game trail. Nevertheless, it headed in roughly the correct direction and likely connected to the chain of small lakes at the headwaters of the Thlewaiza River, marking the beginning of stage 5 of the journey.

The amount of gear to be hauled across the portage was daunting. There were still twenty-seven days of food, supplies, and equipment, plus the boat, a combined weight of at least 250 pounds.

First, I carried the hundred-pound food bag, holding the shotgun in my hands in case I surprised a bear in the bushes. My feet slipped backward in the sand as I trudged uphill. Choosing between the many animal trails in the regenerating vegetation was tricky and required a mix of intuition and compass work. After ten sweaty minutes, I dumped the load at the foot of a distinctive birch tree that would hopefully make it easier to find my gear in the dense shrubbery.

On the second carry, I carried two packs: a heavy bag with all my cooking and camping gear on my shoulders and a second, lighter backpack turned sideways on top of that first pack. I trudged up the trail with my arms full of paddles, ducking under branches and stepping over deadfall.

The third and final load was the lightest—I only had the 55-pound canoe and a 20-pound backpack on my shoulders—but it was also the most challenging carry by far. It was hard to crash the boat through the bushes, and it kept getting snagged at the worst times. I staggered along as though drunk.

I continued up the hill in stages, following game trails through the burned tree skeletons and proliferating bushes. The GPS assured me I was roughly in the right place and heading in roughly the right direction, which was reassuring because this was easy terrain to get lost in.

Near the top of the sandy hill, the different trails merged into a more distinct path that ran east through the open forest. This part of the portage had clearly been used by native hunters on their long-distance winter Ski-Doo treks and was marked by occasional axe blazes on the trees. I was grateful for this ancient path, maintained now by snowmobile. It was possible to walk faster now, which made it a little harder for the black flies to swarm my exposed flesh.

After 3½ hours of sweating, the trail divided. The Ski-Doo trail continued straight, but a smaller path plunged down a steep mossy slope toward the water. I skidded down the steep path and came to the southernmost tip of Lovell Lake, the first in the chain of small, elongated lakes connecting the Cochrane and Thlewieza rivers.

I was covered in sweat, grime, mosquito repellent, blood, and dead bugs, so I dropped my bags and marched fully clothed into the muddy yet refreshing water. That neck-deep water felt like victory. After weeks of difficult traveling, I was now in the headwaters of a river system I had wanted to explore for decades.

The chain of lakes that led to the Thlewiaza River ran alongside an extensive esker network. It was as if a giant deity had run its fingers through the sand at the beach: the little sand ridges between its fingers had become the eskers, and the divots between the ridges had become the narrow lakes I would paddle along.

Back in the boat, I paddled north on Lovell Lake, where the glass-smooth surface reflected an upside-down vision of the world. Then that mirror was disrupted by concentric rings emanating from the first raindrops falling from the darkening sky. Studying the raindrops on this small lake felt intensely intimate, and I knew I was lucky to be there.

Soon, it was time to portage to the next lake along a tidy trail that started in a little wetland and wound up to the top of the esker. The portage was almost finished when a massive thunderstorm rolled over the landscape. I set up the tent in minutes and hastily flung my gear into it. Sheets of rain started to pound the forest, and I cozied into the tent for the rest of the evening, emerging only once during a lull in the storm to cook a quick dinner.

The next few days would involve much portaging, which would be a different form of exertion than paddling hour after hour. I hoped this break from canoeing might allow damaged muscles to recover and make paddling somewhat less painful by the time I reached the Thlewiaza River.

The rain drumming on the tent drove home the growing realization that I was finally in the Thlewiaza watershed. "Well, that took a bloody long time," I said to myself.

As a young man, I spent a lot of time on rivers. I raft guided in the Yukon, floated down Northwest Territories rivers for biology research, and canoed different routes from Alberta to Quebec. Their names still roll off my tongue like an incantation: Missinaibi, Albany, Kenogami, Spanish, French, Pickerel, Nottawasaga, Nahanni, Anderson, Aguasabon, Tatshenshini, Churchill, Batiscan, Cochrane, Athabasca, Fond du Lac, Seal.

I first read about Nueltin Lake in my twenties and was intrigued by this giant body of water that straddled the tree line and lay at the intersection of many possible rivers and routes. It seemed like a miraculous corner of the world, and I made vague plans to get up near there someday.

My romp across the North had been interrupted by adulting, several careers, marriages, mortgages, and kids. No longer could I disappear into the woods with a canoe in May and reemerge in September. Kids changed everything, and my marriage at the time was shaky enough without the added stress of extended solo trips.

To keep my sanity, I often daydreamed about returning to the North someday. I made this distant fantasy a little more tangible by picking a specific route and year: according to that original plan, in 2011, I would descend the headwaters of the Thlewiaza River to Nueltin Lake and then down to Hudson Bay.

I pinned the maps for this trip to the walls and studied the lakes, creeks, portages and rapids while bouncing babies or stumbling to work in the morning after having spent all night working a second job. These maps were a physical reminder that the North was still waiting for me.

During the most challenging parts of marriage and raising children, I counted down to 2011, the designated departure date. *Just nine more years . . . Just seven more years . . . Just five more years . . .* I hadn't given up on my dream; I was just using it to get me through the tough times.

The challenges weren't done yet. Just as 2011—the long-anticipated departure date—came within grasp, all hell broke loose. My marriage crumbled, I got divorced, and I lost both my home and my finances. Much as I wanted to get out of my postdivorce, weevil-infested basement suite, there was no bandwidth for self-indulgent trips; I needed to be there for my kids and rebuild financially.

To make matters worse, I also discovered I was dying of a genetic condition, polycystic kidney disease. My kidneys were shutting down, eventually dropping to a nadir of 12 percent function. The North suddenly seemed very far away.

I kept fighting to claw my way back to normality. Slowly, painfully, I rebuilt my finances. It was a long slog, but in 2014, I said goodbye to apartments and moved into a house of my own again.

Then my brother Christoph offered me one of his kidneys, an incredibly generous gift for which I'll be forever grateful, and on June 9, 2015, it was transplanted from his body into mine. The initial operation was followed by a rough year of additional surgeries, infections, and complications, but the new organ eventually settled into my body.

Finally, after a thousand bad first dates, I found Eva. My final wife is an amazing woman, and it still blew my mind that she allowed me to leave for the Thlewiaza the day after we got married.

It ended up being twenty-six years between long solo trips, from 1993 to 2019. A twenty-six-year drought during which my career, parenting, divorce, financial ruination, and near death conspired to keep me in the South. But that's just the way it goes.

Movement generally beats meditation, and the ability to quickly take decisive action is probably the single most significant determinant of success in life. But this "ready, fire, aim" approach doesn't always work. Life sometimes throws up obstacles that can't be quickly overcome through sheer bullheadedness, and in those cases, you need to temper the speed of implementation with patience. Achieving some goals just takes time, but if it's easy to achieve your goals, then they're probably not ambitious enough.

I was camped above a small lake that looked just like a million other lakes in the North, but this one was special because it was on the height of land into the Thlewiaza. Getting here was the culmination of twenty-eight years of planning, dreaming, and patience. Being here felt like vindication, and the lure of the unknown spaces ahead was palpable.

> In years of roaming the wilds, my campfires seem like glowing beads in a long chain of experience. Some of the beads glow more than the others, and when I blow on them ever so softly, they burst into flame. When that happens, I recapture the scenes themselves, pick them out of the almost forgotten limbo of the past and make them live.
>
> —Sigurd Olson, *The Singing Wilderness*

A CHAIN OF LAKES

July 24, 2019
Start: On the portage at the north end of Lowell Lake
(59°05'15.3" N 101°43'37.6" W)
Finish: On a sandy hill at the beginning of a portage
(59°12'56.1" N 101°34'11.9" W)
Distance covered: 18 kilometers

It's a dangerous business, Frodo, going out your door. You step onto the road, and if you don't keep your feet, there's no knowing where you might be swept off to.

—Gandalf the Grey,
The Lord of the Rings

The small unnamed lake was full of bays, islets, and dead ends. An esker ran down the middle of the water, bisecting it into two hemispheres. The rain was steady, but paddling in my gently swishing waterproof jacket kept me warm. The open spruce forest felt like a strange, new country.

It would take ten portages to cross over the height of land that divided the Cochrane and Thlewiaza rivers, and today, I hoped to complete numbers three, four, five, six, and seven.

The third portage was an easy seventy-five-meter carry to Holmberg Lake. I wondered how this pretty lake surrounded by lichen-clad hills got its name; maybe a Swedish trapper had built a cabin here once, or perhaps a bored mapmaker had named an interesting-looking lake after a long-lost relative. The North contains so many mysteries.

The fourth portage, into Smith House Lake, just half a kilometer long, turned out to be an absolute beast. First, I searched and searched but couldn't find the beginning of the trail. After double-checking the map, I was sure I was standing on top of it, but I couldn't even see a rabbit trail through the bushes.

The paper and GPS maps for this area had last been revised in 1985, making them a minimum of thirty-five years out of date, and heaven alone knows how long had it been since a cartographer had last physically verified the location of these rarely used portages. Unlike the South, where paths are worn deep into the forest duff and marked with metal signs, trails in the remote wilderness respond to the environment. They shift, disappear, and are reborn in response to wildfire, blowdown, the wandering of caribou, or the whims of a snowmobiler.

The forest here was regenerating from a fire, and I assumed the portage must have been entirely swallowed up by the bushy jack pine, dead spruce, and copious deadfall that formed a dense tangle just back from the shore. "This is going to suck," I muttered.

A small esker ran parallel to the old portage route. *Maybe the forest will be less dense up on the drier ridge*, I reasoned and carried my gear to the top of the ridge. Unfortunately, this particular esker was so pitted and hummocky that progress was plodding. After thirty minutes of stumbling, I gave up and slid all my gear back down the steep side slope to the flatter land below.

The jack pine forest here was so densely packed that I could only see a few feet ahead. I crashed through the vegetation, trusting it would eventually become more sparse, but on the other side of every green wall were just more branches with sharp, bushy needles. With the sun hidden behind the clouds, it would have been easy to wander in circles, so I held a compass at waist level and tried to follow a bearing to the northeast. I continually questioned my position and direction; navigating complex terrain is a master class in applied skepticism. I didn't want to suffer for nothing; "Measure twice, cut once," I grunted.

There was a real danger of losing my gear in the endless forest, so every time I dropped my bags and went back for another load, I added a waypoint to my GPS so I could navigate back to it. I also stood the brightly colored backpacks upright and propped the yellow paddle and the red lifejacket high into the branches of a nearby tree to make the gear depot easier to spot from a distance.

Three hours of brutal bush crashing later, I was finally close to the end of the portage. I found the missing trail there; it was a lovely, clear, level path that ran parallel to my own tortured route. It had been so close, only fifty or one hundred meters southeast of where I had been barging through the bushes. I still don't know where on Holmberg Lake this trail begins, but I know it's there somewhere. Finding it earlier would have spared me hours of unnecessary suffering.

The skies darkened as I repacked the boat on the southern shore of Smith House Lake. Just before the storm broke, the drop in barometric pressure roused the black flies to a feverish intensity; they were now so dense that I could kill a hundred rice-sized insects at a time with a single swipe of my hand along my thigh. This achieved nothing because another crawling mass of attackers would replace them just a few seconds later.

I looked down and saw red splotches on my shirt. I idly wondered why there were cherry juice stains on the fabric when I didn't have any cherry juice with me, and then realized those spreading stains were blood. My shirt had come untucked during the portage, and the black flies had crawled underneath it, chewing my stomach into a bloody mess. Thanks to the anesthetic black flies inject into the skin before ripping it open, I hadn't felt a thing, but I knew this wound would itch like crazy in the coming days.

The thunderstorm passed, but the rain continued to fall from a gray and overcast sky. Despite the weather, I was again struck by how pretty these little lakes, eskers, ridges, and sandy beaches were. The forest was becoming more open as I traveled north, inviting me to look for animal sign, native artefacts, and the best places to camp.

Portages five and six once again proved how significantly maps can diverge from the reality on the ground. The map indicated a single 400-meter portage connecting Smith House Lake to the next lake, but the route had since shifted to take advantage of a tiny ear-shaped lake lying between the two other lakes. So instead of a single carry of moderate length, there were now two portages: first, a short hop across an esker, then a two-minute paddle across a pond, and then another short carry to the next lake.

Portage seven was unexpected. The map implied the existence of a small creek between lakes, but instead there was only a forty-meter trail through dry spruce forest. I was so sick of packing and unpacking the boat at this point that I spent ten minutes gathering logs from the forest and building an ersatz boat ramp. Then I dragged the loaded boat over the portage with the wood protecting the hull from the sharp rocks on the ground.

At the edge of the water, I looked out at the next lake. Beams of sunlight breaking through the clouds glittered on the water and caressed the eskers, strange-looking peninsulas, crescent beaches, and lake-bisecting isthmuses created by the sand. This jewel of a lake captivated me, and for a moment, the bugs, headwinds, and endless portages seemed completely trivial. It is these moments of intense beauty that keep me returning to the North.

I camped on a sandy hill at the beginning of the eighth portage that night. The view was great, but the surrounding trees were small, making my aluminum-frame tent the de facto lightning rod for the entire area. If another thunderstorm came through at night, I'd have to break everything down and relocate to a safer place.

Progress had been slow these last three days: I had only covered about fifteen kilometers a day, or one-third of my usual speed. I wasn't discouraged; it's hard to go fast when the lakes are small and the portages frequent.

Crossing into this new watershed felt like a sea change. Things were simple but not easy, and I was now laser focused. Time was either spent traveling or getting ready to travel, which brought remarkable clarity to the days. Many times I had doubted my ability to get here, and yet, here I was. The only question that remained now was whether I could make it down the river all the way to Hudson Bay.

A GLIMMER OF CURRENT

July 25, 2019
Start: On a sandy hill at the beginning of a portage
(59°12'56.1" N 101°34'11.9" W)
Finish: On a beach in Thannout Lake
(59°21'07.9" N 101°23'08.5" W)
Distance covered: 20 kilometers

For all evils there are two remedies—time and silence.

—Alexandre Dumas

Dawn found me trudging northeast on an esker toward Blue Lake. The trail was easy to follow; it was the only logical route between lakes and was worn down by caribou hooves. Sun-bleached caribou antlers lay beside the trail, relics of winters past. This region has two great caribou populations: the Beverly and the Qamanirjuaq herds. These 400,000 caribou spend their summers on the tundra, fattening on the abundant grasses, sedges, and shrubs of that biome, then retreat south in the winter to escape the slashing winds, often crossing the tree line to shelter in the sparse northern forest.

I wasn't just walking in the footsteps of the caribou, but also of the Chipewyan, Cree, and Inuit peoples who had carried their hide-and-bark canoes across this same portage. I'm sure they had also swatted at swarms of bugs and felt a similar sense of relief as they approached the end of the long portage.

Finally, the trail descended the sandy ridge, went through a fringe of swampy forest, and arrived at the water. The long, narrow lake was well sheltered from the wind, and the miles flew by as I paddled in the sunshine. Soon, I was at the far end of the lake, and it was time for another short portage over yet another esker.

At the far end of that portage, I sank into the soft vegetation at the water's edge and crushed a Labrador tea leaf between my fingers, intensifying the fragrance already around me. Labrador tea smells like a pine tree or a juniper berry, but Henry David Thoreau once described the smell as "Being between turpentine and strawberries," which also seems pretty accurate. Despite "tea" being in the name, you shouldn't use these leaves to make actual tea because they contain high levels of toxic terpenes and alkaloids. Many people assume that just because something is natural, it must be good for you, but that's a mistake; cobra venom, radioactive rocks, poisonous mushrooms, and Labrador tea all exist to prove the naturalistic fallacy wrong.

The downriver section of the trip was approaching. Soon, there would be current, whitewater, and far less portaging! I ate chocolate to celebrate while sitting in that sweet-smelling grove above the sparkling lake, remembering one of my mottoes, *ABF, always be fueling.*

The tenth and final portage was into Fort Hall Lake. It was just a fifty-foot hop across a narrow strip of forest. For the second time in two days, I laid forest deadfall across the trail and built a timber trackway from lake to lake. Then, I dragged the boat across to the shore of an intensely blue lake that stretched away to the northeast. A heavy weight lifted off my chest; the journey over the height of land was now complete.

By the standards of the trip, Fort Hall Lake was of modest size, less than eight kilometers long and barely more than a kilometer across. This should have been easy going, but the hills on either side of the lake channeled a headwind that would halve my speed and double my work for the rest of the day.

Despite the wind, the beauty of Fort Hall Lake still shone through. The shore was a thin line between the blue sky and the blue water, sandy beaches were everywhere, and I could see why this lake had once hosted large summer villages for the Dene. Now, the only signs of that long-lost nomadic lifestyle were a few abandoned hunting camps slowly being swallowed by the forest.

The stirrings of a current moved in the small winding channel connecting Fort Hall Lake to Thannout Lake. I stopped paddling and let the moving water carry me downstream. I was giddy—it had been three weeks since I had last traveled with the flow of the water, and that felt like a lifetime ago. The water was finally working with me instead of against me.

The Thleiwiaza here was barely more than a creek, but I knew it would soon grow as countless other creeks and tributaries joined it. The current would plunge into large lakes and seemingly disappear, only to reassert itself at the outflow. The river would flow north across the tree line, onto the tundra, and then down to the saltwater ocean of Hudson Bay. I couldn't wait to see it all.

The creek emptied into Thannout Lake. It was now 7:00 P.M. and time to make camp; fortunately, sandy hills and beach campsites were everywhere. According to P. G. Downes, who traveled this route in 1939, the name Thannout Lake came from the Chipewyan term *Tha-nai-tua*, which translates as, *Sand ridges around the shore*. The name seemed apt.

I pushed toward a small peninsula jutting into the water, hoping this exposed location wouldn't have too many bugs. On the beach were two overturned aluminum fishing boats. Based on how they were buried in the sand, they had been abandoned for quite some time, strange remnants to leave behind, given how expensive it is to ship large items this far into the North.

It might have been a relaxing place to camp had not a disaster been lurking in one of my food bags. Sometime during the day, a one-liter container of olive oil had burst, and the pungent oil had gone everywhere. Food, cooking gear, wetsuit booties, rope, nylon bags, and fuel bottles were slippery. As this oil slowly went rancid, it would release lots of delicious bear-attracting odors. This was a serious problem.

All evening I wiped up oil with a cotton T-shirt, repackaged food into clean bags, and burned anything too greasy to clean. I put the oily gear into the largest dry bag, filled it with hot water and most of the remaining dish soap, and manually agitated it to create an ersatz washing machine. Then, as the sun set and the temperature dropped, I tied all the freshly laundered items to a rope and stretched it out into the lake, where it would bob in the waves to rinse all night. Cleaning up the oil fiasco had taken three hours that could have been spent resting.

The last thing I did before sleep was fire up the portable satellite dish and beam a few photos and stories from the day into outer space. From there, they would get posted on my website and social media accounts. Fussing with electronics in the middle of such a remote setting felt a little discordant, but it was my only relaxing frivolity of the day. It ensured there would be a few moments to reflect on the journey and make sense of it at the end of every day. These dispatches were also my diary, and if my gear and body sank to the bottom of a lake, then at least these digital footprints would survive.

These one-way communiqués also served as a motivational gun to my head. The goal was just crazy enough to justify extreme measures, so before the trip, I had leveraged all my online resources—social media, podcast, email list, and website—to tell my entire audience about the plan. I knew that committing to this big audacious goal out loud would create a situation where I didn't want to disappoint people or invite ridicule, and that would incentivize finding new ways to keep going during the tough times. It was a slightly more intense version of the strategy where you sign up for a 10k race to get serious about running and get back into shape.

Of course, holding myself accountable to an audience could also go too far. If things didn't go my way, of course, I'd then have to pull the plug regardless of what I had announced to the world. I didn't want to do something stupid just because thousands of people were watching. The idea was to use social pressure as a potent goad to my ego to get my ass in gear but stop short of letting my ego get me killed.

I had been traveling for twenty-five days and hadn't seen another person for five days. I was excited to see what lay downstream on this rarely traveled river.

THE LONGEST PORTAGE AND AN ABANDONED LODGE

July 26, 2019
Start: On a beach in Thannout Lake
(59°21'07.9" N 101°23'08.5" W)
Finish: At an abandoned hunting and fishing lodge
(59°31'39.4" N 101°13'49.8" W)
Distance covered: 26 kilometers

My name is Ozymandias, King of Kings;
Look on my Works, ye Mighty, and despair!
Nothing beside remains. Round the decay
Of that colossal Wreck, boundless and bare
The lone and level sands stretch far away.
　　　　　　　　—Percy Bysshe Shelley, "Ozymandias"

A gentle wind and blue sky promised ideal traveling conditions. *This looks like a good day to cover a big chunk of miles*, I thought.

The washing line had been rinsing in the waves overnight, and I couldn't smell any oil on the ropes, bags, neoprene, and other gear. Would the far more sensitive noses of bears be able to detect it? I didn't know.

Back in the canoe, I pushed north again with swift and light paddle strokes. The endless spruce forest on shore was interrupted only by large sand banks wherever the water had cut into a glacial deposit. The Canadian flag has a maple leaf on it, but it should really be a spruce tree since it dominates vastly more of the country.

Somewhere among the trees was the location of historic Fort Hall. This trading post had been built by Herbert Hall in the early 1900s, where he traded with both the Dene and the Inuit. It had been abandoned in the 1930s but was so solidly built that it stood until the 1980s when it was destroyed by fire. I contemplated climbing the sandy terrace to search for evidence of that bygone era among the trees, then weighed that against the weather on Hudson Bay getting worse as the brief arctic summer raced on. I dug the paddle back into the water and continued without stopping.

The lake here was an elongated pond that sometimes constricted into a gently flowing river. When the current sped up, I let the water carry me along, savoring every minute of rest. Then, the river narrowed and curved to the right, indicating that Kasmere Falls was just ahead. These falls are a serious obstacle on the Upper Thlewiaza, and I did not want to blunder into them. I stayed on the outside bend of the river with my senses on high alert, noting every shift of the boat, every rock, the splash of every wave, and every eddy to get off the river.

At first, the low drone of the falls was barely audible, mostly obscured by the waves' splashing and the wind's sigh. Then, the sound of the water smashing into rock at the base of the falls became louder, and finally, the roar reached a crescendo as the river disappeared over a horizon line with mist wafting up from below. Fortunately, there was a large pool of calm water above the falls to pull over and tie up the boat.

After double-checking the knots holding the boat to the shore, I hopped from boulder to boulder to get a better look at the drop. I hoped to avoid the portage by wading or lining the boat down a side channel. After all, in an exciting section of his semiautobiographical novel *No Man's River*, the famous Canadian author Farley Mowat claims to have run this stretch of river in 1947 in a canoe equipped with an underpowered five-horsepower outboard motor . . .

"A fierce current gripped us as we swung heavily into the slick water at the head of the first chute. Man-high waves backing up behind submerged boulders awaited us at its foot. The rock Charles had indicated as our leading mark flashed past, leaving us in a deep trough blocked by a great, curling wave. Charles whooped a warning then we were heeling over between two granite obelisks surrounded by spouting water. I thrust my paddle between the nearest one and the canoe; pulled back for all I was worth; and felt the paddle snap. The engine roared at full throttle and then, the chute was behind us."

Farley had a well-known reluctance to let the truth get in the way of a good story, and as soon as I stood above the falls, I knew he'd been fibbing. The water poured over a steep ledge, plunged down a chute from hell, and then churned into a froth in the gorge below. There was no bloody way that Farley had run Kasmere Falls.

I've crashed down my share of Class IV and even Class V whitewater in playboats and kayaks; on my best day, in a plastic kayak, wearing full protective gear with lots of rescuers standing by, I would still have been apprehensive about running that first drop. But running the waterfall in a wilderness canoe or a small boat with an outboard motor? Ludicrous.

My guess is that Farley and his companion hauled the boat through the forest to circumvent the first significant drop and had only run the bottom section of the rapids. Or maybe he had invented the trip from whole cloth.

Many years ago, I sat at the campfire of a Dene elder on Black Lake in northern Saskatchewan. In our conversation, I mentioned Farley Mowat.

The elder paused, frowned, and then said, "There are some people up here who don't like him very much."

"Why's that?" I asked.

"Well, he came up here, traveled around a bit, and then told a whole bunch of fucking lies."

I understand that the boundary between fact and fiction can get fuzzy at times, but accurately reporting on the navigability of a waterfall is essential.

You don't want some trusting fool swept to his doom because he believed your confabulation of tall tales.

The contour intervals on the map also dispelled dreams of an easy route through the canyon. The steeper a river, the wilder the whitewater will be. Generally, the limit for a wilderness trip is a gradient of about four or five meters of drop per kilometer, and the map showed that the Thlewiaza here dropped twenty-five meters over two horizontal kilometers, more than twice the guideline.

You can think of a downriver trip as starting at a higher elevation and progressing toward a lower elevation; essentially, both you and the water are falling off the land. For the Thlewiaza, I had started at the height of land (375 meters above sea level) and was heading down to Hudson Bay (zero meters above sea level). Kasmere Gorge accounted for roughly $\frac{1}{15}$ of the elevation drop for the entire trip, so no matter how I got around this obstacle, I was getting closer to my goal vertically as well as horizontally!

The portage started in a tiny pond just to the left of the top of the falls, exactly where the map said it should be. The trail headed northeast on an esker, an easy-to-follow line through a carpet of lichen and bearberry plants carved into the soil by thousands of years of tramping. Even the caribou used the Kasmere portage, incorporating parts of it into their idiosyncratic maze of trails that meandered across the landscape like a web spun by a drunken spider.

This was a rich historical spot. There's only one logical route around the gorge, so everyone traveling this river has followed more or less the same path (except Farley Mowat of course). The name of this waterfall comes from the famous Dene chieftain Kasmere, who taxed travelers for using his portage and crossing his lands. If archaeologists excavated here, I'm sure they'd find more than a few arrowheads and spear points. A hundred years ago, a trading post was established here by the Revillon Frères company to bring northern furs southward and across the Atlantic to luxury stores in Paris.

The portage was only two kilometers long but felt much longer when loaded with twenty-five days of food and gear. The first two sweat-soaked carries were tiring, but the third trip was the worst. The edges of the canoe's carrying yoke cut into my shoulders, and I cursed myself for not having carpentered it into a better shape before leaving home. Furthermore, the canoe was forever getting deflected by branches that sent me reeling off the path. It took five hours to get everything to the far side of the portage.

I was glad to be done with portaging and canoeing again. The Thlewiaza River was a delight; I ran small rapids, spotted a mother moose hustling her calf into the bushes, and even enjoyed a temporary tailwind. Any worthwhile expedition is a bit bipolar; once again, I had gone from the brink of exhaustion to the heights of appreciation in just a few hours.

As evening came on, dark clouds crept over the sky. By the time I got to Kasmere Lake, the sun was entirely hidden by the dense gray gloom. Kasmere is a large lake with giant arms that stretch out in the four cardinal directions, and I continued up the lake's southern arm, hoping to get a few more miles under the keel before the inevitable rainstorm.

A rippling circle from a single raindrop appeared on the smooth water ahead of me. Then another, and another. The rain had arrived. The North isn't a place for half-measures, and soon, sheets of rain slashed across the lake.

Had there been a suitable place to pitch the tent, I would have used it; enough miles had been covered and suffering endured to meet the quota. But the shore was inhospitable, and the wall of interlinked spruce denied access to the land beyond. I paddled hard into the horizontal rain, occasionally squinting up in hopes of spying a potential campsite.

My standards dropped as the conditions got worse and my clothing wetter. Soon, any flat area large enough for a tent would have sufficed, but the dense lakeside forest just rolled on without apparent openings.

Through the hammering rain, I thought I saw a rectangular object on a hillside ahead. *Is that man-made?* I wondered. *No, I'm just seeing things; it must be a patch of exposed sand high up on an esker. Keep going!* I lowered my eyes and retreated into a very small world where only the next stroke mattered.

A few minutes later, I looked up, and it became apparent that this object did indeed have human origins. It was a large building on a hill, and at the base of that hill was a beach with a dock and boats. This was almost certainly a fishing lodge. I was so wet, cold, and tired that I decided to pay for a warm room at the lodge, no matter the cost. Fantasizing about warm-water showers, I pushed on into the storm.

There was a large sign on the beach proclaiming this was Kasmere Lake Lodge, but something was wrong. There was no thrum of a generator, no evidence of people, and no lights in the main building. The warped wooden dock dipped into the lake. The boats on shore sank into the sand, and the doors to the boat shed squeaked forlornly in the wind.

It looked like guests and staff had vanished suddenly, leaving behind a scene from a postapocalyptic zombie movie. It was unsettling, to say the least.

I had heard that the Nueltin Lake Lodge Company operated a series of hunting and fishing camps in the area. And I had heard rumors that when the owner had been unsuccessful at selling the company, he had walked away from the whole affair. It now appeared that this was precisely what had happened.

I approached the main lodge building, looking for shelter from the storm. The front door was unlocked, but an unpleasant musty smell, chew marks on the furniture, and a generally creepy vibe convinced me to look elsewhere.

There were other buildings in this ghost town, including smaller cabins for the now-vanished guests. Bears and wolverines had gone to work on most of these cabins, clawing holes through the walls, caving in doors, and smashing the furniture inside.

I was relieved to find a small cabin with an intact roof, windows, and door. It was empty except for a metal bed frame, two chairs, and some old motorcycle magazines. This was an austere environment, but the rain was intensifying, and this seemed like the perfect place to hunker down for the night.

The paddling day was over, but a lot still needed to happen for tomorrow to be successful. Napoleon once said, "An army marches on its stomach," so the first order of business was dinner, the only warm meal of the day. I rehydrated a mix of dried corn, peas, and freeze-dried chicken with cold lake water and brought it to a boil. Then I added dried mushrooms, parsley, green onions, chicken bouillon, spices, and some of my remaining olive oil to the pot and let it simmer.

Then I hung wet clothing to dry on the lines that crisscrossed the room, studied maps that were scattered on every flat surface, and sewed torn clothing. I had been on the go for sixteen hours without any downtime, every minute spoken for.

The last thing I did was write out my daily dispatches in the dying light, then fell into the sleeping bag, throbbing with exhaustion, hoping to sleep quickly because I knew the dawn would return too soon.

Unlike camping alone in the forest, it felt strange to be alone in this abandoned outpost. Every beam, board, nail, and screw in this lodge had been flown in from the South at great expense. Building and operating this lodge had been someone's dream once, but now it was abandoned and—like so many other structures out here—was being reclaimed by the wilderness.

OF LAKES AND RAPIDS

July 27, 2019
Start: At an abandoned hunting and fishing lodge
(59°31'39.4" N 101°13'49.8" W)
Finish: On rocky ledge above serious rapids, 5 kilometers upstream
of Sandy Lake (59°37'05.7" N 100°37'57.1" W)
Distance covered: 56 kilometers

The tide rises, the tide falls,
The twilight darkens, the curlew calls;
Along the sea-sands damp and brown
The traveler hastens toward the town,
And the tide rises, the tide falls.

—Henry Wadsworth Longfellow,
"The Tide Rises, the Tide Falls"

I had intended to sleep as long as possible in my weatherproof cabin to maximize my body's recovery. Unfortunately, the wind's thrumming woke me many times during the night and at 5:30 A.M. I finally admitted defeat. *If I'm up, I might as well be paddling.*

I packed the boat at the water's edge for the umpteenth time, but something was different today. For the first time, all the food and equipment sat *below* the boat's gunwales, which meant I could finally use the black nylon spray deck I had been carrying for weeks.

A spray deck is a fabric cover covering the open areas of your boat. Waves that could swamp you hit the heavy nylon cloth and roll off back into the water, giving you a considerable margin of safety on wavy lakes and in whitewater. Spray decks also keep you warmer by protecting your legs from the wind and the rain.

But spray decks also have their downsides. They're bulky and heavy and are one more thing to carry across portages. Attaching them to your boat with snaps or straps takes time, and they make accessing your gear more difficult. And—worst of all—some designs can trap you upside down if your boat flips.

My stomach sank as I installed the spray deck and realized the tunnel around my waist was a major entrapment nightmare. The material here was held up by two nylon straps that buckled over my shoulder, but disentangling myself from them would be a nightmare if the boat was upside down in heavy seas or bouncing off boulders in whitewater. Fumbling for the plastic buckles with cold fingers underwater seemed like a really bad idea.

This spray deck debacle was entirely my fault; I had received it just a few days before leaving for the trip and hadn't had the time to test and modify it. Fixing the entrapment hazard would have been easy given a few hours with a sewing machine, but in the middle of nowhere, with minimal equipment, there wasn't much I could do.

I compromised by covering the front and back of the boat with the spray deck but leaving the middle section open with the tunnel unattached. If a large wave broke over the bow, some of the water would still find its way into the boat, but much less than if there had been no deck at all.

Heading up the southern arm of Kasmere Lake against the unrelenting wind was a real slog. I could only maintain a speed of one or two kilometers per hour, even while paddling as hard as possible. The only way to take a break was to tuck the canoe into the wind shadow of a promontory or island, but after resting my arms and choking down some nuts and chocolate, it was always time to leave the harbor and head back into the gale.

It's sometimes possible to interpret struggle and suffering in a positive light. For example, on other days, I had successfully reframed the wind as an interesting challenge, a great workout, or a bridge to all the other travelers who had struggled across this land before me.

Those reframing tricks didn't work today. My mentality was grim, and I was in a hostile, negative place . . .

Why the fuck am I even doing this?

Let's just get this fucking over with.

I fucking hate this goddamn wind.

This negative mindset probably came from being severely worn down and was exacerbated by an acute sleep deficit. Our psychology doesn't exist separately from our physiology, and what happens in our bodies affects what happens in our minds.

Things got a bit better around noon, after four hours of battling brought me to the north shore of the lake where the wind had less distance to gather its fury. I was unbelievably tired, so I paddled in short bursts from island to island and peninsula to peninsula. Eventually, the lake narrowed, the current picked up, and I was back on the Thlewiaza River. Navigating Kasmere Lake had been some of the most brutal paddling of my life.

The river was noticeably bigger now because all the many small creeks flowing into Kasmere Lake had joined the Thlewiaza at the outflow. I was still in a dour mood but grateful for the downstream current and the riverbanks that provided some shelter from the wind. I hoped it would now be possible to make good time.

Below Kasmere Lake, the river twisted and turned like a beaded necklace fallen on the floor. Every bead was a new irregularly shaped lake with its own cryptic name: Graves, Sucker, Sandy, Downes, Tuninili, and Nahili. Each lake was a new route-finding puzzle where I had to balance navigating around extensive sandbars close to shore and the large waves being raised by the wind in the center of the lake.

As the river wandered left and right, the wind shifted; sometimes it pushed me backward, but a minute later it pushed me from behind.

Consequently, my existence alternated between two extremes: grueling paddling one minute and easy cruising the next.

Between every two lakes was at least one stretch of whitewater. The first rapids between Kasmere Lake and Graves Lake were minor, but after that they continued to grow in intensity and consequence.

To vastly oversimplify things, there are two types of whitewater: boulder-controlled and bedrock-controlled rapids.

In boulder-controlled rapids, boulders on the riverbed create waves, eddies, hydraulics, and other river features. These rapids are often prolonged and continuous because, over time, the steeper sections tend to get flattened as the relentless force of the water rolls cobbles and boulders downstream. Spend enough time in boulder-controlled whitewater, and you'll become familiar with its characteristic style and rhythm.

Bedrock-controlled rapids are something else entirely. They are much less predictable because the whitewater reflects the shapes frozen into the rock a billion years ago and then resculpted by massive glaciers and millennia of erosion. Whitewater here tends to pool and drop; the river might flow languidly for miles and then suddenly convulse into a significant rapid.

The Thlewiaza had both bedrock and boulder-controlled stretches, as well as rapids that combined the uncertainties of both. The map only provided the most subtle hints about the type of whitewater ahead—every rapid still needed to be individually assessed.

After Graves Lake, the rapids mainly were long wave trains flowing over a bouldery river bottom. Hidden in the waves were large hydraulics where water poured over giant boulders to create vertical whirlpools. These hydraulics had the potential to submerge and trap even quite large boats; I tried to imagine going around and around in this frothy hole, never quite making it to the surface because of the less buoyant aerated water, and shuddered.

I spun into an eddy and looked for trouble downstream. There was a lot of big water, but fortunately, the route was obvious. I ran the rapids conservatively, tight against the shore where the boat could stay out of the biggest waves.

An Ancient Greek saying attributed to the poet Archilochus of Paros goes, "We don't rise to the level of our expectations; we fall to the level of our training." Many days spent playing in low-stakes rapids down south had sharpened my whitewater-reading skills so they functioned even when I was worn down and sleep-deprived.

Learning how to make the right decision quickly can take a long time. Consider learning how to drive . . . The first time you drove in traffic was probably terrifying, and basic maneuvers like lane changes and left-hand turns required all of your attention. However, after hundreds of hours, the car became an extension of your body; turning the wheel, operating the signals, and pushing the pedals became instinctive.

Time spent working on the basics allows you to react automatically when an emergency happens. If a sheet of plywood flies out of a pickup truck in front of you, then you swerve without thinking. If a car runs a red light, your foot hits the brake before you fully register what's happening.

Similarly, if you're a skier, it takes a thousand easy turns to pull off that one turn at the brink of a cliff you absolutely must make. Your ability to perform under pressure and make the correct split-second decisions comes from perfecting your craft beforehand. The days of practice create a repository of knowledge and context that enable correct instinctive reactions when the chips are down.

But it's not as simple as only ever doing easy repetitions. Acquiring high-level skills is a scaffolded process. It requires a stepladder of progressively more significant challenges, with each step being difficult but achievable.

In whitewater paddling, you first start by running Grade I rapids. Once this is comfortable, you move on to Grade II and then to Grade III. Each time you head back to the river, you deepen your skills, learn more, and test yourself against progressively more demanding challenges. And then, one day, you're doing things that most people would consider insane.

Each escalation ramps up the difficulty level, forcing the body and mind to adapt. But you have to walk a fine line: your challenges must be both difficult and achievable. If the challenges aren't difficult enough—if there isn't a real risk of failure—your improvement will be glacial and you won't get tougher mentally. But if the steps on the ladder are too extreme and you fail too often, you'll destroy your body and confidence. That's why you have to push yourself intelligently, taking on difficult things while still ensuring that successes are built into the process.

> In days of peace the soldier performs maneuvers, throws up earthworks with no enemy in sight, and wearies himself by gratuitous toil in order that he may be equal to unavoidable toil. If you would not have a man flinch when the crisis comes, train him before it comes.
>
> —Seneca the Younger, *Letters from a Stoic*

The most challenging whitewater of the day came later, between Sucker Lake and Sandy Lake. The map showed thirty-five feet of elevation drop between the two lakes, with most of that drop occurring in the first three rapids. Steep whitewater is fun in a small whitewater kayak but presents a serious challenge for a heavily laden wilderness canoe. I was on full alert as I approached this stretch of river.

At the lip of the first rapid, I gently broached the boat sideways on a rock and let the current hold it in place. This gave me time to scout the whitewater; I studied how the current below accelerated into a frothy mess of waves, rocks, and channels. The line through the whitewater was tricky, but the dealbreaker was that the river surged around a corner at the bottom of the rapid; there could be a waterfall, a rock weir, or a giant logjam hiding there.

Charging downriver here would have been stupid. The whitewater was one thing, but not knowing what was around the bend made the risk level too high. There were two alternatives: carry everything up a steep bank and portage it through the bug-plagued, ankle-breaking muskeg or line the boat tight along the left shore. I didn't want to get wet again, but it was still an easy choice; I slipped into the cold, waist-deep water and uncoiled the ropes.

Shivering slightly, I set up for the first shot. I aimed, pushed the heavy boat between two rocks, watched it career through the waves, and reeled it back like bringing a huge, unruly dog to heel on a leash. Then, I trudged downriver to reclaim the boat and repeat the process.

I snuck the boat past the most difficult whitewater, one rope length at a time. Once around the corner, I could see only friendly haystacks downstream. I slowly clambered into the boat, water seeping from my clothing, and let the current carry me to the bottom of the rapid.

The sun was now low in the sky, and rain clouds were again inbound. It didn't make sense to stop because there were only a few kilometers before the next rapid; better to camp there and only pack and unpack once.

I was delirious with fatigue. I had been paddling for twelve hours straight and had never really recovered from the knock-down drag-out fight against the wind on Kasmere Lake at the beginning of the day. It was habit, not willpower, that kept the boat going forward.

Eventually, the river narrowed into a giant flume that thundered through a fracture in the bedrock. There was no way to run this drop, so I unpacked the boat and set up the tent on the rock slabs at the brink of the rapid. I wolfed down a simple dinner and crawled into the sleeping bag as distant thunder prophesied rain.

RIVER CHANNELS GREAT AND SMALL

July 28, 2019
Start: On rocky ledge above serious rapids, 5 kilometers upstream of Sandy
Lake (59°37'05.7" N 100°37'57.1" W)
Finish: On the beach of a small island in Nahili Lake
(59°43'20.0" N 100°10'30.8" W)
Distance covered: 37 kilometers

There was a little girl in my class. Every day I went over the questions and answers with her alone. You know, there is a part in our catechism where the question is asked, "What is the most beautiful thing that God created?" The answer is: "Man and all the angels." Every time I asked, she would look up at me and say: "Idthen!" the caribou!
—Father Egenolf to P. G. Downes,
Sleeping Island: A Journey to the Edge of the Barrens

It rained during the night, but I didn't notice it. Total exhaustion and the white noise of the roaring cascade had knocked me out. I emerged into the cool morning and realized I had just slept amazingly. For the first time in days, I felt refreshed, renewed, and optimistic.

After a bad night at the abandoned lodge on Kasmere Lake, it had taken everything I had to keep grinding forward. But now, after an excellent night's sleep, I had a totally different mindset. The dependency of your mental state on the quality and quantity of your sleep shows how subjective reality is. We are all just bags of chemicals, and getting your biochemistry right depends on getting enough sleep.

The morning was mostly overcast, but scattered patches of blue sky promised better weather to come. It was cold enough that no bugs were in the air, which meant wearing more clothing but less slapping at mosquitos and black flies.

After less than five minutes of paddling, mist rising from a sharp horizon line announced the next rapid. A bedrock ledge stretched 400 feet from bank to bank, with most of the current going to the right, where it poured over the shelf and then fell back upon itself to create a frothy white foam that would swallow any boat. Going right was out of the question, but about thirty feet from the left shore, a small bedrock island protruded above the water at the steepest part of the ledge.

I floated cautiously downriver, then climbed onto that rock slab. The slanting rock was a perfect ramp to bypass the ledge, but the stone's surface was rough, and dragging the boat across it would have destroyed the hull. I noticed three logs pinned underwater against the upstream end of my little island. I pried the wood free and laid it on the rock to form a roller system. I eased the canoe onto the wet wood and slid it downhill toward the bottom of the ledge. The entire operation took only ten minutes, and I launched from the downstream edge of the island, having circumvented a serious obstacle without unpacking or portaging.

Having saved an hour of effort made me very cheerful. In my well-rested state, the rapids became interesting puzzles to be solved rather than interminable trials to be grimly endured. Furthermore, the green landscape was now bathed in the bright morning sunshine, and I was mostly protected from the wind by the narrowness of the river channel. Life was good! Oh, what a difference a day makes!

To avoid Sandy Lake and its extensive shoals, I curved the boat into a small creek that ran through the swampy lands north of the lake. This route bypassed the wind-whipped waters entirely. A Canada goose mother hustled her goslings off the river and into the bushes for safety as I headed down this bypass. The low reed-lined banks were usually less than a hundred feet apart and provided considerable protection from the wind.

A large log, fuzzy with vegetation, floated ahead of me in the channel. Suddenly, the log convulsed and emerged from the water to reveal a large head with wide, flat antlers. It was a thousand-pound moose that had been foraging underwater for nutritious aquatic vegetation; its head had been completely submerged, yet it had still somehow sensed my approach.

We eyed each other warily as the current slowly carried me toward him. Moose aren't typically aggressive toward humans, but they are unpredictable, and he could have smashed my boat as an afterthought. He snorted, then retreated to the shore, trotting across the uneven swampy terrain as smoothly as a horse cantering in a riding arena. This enormous animal, the largest member of the deer family, bursting out of the water at close range was the highlight of my day. As climate change warms this region, moose have expanded their range, moving further north than any native elder can remember.

Eventually, the small channel rejoined the main river, which surged down to Downes Lake in a series of easy wave trains. The lake was small, with many bays, islands, and tall hills on the eastern shore. It was named after P. G. Downes, an American schoolteacher who traveled through this area in the 1930s. Downes recorded his journey in the classic adventure book *Sleeping Island: A Journey to the Edge of the Barrens*, which I read multiple times to prepare for this trip.

Amazingly, Downes and other early travelers traversed this country without detailed maps, relying instead on rough, hand-drawn sketches and a few oral accounts from Cree and Dene natives they encountered along the way. It's one thing to struggle against the wind and the current, knowing that you're going the right way, but to do all that work without knowing what's coming next is incredible.

Below Downes Lake there were extensive swifts and wave trains as the river lost more elevation in its relentless plunge to the Bay. I mostly floated down the middle of these easy, boulder-controlled rapids, taking an occasional stroke to move the boat around rocks and shallows. The easy paddling ended when the river widened into Tuninili Lake, where a headwind ripped across the water. This lake was only six kilometers long, but covering this short distance took hours of intense slogging. It was five in the evening when I finally put it behind me.

The current picked up past Tuninili Lake, a series of Class I to Class III boulder gardens through Stonehenge-sized blocks of stone. I was in the zone and ran everything on sight, scouting from my boat and dragging the boat through the shallows for the more challenging sections.

As the river approached Nahili Lake, it fanned out to become much broader and shallower. The challenge soon became finding water deep enough to float the boat, and I bumped my way down to a lovely bay on the lake's western side.

Some people think that running rapids in the wilderness should be avoided at all costs. "Nobody ever drowned on a portage," they say, which might be true, but you can easily break your ankle stumbling across uneven terrain. You might also starve on some trips if you took the time to carry around every rapid. On northern rivers, you need whitewater skills with the paddle, lining skills with ropes, willingness to wade in hip-deep water, an iron back to portage your gear, and the wisdom to choose among those modalities.

A giant beach beckoned about a kilometer to the south. It would have felt so good to lie down on that sand, but I was heading east and was unwilling to divert from my direction even for a nice campsite. Instead, I set off toward a group of islands in the middle of the lake. The wind was now at my back, and the waves grew in size as I got father out from shore.

This was an "overtaking sea" where the waves come from behind and travel faster than your vessel. The biggest danger in an overtaking sea is getting turned sideways by a breaking wave hitting your boat from behind. Once you're parallel to the breakers, your boat gets hammered again and again as you struggle to turn it downwind again, making tipping quite likely.

My entire focus became controlling the boat's angle and refusing to let it broach in the waves. My ears strained to hear the sound of waves breaking behind me. The skin on my face registered every gust of wind. My eyes watched for the slightest deviation of the boat's angle relative to the waves. My hands felt the water through the shaft of the paddle, and I instinctively adjusted the blade's path through the water two or three times every stroke. For every sensory input, there was an appropriate response: a specific paddle stroke, rudder adjustment, hip tilt, body lean, or a combination of them all. It was exhilarating, as much a mental as a physical challenge. All my senses were engaged, and I felt wholly and completely alive.

The steepest swells on Nahili Lake sometimes lifted the back of the boat so high that the narrow bow plunged underwater. This would have been a dire situation in an open canoe without a spray deck, but my canoe-kayak hybrid was built for this. After each dive, the spray deck shed the water left and right, and the boat's buoyancy lifted the bow triumphantly back to the surface. Still, if the waves had been any bigger or the distance to the islands had been any longer, I would have had to abandon the crossing.

After three kilometers in the waves, I made it to the shelter of the islands and camped on a small gravel beach that jutted into the water. It was a cold but beautiful evening—the sinking sun added colors to the clouds that any Impressionist painter would have been proud to have on his canvas.

Dehydrated homemade chili simmered on the fire. It was time to do laundry. I took my stinkiest clothing, walked knee-deep into the lake, and pinned each item underwater with a large rock. Buffeted by the waves, the pants and the shirt danced like a roadside inflatable tube man, which rinsed some of the sweat, blood, and dirt from the clothing. Later, I hung the clothes on a line before a bonfire to help dry the fabric.

The fire took the chill out of the evening air as I ate my dinner and admired the sunset. It had been a good day—tough, but good. Eight days had passed since I had last seen anyone, and tomorrow, I would hopefully reach Nueltin Lake to begin the next stage of the journey.

As I sat by the fire, my mind drifted back to all the martial arts training I had done over the decades. Even now, I could still smell the sweat and hear the thud of bodies against the mats in my first judo class at the Hatashita Dojo in Toronto. I could feel my thighs quiver as I stood in a deep Kung Fu horse stance. I could feel the impact of fists and feet on my body as I trained in Kajukenbo with Philip Gelinas in Montreal. I had a visceral sense of getting crushed on the bottom during countless jiu-jitsu classes with Marcus Soares in Vancouver.

That training was now translating to overcoming challenges in an entirely different setting. It had made me tougher, stronger, and more able to solve problems under pressure, essentially a form of mind, body and spirit unification that is usually the topic of earnest homilies in candlelit yoga studios.

All the endurance of a triathlete and the athleticism of a gymnast won't help if your adrenaline-soaked brain isn't thinking clearly. Knowing every technique in the book won't help if you crumble at the first sign of adversity. And willpower is far more effective if you've developed the physical attributes to back it up. You need all three: mind, body, and spirit. Miss any one of these, and you have a weak link.

Even here, in the lonely windswept waterways of the northern boreal forest, that training was still helping. I felt grateful to my teachers and training partners who taught me how to handle high-pressure situations with real consequences.

> Most people have the will to win, few have the will to prepare to win.
>
> —Bobby Knight

A CLOSE BEAR ENCOUNTER

July 29, 2019
Start: On the beach of a small island in Nahili Lake
(59°43'20.0" N 100°10'30.8" W)
Finish: On a low gravel ridge separating Nueltin Lake from a smaller,
unnamed lake (59°57'40.0" N 100°01'44.6" W)
Distance covered: 39 kilometers

Island Lake . . . at the part we crossed, was about thirty-five miles wide: but from the North East to the South West it is much larger, and entirely full of islands as to make the whole Lake resemble a jumble of serpentine rivers and creeks; and it is celebrated by the natives as amounting with great plenty of fine fish during the beginning of the Winter.

—Samuel Hearne describing Nueltin Lake in
A Journey to the Northern Ocean

The current accelerated down the channel and then turned right. The waves were small, and the rapid ranked no higher than Class I, but they still had my full attention. Around that corner, the entire river poured over a series of bedrock ledges called Nahilin Falls.

The portage started in a small oxbow lake at the waterfall's brink. The path was clear initially, but then splintered into a confusion of game trails, which all seemed to lead into dense forest and swampy areas. I dropped all the gear and scouted ahead—feet squishing through the mud—to find the one good route that led in the right direction. This reconnaissance saved at least an hour of floundering about in spruce and Labrador tea shrubs. I was learning!

The trail climbed high onto a sandy hill where the deeply scoured track became easier to follow, then descended through open forest to terminate at the base of the rapids. I looked back up at the river thundering down the final rock staircase.

Every canoeist in this situation asks the same question, *How would I run this drop if my life depended on it?* Most of the water pulsed down the right side of the river, so I looked for a path on the left. I visualized gathering momentum above the drop, then driving the boat onto the slabs of bedrock barely covered by water. I felt myself grating down the bumpy bedrock, wet from the spray of the rapids, until I slid to the bottom. Then I sighed and snapped back to reality; if the waterslide-from-hell didn't kill me, it would still be a pyrrhic victory because the boat would have sustained so much damage it would likely snap in half later.

Below the whitewater were the quiet waters of a small bay at the southwesternmost corner of fabled Nueltin Lake. The waves glinted in the sunlight, sandy beaches lay along the shore, and loons tremoloed their welcome. The vast majority of the lake lay out of sight beyond the confines of this bay, but this first impression was very promising.

Nueltin Lake is a subarctic crossroads. It lies between the forest and the tundra, the Dene and the Inuit. From here, you can continue to the Thlewiaza River, cross over to the Kognak and the Tha-Anne Rivers, connect to the Kazan River, or descend to the Caribou and Seal River systems. Many of the explorers I admire most had crossed Nueltin Lake, including Samuel Hearne, Oberholtzer and Magee, and P. G. Downes. I had read everything they had written and looked forward to seeing this country in person.

After eating some energy balls and dried fruit, I was soon paddling through the many islands of southern Nueltin Lake. The southwest wind was gentle, perfect for the larger crossings ahead.

Given the idyllic natural setting, it was shocking to paddle around a corner and discover a flotilla of aluminum fishing boats on a beach below a cluster of cabins. This was another fishing camp—Nueltin Lake Lodge—just as deserted as Kasmere Lake Lodge, the other camp I had explored a few days earlier.

It was amazing how much equipment remained at this camp. Eleven fishing boats were half-buried in the sand. A perfectly serviceable canoe sat in the forest. Animals had ransacked the boat shed; every last life jacket, fishing net, and fuel tank had been pulled off the shelves and thrown on the floor. Another shed contained at least forty outboard motors. A fully equipped workshop was stuffed with tools and an ATV. Millions of dollars of material and equipment, entirely abandoned.

It was too early to make camp, but I wanted to explore the ghost lodge. I wandered up the gently sloping hill, studying the row of guest cabins with ripped-open walls, caved-in doors, torn-apart mattresses, and demolished furniture in the rooms. There were bear prints in the sand, but they were old, suggesting it had been some time since a bear had last wandered here.

The main lodge building sat on a sand ridge overlooking the azure lake. Unlike the cabins, the lodge was in good condition, built with sturdy logs instead of the more fragile plywood. Furthermore, every doorway of the lodge had a sheet of plywood studded with many upward-pointing large nails in front of them. These "bear boards" are often used to protect northern buildings from unwanted animal intruders.

I came to the main entrance and noticed that the bear board had been pushed to one side. *Oh man*, I thought, *Who would do that? That'll let the animals in to ruin the joint.*

Then, in the next few seconds, I realized three different things . . .

First, the front doors to the lodge had been smashed in, creating a direct route into the interior of the building for any large animal.

Second, there was a *lot* of bear scat all around me, maybe twenty-five different heaps in a thirty-foot circle around the lodge's front door.

Third, something large was growling and snorting at me inside the lodge. It sounded like a giant baritone dog was clearing its throat in the darkness.

The hair at the back of my neck rose, and my stomach sank. A black bear or a grizzly was inside the abandoned building about thirty feet from me. *Holy shit*, I thought.

This was almost certainly his home. There's a big difference between disturbing a bear in the forest, where it can simply run away, and cornering that same animal in its den, where it feels the need to protect itself. It knew I was there, and I was in genuine danger of getting mauled by its defensive attack.

My bear spray and shotgun were back at the boat, more than 500 feet away. Bears can run thirty-five miles per hour, so if it charged now there'd be no chance of getting my hands on those weapons before the bear flattened me into the earth.

I resisted the urge to turn and run; that would just trigger its hunting reflex. Instead, I backed away for a minute, then retreated at a brisk walk while looking back over my shoulder often. I returned to the boat on a different path and saw *tons* of bear tracks. Some prints were so fresh that the sand was still moist around the claw marks. The Nueltin Lake Lodge bear had been surveying his kingdom less than an hour ago!

Fortunately, the bear remained in his wooden palace, apparently content that he had frightened away a potential rival. At the beach, I cast a final anxious glance behind me, then jumped into the boat and headed out into the lake. This felt safer; I couldn't outrun a bear on land, but could almost certainly out-paddle one on the water. Passing the seaward side of the lodge, I half expected the bear to be leaning on a railing and watching my retreat. This bruin had an entire building all to himself, complete with a stunning view of the lake, doubtless the nicest den for 1,000 miles in any direction.

I had made a mistake that got me into trouble, but I had also stayed calm and kept thinking. I was happy with that; panic rarely solves anything.

A retired fire chief once told me, "When I arrive at a fire and get out of the truck, I first take a big breath. And if it's a really big fire, then I take a really big breath." He didn't want to react blindly to emergencies, so instead he'd take a moment to collect himself and gather relevant information. Then, he prioritized his problems; determining what the most critical issues were and which headaches could wait for later. Finally, he'd come up with a plan using all of his available resources. Only once the planning was done would he rush into execution. He called this approach Think, Plan, Act.

It can be overwhelming when a thousand different things compete for your attention, so instead of uselessly flapping around, take a deep breath, list and prioritize your problems, consider your resources, and then act. As British paratrooper and adventurer Andy Torbet once said, "Deal with the crocodile closest to the canoe."

My surprise bear encounter was a good reminder that complacency kills. I should have been prepared for trouble and had my 12-gauge with me, or at least should have doubled back to get my gun the first time I saw a cabin door with claw marks in the plywood. Many bear problems happen around hunting camps and fly-in fishing sites because the bears get used to finding offal and garbage there.

The lesson was that I always needed to be on alert from now on because the bear situation would only worsen as I continued north. I didn't know if this had been a black bear or a grizzly. Black bears can be dangerous, but they usually behave like large dogs that you can intimidate into retreat. However, this close to the tree line, their range overlaps with the larger, grumpier, and more aggressive tundra grizzly that is much more dangerous. And closer to Hudson Bay, the hypercarnivorous polar bear would be the greatest threat of all.

Back on the water, I climbed up the lake on autopilot, kilometer after kilometer. The relentless headwinds of the past week had finally blown themselves out, and I was using the fantastic weather to make as much progress as possible.

Nueltin is an extraordinarily gorgeous lake with thousands of islands, bays, and beaches. White clouds swirled in the lapis sky as if a celestial impressionist was reworking the heavens with a giant brush. Losing myself in that sky helped induce a trance that detached my mind from my aching body.

Yet another forest fire erupted behind me in the South, its smoky mushroom cloud billowing higher and higher into the sky as the afternoon got warmer. This wasn't the same forest fire I had dueled with on the Cochrane

River the previous week; that fire was now one hundred kilometers to the west. I had no concerns about this most recent fire. There were an infinite number of islands to retreat to if it got close, and within a few days, I'd be out on the tundra where there are no trees to burn.

Making the most of the weather, I kept going until 7:30 P.M., when I spotted a lovely gravel ridge separating gigantic Nueltin Lake from a small pond just inland from the shore. The sky threatened rain, and the breeze now felt slightly different on my face. It was time to hunker down. I set up the tent and then attached the tent's guy lines to small logs buried in trenches dug perpendicular to the direction of the pull. These deadman anchors work even in the loosest soils and would hopefully prevent the tent from getting blown away if the winds picked up.

I took extra care in setting up the perimeter wire for the bear alarm, testing it twice by deliberately walking into the tripwire to set off the wailing siren. If something large and furry approached the tent at night I would know about it.

KILLERS AT THE TREE LINE

July 30, 2019

Start: On a low gravel ridge separating Nueltin Lake from a smaller, unnamed lake (59°57'40.0" N 100°01'44.6" W)

Finish: On a small tundra island in Nueltin Lake

(60°12'01.0" N 99°43'50.2" W)

Distance covered: 45 kilometers

Put to sea on a small open boat and you meet it intimately. Every sense springs to life, vibrant and tingling. Drop your hand over the gunnels, your fingers touch the icy waters. You hear it and feel it slap the bow, rumble under the keel, and gurgle behind the stern. When the salt spray bites your face and stings your cheek, and salt air fills your nostrils, pure and sharp—undiluted by distance—you're as close to being at sea as you'll ever come.

—David Conover, *Once Upon an Island*

Before my eyes opened I could hear the rain drumming on the tent, whitecaps lashing the shore, and the wind shaking the trees. There was no safe passage on Nueltin Lake in these conditions.

Well, I guess this is finally a rest day, I said to myself. I covered my head with clothing to shut out the light, and was unconscious again in seconds. The ease with which I fell back asleep indicated how deeply fatigued my body was. Twelve-hour paddling days had become the norm, barely leaving time to prepare and eat a single warm meal in the evenings. I had maintained this pace for thirty days with only a few half days of rest. The cumulative physiological and endocrine load was catching up with me.

I awoke again at 9:00 A.M., a scandalously late hour, still feeling drained and fatigued. Stiffly observing the lake, I noted that the wind had calmed a bit, and the waves were a little smaller. Maybe there'd be a way to progress northward today after all. To coax my zombie body into cooperating, I told myself, "Right, let's just go a few kilometers, just to say we did something today." This was a lie; the first few kilometers would be hard, but momentum would keep me going after that.

Paddling was automatic now, but that didn't mean it was painless; my back ached, my shoulders throbbed, and it felt like a needle was being pushed through one of my shoulder blades.

Today's wind was strong and gusty, which required hugging the shore and only allowed intermittent use of the sail. The word "sailing" probably conjures up visions of leisurely steering a yacht through Caribbean waters while admiring the bikinis on the foredeck. Well, that's not the kind of sailing I was doing on Nueltin Lake. Instead, I was on high alert, forever monitoring the wind, the waves, and the exact angles of the sail and boat. There could be no capsizing here as help was now much too far away.

Nueltin is the most complicated lake I've ever been on, with thousands of small islands, crooked bays, and narrow channels bending and stretching in all directions. I was fairly sure about my position, but succumbing to wishful thinking here could result in getting very, very lost. "Could I be wrong about where I think I am?" I asked, then double-checked my position by cross-examining the lines on the crinkling map and comparing them to the labyrinthine landscape around me.

Some form of mapping is essential in the wilderness, but the irony is that trusting your maps too much can also get you into trouble. As I had learned from portages disappearing, maps can be just plain incorrect. Furthermore, even if the map was accurate when it was made, seasonally changing water levels on a lake can completely hide islands or reveal new ones that were previously under the surface, dramatically changing what you see. Any map is more of a guideline than a rule, and you must be skeptical about everything on it.

Technical aspects of navigation include taking bearings, adjusting for magnetic declination, operating your GPS, and visualizing a landscape based on the squiggly lines on a map. Of course, you should know all that, but navigation also includes using every hint that nature gives you, including the steepness of the waves on a lake . . . the shape of a distant hill . . . the presence of tree patches on the tundra . . . how reeds bend above and below the water . . . the absence of a beach where one is expected . . . the roar of a rapid where none is expected . . . and how landforms appear in shadow and sunlight. This style of observation is harder to teach and not widely appreciated, but it is incredibly useful for both navigation and deepening your connection to nature.

I crossed the Manitoba-Nunavut border late in the morning at 60° North. In theory, this was a significant milestone, but I was too focused on paddling and navigating to give much thought to celebration. More interestingly, as I crossed this border patches of tundra first started appearing on exposed hilltops. There isn't a sharp line where the trees stop; instead, the tree line is a broad transitional zone—about fifty kilometers wide—where the trees gradually begin to thin out, and patches of tundra get larger. As you go farther north, the trees retreat to sheltered areas like gullies and ravines, eventually disappearing altogether.

The tree line occurs at different latitudes in North America. In Alaska and the Yukon, trees can grow above 67° latitude. As you head east across the continent, the weather at a given latitude becomes harsher, and the tree line comes farther and farther south. In the Nueltin area, the tree line is at about 60° latitude, and in Quebec and Labrador, it comes even farther south than that.

I spotted a grizzly bear—the sixth bear of the trip—eating crowberries on a sandy ridge. I was only able to see him because the trees were thinning; a little bit farther south and this giant animal would have been completely hidden under the canopy of spruce, larch, and birch trees. Grizzlies can lose hundreds of pounds of fat and muscle during their winter torpor, so gaining weight during the summer is a survival necessity. A University of Calgary study found that grizzly bears can eat up to 200,000 berries a day to prepare for winter, so this fellow had his work cut out for him; he was busy and paid no heed to my passage.

By midday, a brilliant blue sky was directly overhead, but rows of thunderclouds formed dense walls on both the eastern and western horizons. These storms swept northward on either side of me, flashing and thundering as I crossed from island to island. Behind me, the forest fire flared up again in the heat of the day and sent a giant smoke plume up to the heavens, adding a dash of apocalypse to the day.

Then things got even more bizarre . . .

The GPS beeped as a series of 160-character satellite texts with concerning news from my wife. The details were still fuzzy, but it looked like two armed teenagers had gone on a killing spree in northern British Columbia, murdered three people, fled halfway across the country, stole a boat, and were now somewhere in northern Manitoba. Eva was justifiably very concerned about my safety and urged me to take all possible precautions.

A few hours later came another satellite text update with more information—the fugitives had last been seen in Gillam, Manitoba. I exhaled and relaxed; there was almost certainly no danger. That town is quite remote, but it was still 500 kilometers south of where I was.

If the killers were on foot, they'd never make it through the dense bush to get near me. They'd never make it over the portages if they had a motorboat. And if they were in a canoe, they would take a month to get from Gillam to Nueltin Lake. Still, had I run into other paddlers on the lake that day, it would have been a very tense few minutes as everyone tried to figure out whether the other boat was full of murderers on the run from the law.

Escorted by thunderstorms, I entered the narrows where the northern and southern basins of Nueltin Lake meet. The topography here is a dense tangle of islands, isthmuses, and deeply involuted bays. Without my maps,

I would have taken days or weeks to find the way through this maze and get to the second, larger part of the lake. The difficulty of route-finding through this insanely complex area further increased my respect for the natives and the early explorers who had traveled this land before me.

I spotted a building on a low hill among the last islands of the Narrows. This was yet another outpost run by the now-defunct Nueltin Lake Lodge Company. This particular camp was smaller and less grand than the other two earlier lodges but might be much more helpful because the knob to spool and unspool my bear perimeter alarm line had broken. The device still worked, but it took an additional thirty minutes to set it up and break it down every day because I had to laboriously coil the monofilament line around a stick. All I needed to fix the knob of the alarm was a little piece of metal about ⅜" in diameter; maybe something appropriate could be pilfered from this abandoned lodge.

I landed on the beach and—still spooked by the close call with the bear yesterday—took every possible precaution. I pointed the boat back out into the lake to facilitate a quick getaway. I chambered a shell into the shotgun with a loud *clack-clack* and nestled the butt of the weapon into my shoulder. Then I swiveled and cross-stepped my way through the shrubs and up toward the outpost camp, calling out loudly and aggressively as I went. I was absolutely determined not to be surprised by large and potentially aggressive animals again!

The safeguards were all unnecessary. There were no bear tracks, bear scat, or actual bears. Some of the buildings had been torn apart, but the damage did not look recent.

Once again, it looked like everyone who had worked there had been suddenly teleported away. The lodge workshop was unbelievably well stocked, with enough tools there to strip an engine or build a house. I scavenged only a few lengths of aluminum tubing, a handful of nuts and bolts, a heavy-duty nail, and a hacksaw blade; enough materials to fix the broken knob of the bear alarm in three different ways.

I briefly considered spending the night in the main lodge building. The kitchen and dining area were intact and not yet ravaged by animals but were permeated by that musty smell shared by all abandoned buildings. Better to sleep in a tent away from all of this.

A half-hour later, I made camp on a small island, nestling the tent between spruce trees, low birch bushes, and large rocks. Most of the spruce were dwarf versions of their southern selves, pruned into a dense mat of branches between one and eight feet high, known as "krummholz," the German word for crooked wood.

In the tent, I improvised a new knob for the bear alarm using a roofing nail, a short length of aluminum tubing, and some duct tape. I tested it several times, then strung the tripwire from bush to bush around the tent. It had been a worthwhile plundering! Despite the late start, I had still covered forty-five kilometers in nine hours today. I was now one-third of the way to the top of Nueltin Lake.

As darkness crept across the low arctic tundra, I thought again of Peter and Mathew, my brothers who had stumbled across the line between life and death much too early. I was very aware that only modern medicine and luck had kept me from joining them. They still lived in my memories, vibrant and young, and I was grateful that I could bear witness to their brief lives. They would have liked this part of the world, I thought.

EVALUATING THE ODDS

July 31, 2019
Start: On a small tundra island in Nueltin Lake
(60°12'01.0" N 99°43'50.2" W)
Finish: On a rocky headland above Nueltin Lake
(60°27'04.6" N 99°39'02.0" W)
Distance covered: 31 kilometers

And you, to whom adversity has dealt the final blow
With smiling bastards lying to you everywhere you go
Turn to and put out all your strength of arm and heart and brain
And like the Mary Ellen Carter rise again.
　　　　　　　—Stan Rogers, "The Mary Ellen Carter"

reaking camp in the early morning light was done in a well-rehearsed sequence. Before leaving the tent, I put all the clothing, my sleeping bag, and loose gear into their waterproof bags and chucked them out the door.

When nothing remained in the tent, I stepped outside to put away the bear alarm and retrieve the food bags from their hiding spots. Then, I filled a Ziplock bag with the day's food and mixed dry muesli with water in a pot for breakfast. While breakfast soaked, I collapsed the dew-wet tent and stuffed it into yet another bag.

With everything packed, I ate breakfast at the water's edge. I felt the first mosquitoes of the day pinch my neck, so I applied DEET insect repellent to my head and hands to swallow the cold cereal mostly unmolested. The biting horde that swarmed me anytime the wind dropped made me respect the native peoples even more; after all, I had chemicals and mosquito netting, but all they had were smudge fires, bear grease smeared on the skin, and the stoicism to endure nonstop bites for the summer months.

Loading the boat was more manageable now that only twenty days of food were left. Everything slid into its proper place and was covered by the spray deck. With the map case, compass, paddles, ropes, and sail strapped to the top of the deck, I waded the boat out into knee-deep water. I gingerly lowered myself into the seat and began paddling north again.

There were ninety kilometers left to the top of Nueltin Lake by the most direct route, but the deep bays and large islands meant that it was not as simple as going directly from point A to point B. There were always multiple ways to get somewhere, and the risks and benefits of each route needed to be carefully weighed and then reevaluated every time the weather changed.

The morning was still, with not a breeze in the air nor a wave upon the water. This made some larger crossing possible, the biggest of which—and the only one that made me nervous—was a five-kilometer stretch of open water between the tips of two jagged peninsulas. That was a lot of exposure, and I resolved to instantly turn around if the wind picked up before the halfway mark. My children—Wolfgang, Uma, and Zenya—did not deserve a dead father. Muttering incantations to the weather gods, I struck out for the faraway shore, paddling hard because going fast was the best way to minimize the risk. My luck held, and I finished the crossing just as the day's first gusts scuffed the lake's surface.

The idea of deciding on turnaround criteria before embarking on a hazardous crossing is an idea I stole from mountaineering. Everest is the tallest mountain in the world, and getting to the top is usually a multiday slog from camp to camp, followed by a big push to the summit on the last day. That final heave is through the death zone, the elevation above 26,000 feet (8,000 meters), where oxygen levels are so low that it makes people physically feeble and mentally incapable and kills them inch by inch. If you stay in the death zone long enough, your frozen body will become a permanent part of the landscape.

Most fatalities on Everest occur on the *descent*, when climbers are exhausted, darkness is coming, and temperatures are dropping quickly. To mitigate this, many mountaineers decide on a time of day—often 2:00 P.M.—when they'll turn around regardless of whether they've summited. Theoretically, if 2:00 P.M. strikes, they'll go back down even if they're only a couple hundred feet from the summit.

Jon Krakauer's excellent book *Into Thin Air* depicts in detail what happened when mountain guide Rob Hall broke his own rule and tried to get a client to the Everest summit after the turnaround time. Both of those climbers died, as did six other people that day.

The turnaround time on Everest is a heuristic to make difficult decision making simple when your brain is addled by lack of oxygen. In this way, climbers do their thinking in advance and avoid being tempted to make stupid, impetuous decisions later when they're caught up in the moment.

There weren't many mountains on the 1,000-Mile Solo, but deciding to turn around the instant the wind picked up was only one example of setting my turnaround criteria in advance. I had many heuristics and predetermined benchmarks for taking action, plans that would automatically activate if thunderclouds loomed on the horizon . . . if my health deteriorated . . . if I started shivering uncontrollably . . . if the rapids ahead were obscured by a bend in the river . . . or a hundred other circumstances.

It was much safer to formulate my plans when I was still thinking clearly and avoid trying to make decisions after my brain was overwhelmed by fatigue, surprise, adrenaline, testosterone, and ego. Less can be more, and sometimes it's simpler to have automatic responses rather than weighing every decision on its merits.

Brave Sir Robin ran away, bravely ran away, away.
When danger reared its ugly head, he bravely turned his tail and fled.
Yes, brave Sir Robin turned about and gallantly he chickened out.

Swiftly taking to his feet, he beat a very brave retreat.

Bravest of the brave, Sir Robin!

—"Brave Sir Robin," *Monty Python and the Holy Grail*

Thunderstorms blew in from the North at midday, and open water crossings suddenly became much more dangerous. The winds were still low at the moment, but these storms can generate unpredictable gusts that can be just as hazardous as a bolt of lightning. For the rest of the day, I shunned the open water and snuck from island to island to always be close to refuge.

This caution paid off a few hours later when the calm conditions degenerated without warning. The wind crescendoed from nothing to formidable in just a few minutes, bringing progress to a screeching halt. I battled with my paddle for twenty minutes but was stuck in place—I could not make headway no matter how hard I worked. There was nothing to do but pull over to a craggy shore and wait out the weather.

The wind never did die down and I was stuck there for the night. Making camp here was challenging because the hillside was covered in tightly packed boulders ranging from football to fridge-sized. I rotated a mental image of my tent amid the rocks, but there just wasn't a flat space large enough to sleep on. In the end, I had to rearrange the landscape by prying boulders out of the dense soil and rolling them aside to make enough room for the Hilleberg tent.

As the tent groaned in the wind, I put the finishing touches on the bear alarm using the parts liberated from the abandoned workshop. I journaled about the day and sent a short message with a few pictures to the outside world with the portable satellite dish.

Keeping the electronics charged with a single solar panel was challenging. The panel worked best in direct sunlight but produced only a trickle of electricity when the skies were overcast or the sun was at a low angle, meaning that the cranky battery was almost empty most of the time. To save electricity, I hadn't listened to music or podcasts in over a week.

The electronics and their padded waterproof bag weighed about twenty pounds. I often wondered how much faster I could have gone without it;

every extra pound slowed me down, both on the water and portage trail. At more than one trailhead, I fantasized about throwing all my electronics into the water instead of carrying them through the bush. Still, this additional weight significantly improved my survival odds if a severe accident happened, so, despite my grumbling, I was better off with it than without it.

GRINDING NORTHWARD

August 1, 2019
Start: On a rocky headland above Nueltin Lake
(60°27'04.6" N 99°39'02.0" W)
Finish: On a small tundra island on Nueltin Lake
(60°41'31.8" N 99°15'39.1" W)
Distance covered: 42 kilometers

In every landscape, as in every mathematical proof, there are countless routes one can take to the solution, but some are elegant and others are not.

—Robert Moor, *On Trails: An Exploration*

Clouds charged across a blue sky, but at lake level the wind was weak and the waves were small. The bone weariness from the day-after-day grinding was taking its toll, and it felt like lead sinkers were attached to my eyelids, pulling them down. I paddled with my eyes shut most of the morning while silently counting strokes. Every time I got to ten, I briefly opened my eyes to ensure the boat was still going in the right direction, then closed them again. These micro-rests felt like nodding off in a car on the highway, albeit with less disastrous consequences.

My body was breaking down. My back, shoulder, and arms had been in constant pain for weeks, but today, it was all much worse. Everything ached even more, and new pains appeared regularly. It felt like a stiletto was being jabbed into my trapezius muscle. I wondered if this was an old pinched-nerve injury flaring up; after I'd sustained that in jiu-jitsu years ago, it had left my left arm almost useless for months. Hopefully, it wouldn't get that bad this time.

The anti-inflammatories in my dical kit only helped slightly with the discomfort. To dissociate mind and body (and to avoid brooding on the pain), I let my mind fixate on the clouds folding into new shapes above me. But dissociation only went so far—it was undeniable that my strokes were becoming slower and less powerful. I caught myself procrastinating by constantly rechecking compass bearings and then applying sunscreen for the third time in an hour. My subconscious was trying to figure out how to have me take more breaks.

The numbers clearly showed that my pace was slowing; it took longer to cover the same distance each day. To compensate, I simply had to spend more time in the boat. High-tech boats and carbon fiber paddles don't take you anywhere on their own; ultimately, you still have to grind across the lake yourself.

The landscape along the western shore of Nueltin Lake was now reminiscent of the alpine tundra you find on mountaintops, where the harsh and cold environment encourages very similar plant assemblages. Krummholz grew in small, protected clumps in gullies or on leeward slopes where they found some protection from the harsh winter winds.

Ahead of the boat, the water welled up, and an enormous lake trout broke the surface before whooshing back into the depths. If I had a fishing rod in my gear, it would have been tempting to break it out; giant trout fillets fried in my remaining oil would have been a welcome break from the routine. But to the dismay of all my fisherman friends, I had decided to eschew fishing on this trip. Fishing would have taken extra time, and I wanted to maximize the paddling hours, so when I wasn't in camp I was in motion. Also, the last thing I needed was bears lured to my campsite by the smell of food, so keeping the fish oils off my hands, clothing, and cooking gear was a priority. The trophy fish of Nueltin Lake were safe for another day.

Forty kilometers later, I found a tent-sized spot on an island mostly covered by waist-high spruce. Mosquitos filled the air, so I donned a bug jacket and leather gloves and tucked my pants into my socks. Zipping up the mesh hood made me feel like an astronaut sealing his helmet—it had to be fully closed to protect against the outside world. Being in the Arctic and hating the bugs is like being in space and hating the vacuum; you just have to dress for the environment. A space suit allows you to survive the vacuum, and wearing the correct clothing allows you to withstand the relentless assault of biting insects.

These protective layers allowed me to set up camp in relative comfort. Still, the thick cloud of insects followed me everywhere. Dinner was eaten in single spoonfuls slid into my mouth during brief unzippings of the mesh hood.

Getting into the tent without inviting hundreds of mosquitoes in required another trick—I backed up fifty feet and then sprinted back toward the tent. This temporarily left the bugs behind and created enough time to unzip the door, hurl myself inside, and then seal the door as fast as possible. It still required a few minutes to kill the stray mosquitoes that had hitched a ride inside on my clothing, but after that, I had a bug-free zone for the night.

I hadn't seen anyone at all for twelve days; hopefully, this wouldn't change until the end of the trip. I wasn't worried about the murderers anymore—their escape attempt had ended in a fusillade of police bullets so they were no longer a threat. Instead, I was now in a groove of solitude. It felt completely normal to be alone, and running into other people would have interrupted that flow.

People often wonder if I'm an introvert, which comes down to definitions. I think introverts and extroverts are characterized by how they recharge their batteries.

Introverts recharge alone. When introverts are tired, stressed, or feeling drained, then being in large groups just tires them out more. They replenish their energy by spending time by themselves, curling up with a book, sequestering, or briefly hiding from the world.

Extroverts recharge by spending time with other people. They hang out with friends, go to the bar with coworkers, dance at a party, or watch the hockey game with buddies. The stimulus of social interactions recharges them.

In general, I think introverts do better on solo trips than extroverts, but being an introvert doesn't mean spending all your time rocking back and forth in a darkened corner. In public settings, introverts can be quite friendly and social; I spend a lot of time doing jiu-jitsu with training partners, teaching seminars, playing with my kids, and working among in a perpetually gregarious fire hall. All that social stuff is great—I enjoy it—but when I'm run down, there's nothing I like more than having a quiet room to myself for a while.

Thus, while my longer solo trips are among some of the toughest physical things I've ever done, they have also been periods of intense mental and emotional rejuvenation.

I was grateful for the good weather of the last few days. There had only been one windbound morning and I had made good progress every day. The fine weather had also revealed the lake's dramatic, complex, and infinitely varied splendor. Nueltin is the most beautiful lake I have ever been on. Still, I was also looking forward to reaching its northern terminus, returning to the Thlewiaza River, and following the current downriver again.

WIND AND WHITEWATER ON THE LOWER THLEWIAZA

August 2, 2019

Start: On a small tundra island on Nueltin Lake
(60°41'31.8" N 99°15'39.1" W)

Finish: On the tundra along the south side of Seal Hole Lake
(60°48'41.2" N 98°47'22.0" W)

Distance covered: 39 kilometers

The Barrens, or as they are more properly called, the Barren Lands, is a name for the vast area about the sixtieth parallel crossing in a great arc northwest from Hudson Bay to the mouth of the Mackenzie. It is the North in which the endless spruce forest at last grudgingly gives way to dwarfed clumps and then to a vast land of rolling treeless moss and sedge—the tundra. Just why this desolate frozen sea of emptiness, this desperate land of sullen, gray rock should call me so, I hesitate to analyze. Perhaps the narrative may give some hint. But I knew that whatever my course, somehow I would get back to the Barrens.

—P. G. Downes, *Sleeping Island: A Journey to the Edge of the Barrens* espite the localized squalls that periodically peppered the lake with cold rain, I had a mild tailwind. For the first time in days, I hoisted the sail, which pushed the boat through the water at about three kilometers per hour. With some light paddling, I could increase this to six kilometers per hour, which gave my beaten-down body a bit of a rest while still chewing up the miles.

The sea of islands in the northeastern corner of Nueltin Lake was unbelievably dense; I passed within two kilometers of more than 120 islands during the final thirty-kilometer stretch; some were little more than heaps of boulders, others were covered with dense green tundra vegetation. No wonder Samuel Hearne called this "Island Lake" when he passed through this country 250 years ago.

The clouds darkened and the rain intensified as I approached a small bay identical to 10,000 other shoreline indentations. This cove was distinguished only by ripples and small haystacks in the water, evidence of current leaving the lake. This was the northernmost of three channels draining Nueltin Lake into the Lower Thlewiaza. Stage 7 of the trip, the final descent to Hudson Bay, had begun.

The map promised plenty of rapids ahead, so I pulled onto the gravel shore and ran down the mental pre-whitewater checklist. I ensured that my PFD was tightly buckled, that all the bags were tied into the canoe, that the spray deck was fastened, and that a spare paddle was within easy reach. I checked that the carabiner of the rescue pigtail was clipped low onto the right panel of my PFD so my dominant hand could grab it and that my river knife was mounted on the left side of my chest with the blade facing outward so that if I ended up entangled in a rope underwater, I'd know exactly where the sharp edge was to slash my way free. Were the compass and GPS still in the chest compartment of the PFD, secured by short lanyards? What about the lighters, matches, a fire-starting magnesium block, a space blanket, bug dope, and a small mosquito headnet? Yes, yes, yes.

I punctiliously checked these things before every major rapid. Ironically, I'm not the world's most neat and tidy person in daily life; my organization skills are lacking, and I spend too much time every day searching for my keys, wallet, and phone. However, a change comes over me in the wilderness, and I become obsessive-compulsive about my equipment. Suddenly, there are systems, routines, and specific places where everything is supposed to be.

I have a whitewater routine, a packing routine (color-coded bags where everything goes into the same bag every day), a camping in bear country routine (knife, headlamp, and bear spray go into the right corner of the tent beside my head, and the shotgun gets laid on its case to the left of my body), and many others.

Having these routines where everything goes in the same place every day means that you can access your equipment quickly under stress. It also means you're less likely to lose stuff; packing and checking your bags become instinctive, and an alarm goes off in your head if something isn't in the right place. Something as simple as leaving your tent poles behind is much more serious when you're hundreds of kilometers from the nearest town.

I use similar procedures every day as a firefighter. At the beginning of the shift, the tactical radio goes into the left chest pocket of my turnout gear with the antenna on the left side and the knobs to the right. A flashlight gets mounted on the right side of the chest, and the infrared search camera dangles beside it. Each pocket of my turnout gear holds specific tools, including medical gloves, a waterproof notepad, pens, a flashlight, wirecutters, sixty feet of static cord, ten feet of webbing, and a folding wrench. The more serious the situation, the more critical that everything is systematized.

The quickening current carried me downstream toward the first horizon line. The rapids were a simple combination of eddies and haystacks, a fun, bumpy warmup for the more significant water to come. The second rapid featured bigger haystacks, more rocks, and more curling waves. Not knowing what lay downstream, I threaded the needle between the haystacks in the middle and the calmer waters along the left shore, scouting from the boat as I went. The third rapid looked impressive from above, with large waves curling at the horizon line. However, after those initial waves, the rapid dissipated into a large boulder garden where the main challenge was finding a route deep enough to float the boat.

After thirty minutes of riding the waves, I pulled into an eddy. It was a relief to successfully run these rapids because I had read multiple accounts about how tricky they were. It had been easy paddling so far; this didn't make me a whitewater god, but merely demonstrated how whitewater is inherently subjective. Two people will often rate the same rapid very differently based on their paddling skill, the boats they're paddling, and their familiarity with that flavor of whitewater.

Water levels also make a huge difference. Some rapids are harder to run in high water, and others are more difficult in low water. Rapids can also be substantially reshaped, especially during the spring melt when massive amounts of ice and water charge down the channel, radically shifting a bouldery riverbed. What was an easy Class I riffle one year can mutate into a serious Class IV boat-destroyer in just a few seasons.

No matter the river, you need to be skeptical of other people's descriptions and assess every stretch of whitewater for yourself before you slip past the point of no return. You'd be a fool to ignore what other people say about a rapid, but you'd also be a fool to take it as gospel. Any rapid can be completely different from what was advertised, and getting complacent about a drop can kill you.

At 4:00 P.M., I came to Seal Hole Lake, which was ringed with hills, cliffs, and rock outcrops. The crash of a waterfall in a narrow gorge echoed across the water—this was one of the more southerly channels draining Nueltin Lake, and I was glad I had not gone that way!

I was heading along the shore when—in a few minutes—the wind escalated into a face-punching gale that completely transformed the day. It was soon too windy to paddle, so I tried walking along the bouldery shore and tracking the boat into the wind using ropes. This proved impossible because the breaking waves continuously threatened to overturn the boat. I was only four kilometers from the lake outlet but I just couldn't get there. I could go no further, so I reluctantly made camp after eight hours of paddling.

To pitch a tent in fifty-kilometer-per-hour winds on the tundra is challenging. You can't use regular tent pegs because those would be ripped out of the ground in seconds, and the tent would whirl away across the landscape like an out-of-control kite.

The first task, therefore, was to build sturdy anchors. To this end, I gathered hundreds of pounds of rocks, choosing jagged and oblong boulders that were easy to tie ropes to. These were arranged in four piles, and the tent was laid flat in the middle of this proto-Stonehenge. Each corner of the tent was tied to a large rock using a short extension rope and then piled with many additional stones to hold it in place.

Only when everything was securely fastened to these ersatz deadman anchors did I insert the tent poles and raise the tent. The Hilleberg Keron tent has twelve attachment points on its waterproof fly, and I connected each of those points to a new rock pile using more lines. My shuddering tent was now the spider at the center of a rope web, secure even if the wind got worse or shifted directions.

Cooking in this gale was problematic—the wind carried the burner's heat away so quickly that it was impossible to boil water even with the stove's windscreen in place. Ultimately, I stuck the pot and stove deep into a bedrock crack and built a boulder wall around the fissure. Crouching low, I coaxed the cold water to a reluctant boil and cooked my pasta dinner, served with a rehydrated ground beef and mushroom tomato sauce, topped with grated Parmesan cheese.

The whitecaps danced on the lake, and the wind became even more furious as the evening went on. I retreated to the tent and tugged the down sleeping bag around my neck, hoping to get an early jump on the day tomorrow.

Conditions were ugly today, but there was much worse to come; six of the next eight days were destined to have absolutely dreadful weather, making for some of the toughest traveling of my life.

DAY 34

A STORM ON THE TUNDRA

August 3, 2019

Start: On the tundra along the south side of Seal Hole Lake

(60°48'41.2" N 98°47'22.0" W)

Finish: A muddy riverside campsite

(60°41'02.4" N 98°38'19.8" W)

Distance covered: 18 kilometers

The clouds poured out water: the skies sent out a sound: thine arrows also went abroad. The voice of thy thunder was in the heaven: the lightnings lightened the world: the earth trembled and shook. Thy way is in the sea, and thy path in the great waters, and thy footsteps are not known.

—Psalm 77

The screaming wind shifted directions all night long, probing my fortifications for a weakness. In hazy periods of wakefulness, I pondered what to do if the tent fabric ripped or a pole snapped and decided there weren't many options other than sitting huddled in the flapping tent material and waiting for dawn.

The tent was still standing at daybreak, but the wind had not abated. The simplistic weather forecast on the GPS wasn't encouraging; it suggested that the wind would remain high. I burrowed back into the sleeping bag and tried to compensate for weeks of missed sleep.

I dozed, ate, and sewed a backpack strap back on for most of the morning. At least there were no mosquitoes or black flies aloft over the tundra. Every winged insect for a hundred miles was burrowed into the vegetation, hanging on for dear life against the wind.

In the early afternoon, I grabbed the shotgun and went into the hills above camp, looking for caribou, edible berries, and bears.

Signs of caribou were everywhere: footprints, scat, and shed antlers. Whether I met the herd depended on whether their migration route overlapped with mine. Encountering the herd was the difference between survival and starvation for the traditional Dene and Inuit people who lived here before European contact. Caribou are the plains buffalo of the Arctic, a migratory herd animal with entire human cultures built around them, providing meat for food, furs for clothing, leather for shelter, and bones for tools.

It was August, and a different sort of Arctic bounty was finally ripening. The tundra was dense with edible berries: orange cloudberries, dark blue blueberries, black crowberries, and red bearberries. Their bright flavors exploded in my mouth—a welcome variation from the dried food I had been subsisting on for weeks.

The abundance of berries also meant the possibility of bears. Grizzlies are omnivores, and although they'd prefer meat, they're also flexible enough to devour any calorie that comes their way. I had already seen a giant bear with its muzzle in the ground, working its way across the land above Nueltin Lake, methodically harvesting these berries. The old saying, "There are only two things in the world: grizzly bears and grizzly bear food," has much truth.

In addition to tundra grizzlies, there was also the possibility of encountering polar bears. Most polar bears stay close to Hudson Bay waiting for the winter ice to come in so they can head out onto the floes to hunt for seal. The longer summers and shorter winters now make running into a wanderer looking for food inland more likely than in the past. Fortunately, the rolling landscape made it relatively easy to watch for bears of all colors because there weren't many dips, bushes, or rocks large enough to hide an animal of that size.

On a hilltop, I did some shotgun drills, including rapid reloading, clearing misfires, and shooting at a target while sitting to simulate shooting at something from inside a tent. I thought about my friend Bill, who—years ago—had a polar bear come into the vestibule of his tent. He seized his shotgun and blasted buckshot into its throat at point-blank range, firing right through the mesh of the inner tent door. That didn't kill the bear, and it took a second shot to finish it off, which shows you how tough they are. Bill had been in a terrible situation and made the correct decision in a split second. At least the animal didn't suffer for very long.

My time in the hills was interrupted by a drumroll of booming thunder-claps. I turned around and ran, scrambling under cover just before the mother of all rainstorms hit. The rain blasted the camp as if trying to wipe it off the landscape, but my top-quality tent stayed upright and kept the water out despite the insane conditions.

It was tough to get blasted by this infernal storm, but it was nothing compared to the difficulties I had experienced before the journey. Between the first Nueltin Lake daydream and the first paddle stroke of the trip decades later had come a godawful amount of work and suffering.

The thing is that work and effort are things you *can* control. Some people are born rich, others are born intelligent, and others are born blessed with physical gifts, but you can't pick your parents, so you have no control over that. That leaves you with work. If you have a goal, you need to decide what you're willing to sacrifice to get there, then roll up your sleeves and get to work.

There's a lot of wishful thinking out there. In the self-help section of the library, between Kabbalah studies and crystal healing, are books that espouse the importance of following your dreams. These authors would have you believe that achieving your goals is simply a matter of belief; with enough conviction, the universe will magically manifest your heart's desire. If only life were so simple. If you want to achieve more than a basic existence, simply "following your dreams" doesn't get you to the promised land. Your dreams are not a mother duck, and you are not a duckling.

What those half-wit self-help writers won't tell you is that you have to force your dreams into existence using willpower, stubbornness, focus, and every tool available to you. You must be prepared to bleed through your eyeballs to make them happen. The universe won't shit out your dream for you any more than a canoe will paddle itself across a lake.

Furthermore, you have to pick your critics very carefully. You should keep a very small circle of friends whose criticism and input you take seriously when you're trying to achieve something of significance. For everyone else who doubts you or bravely criticizes you from anonymous online accounts, I leave you with President Theodore Roosevelt's advice . . .

> It is not the critic who counts; not the man who points out how the strong man stumbles, or where the doer of deeds could have done them better. The credit belongs to the man who is actually in the arena, whose face is marred by dust and sweat and blood; who strives valiantly; who errs, who comes short again and again, because there is no effort without error and shortcoming; but who does actually strive to do the deeds; who knows great enthusiasms, the great devotions; who spends himself in a worthy cause; who at the best knows in the end the triumph of high achievement, and who at the worst, if he fails, at least fails while daring greatly, so that his place shall never be with those cold and timid souls who neither know victory nor defeat.

The storm subsided a little at around 4:00 P.M. I didn't want to be overly hopeful, but I had an early dinner and started packing up the loose items just in case the wind continued to die down.

By 5:00 P.M., conditions had improved just enough to get back on the water, so I set off, fighting my way to the far end of Seal Hole Lake one foot at a time. Two tiring hours later, I reached the outflow. A dilapidated orange cabin sat on a beach. The windows had been smashed, and empty fuel drums littered the area, so there was no temptation to explore the site. Besides, there were still a few hours before darkness, and I was eager to make progress again.

Initially, the rapids at the outflow of Seal Hole Lake were fun swifts that required only corrective steering. Riding them was much easier than struggling against a constant headwind on the lake. Then the gradient increased and the waves grew large enough to be a real threat. I spun the canoe into an eddy to avoid blundering into the whitewater chaos below and searched for a line. There it was, a band of slower water threading the needle between the rocky shore and the wild tumult in the middle of the river. I bumped the boat downriver in that slower water, feeling the hull grind over the shallow boulders.

My canoe was not a whitewater boat. The *Sea-One* was designed primarily for covering long distances on flat water. It turns relatively slowly because it's long and doesn't have significant upward curvature along the bottom of the hull. Fortunately, it handles reasonably well in waves because if the bow dives underwater in a bigger swell, it usually bobs back to the surface.

In rapids, the sea kayak rudder at the back of the *Sea-One* was a double-edged sword. When the boat had speed relative to the water, the rudder made turning easier. But when the boat wasn't moving forward, the rudder anchored the stern to the water, making spins more difficult. In deep water, I typically kept the rudder down to help maintain the correct alignment, but I hoisted it up using a control line in shallower water where the rudder might get smashed by rocks. Adjusting the rudder became yet another plate to spin while running whitewater.

The swifts and rapids continued, carrying the boat through the tundra. Many of the channels indicated on the map had dried up and were filled with nothing but boulders. It seemed likely that the maps for this section of the river had been transcribed from aerial photographs taken during the spring thaw when every river channel was flooded.

The wind that had been so violent for two days kept weakening, and by 8:00 P.M. the evening became entirely still. The formerly windbound mosquitoes rose in droves to search for their blood meals. They swarmed my face and hands on the slower sections, but I could temporarily leave them behind in the swifts.

I made camp on a small mud patch just feet from the water's edge—this was the best I could do before the sun disappeared. There was no time to cook, so I ate one more energy ball and retreated into the tent. There had only been eighteen kilometers of progress today, which wasn't much, but it was still better than nothing. I hoped for better weather tomorrow.

DAY 35
A SLOW SORT OF COUNTRY

August 4, 2019
Start: A muddy riverside campsite
(60°41'02.4" N 98°38'19.8" W)
Finish: On a small sandy beach fringed with krummholz
(60°38'01.3" N 98°17'01.8" W)
Distance covered: 25 kilometers

This earth is being overrun by mankind and his machines. There will always be a need for quiet places that can only be reached by physical effort, skill and endurance.

—Bill Mason, *Song of the Paddle:*
An Illustrated Guide to Wilderness Camping

The morning brought light rain and wind from the north. Once on the river, the swift water helped make the riverbanks fly by. But this easy state of affairs only lasted a few hours; by midmorning, the weather deteriorated precipitously again. The cold wind pushed my boat sideways across the river. A thick fog moved in, making the air heavy with moisture. The drizzle then became a downpour, making it hard to see ahead. It felt like I was canoeing by braille.

Through the mist came the unmistakable grumble of a significant rapid ahead. I slipped cautiously along the left shore and stopped at the brink of a series of large bedrock shelves. Each of these steep drops was immediately followed by a boat-eating hydraulic, which would have trapped the boat in a watery hamster wheel of death.

Looking at the rapids, I groaned—I had committed to the left side of the rapid, which was not passable at this water level. It was hard to tell through the gray fog, but it looked like there might be a relatively safe route along the far shore. However, getting to that far side required crossing a hundred meters of swift water just above the first ledge. I did the river math in my head—speed, current, angles, distance—and concluded that the crossing should be possible.

I angled the boat about thirty degrees upstream and started paddling like crazy. If I maintained this pace, the boat should ferry sideways across the river and stay out of the worst whitewater. But if I made a mistake or got spun by the current, I'd be pushed into the worst part of the rapid . . .

I could only look downstream occasionally, so I listened carefully to the drone of the rapids. If the tumult got louder, that meant the boat was slipping backward. Powered by fear, the canoe cut across the river and finally bumped into the far shore without getting sucked downriver. Just as I had guessed, there was an easy route down through the whitewater, just off the right-hand shore.

If I had miscalculated and been unable to complete the ferry, my backup plan was to spin the boat downstream and try to punch through the giant breaking waves, which probably wouldn't have turned out well. Ferrying was a maneuver I had gained confidence in by performing it thousands of times on many different rivers and in many different boats, but performance under pressure is always tricky.

Being able to do something in a tranquil environment is very different from being able to perform that same skill in a stressful situation. And the more stress you're under, the greater the risk you'll choke and forget everything you've ever learned.

We might live in big cities, drive cars, and have digital arguments with virtual friends, but we essentially have the same brains as our stone age ancestors who painted caves in Southeast Asia 40,000 years ago. Our neurology and physiology are primed to help us with stressful gross motor activities like chasing woolly mammoths and fleeing saber-toothed tigers.

The fight-or-flight reflex is always lurking just below the surface. When things get sufficiently stressful, our hormonal system dumps enormous amounts of adrenaline into our bloodstream, and—BOOM—suddenly we're ready for action.

That adrenaline serves a purpose: it elevates your heart rate, makes you much stronger, more pain tolerant, and able to ignore injury. If you ever have to lift a car off a child, you don't want to be calm. Instead, you want to be mad, scared, enraged—whatever it takes to get into that adrenaline-soaked state of high arousal to lift the damn car with your bare hands.

But that superhuman strength comes at a cost; as adrenaline floods your system, you lose a significant amount of fine motor control and higher brain function. Take whatever IQ you started with and cut it in half.

If Thrag the caveman was about to get trampled by an angry mastodon, he didn't need to dial 911, stay calm, or talk about the mastodon's feelings. He just needed to run faster, jump farther, and climb higher. He needed gross motor solutions to gross motor problems. Thrag probably spent more time in dangerous situations than we do today in our pampered, cosseted, cubicled lives. So, ironically, he had more experience dealing with (and staying intelligent during) those highly adrenalized moments.

We rarely need to deal with stampeding mastodons today. And when things get stressful at work, it's generally frowned upon to use your newly found super-strength to flip desks and throw computers out the window. Instead, most stressful situations in our modern lives require thinking, communicating, and fine motor skills. To meet deadlines, you should sit more and type faster.

You can use progressively increasing exposure to stress to become better at performing under pressure in any field, from paddling to firefighting to being an air traffic controller. To become comfortable paddling high-consequence rapids in the tundra, you first need to become comfortable in relatively safe whitewater. Start by honing your technical and adrenaline management skills in easier whitewater, on warmer rivers, close to a road, with full safety measures in place. Then gradually increase the level of challenge and keep trying to harness those adrenaline surges to your advantage. If you train enough and persist in pushing your boundaries, you'll inoculate yourself to stress so that you'll swing into action during high-pressure emergencies instead of freezing.

Finally, acting as if you're calm even when stressed out can keep *other* people calm and prevent a runaway panic reaction within the group. This is another cultivated skill; anyone can be calm while reclining on the beach, but the real virtue is being calm when everything is going to hell.

The best captain I ever had in the fire department was always calm during big emergencies. Regardless of how stressed he was inside, his mannerisms and tonality suggested he was about to fall asleep. This calmness was contagious among all the responders at the incident; "Things can't be that bad if the captain is talking low and slow."

Back on the Thlewiaza, the big ledges were followed by gentle currents, swifts, and easy rapids. On a normal day this would have been quite pleasant, but the rain intensified into a horizontal blast that stung the skin and forced me to paddle with my eyes nearly completely closed. The fog thickened, making it hard to find safe routes through even the most straightforward rapids. Worst of all, the incessant wind brought forward progress to a halt. It was, to quote Lewis Carroll's Red Queen, a *slow sort of country*, where it took all the paddling I could do to stay in the same place.

There was no point in remaining on the water. In four and a half hours, I had covered twenty-five kilometers, but to continue now meant risking capsizing and hypothermia.

I pitched the tent on a small sand beach, partially protected from the wind by a low sandy scarp and a fence of krummholz. I crawled inside and dozed. The weather never did improve, so I spent long hours studying the maps to extract any hint about how to best proceed downstream when conditions got better.

This was now the third day in a row where I'd been forced off the water by a violent storm. It was frustrating, but there was nothing to be done; the weather always has the deciding vote in the Arctic.

In the late afternoon, I received a satellite text informing me that my wife had unilaterally added a kitten to our household. Normally, we would have discussed this, but if unauthorized cat acquisitions were the price of roaming across the subarctic unattended, it was well worth it. Besides, I knew she had good taste, and I wanted to meet the little fella when I got home.

THE PERFECT DAY

August 5, 2019
Start: On a small sandy beach fringed with krummholz
(60°38'01.3" N 98°17'01.8" W)
Finish: On a small sandy beach just upstream of Edehon Lake
(60°29'58.3" N 97°24'59.3" W)
Distance covered: 70 kilometers

Tell me father, is it like the land of little sticks when the ice has left the lakes? Are the great musk oxen there on hills covered with flowers? There will I see caribou everywhere I look? Are the lakes blue with summer? Is every net full of great fat whitefish? Is there room for me in this land like our land, the Barrens? Can I camp anywhere and not find someone else has camped? Can I feel the wind and be like the wind? Father, if your heaven is not all of these, leave me alone in my land, the land of little sticks.

—A Dogrib Indian to an oblate priest,
Sleeping Island: A Journey to the Edge of the Barrens

My first conscious thought was, *Hey, the tent isn't getting bent in half by the wind. This is good.* Things got even better when the clouds split to reveal an alluring blue sky beyond. I broke camp hurriedly, eating only a few energy balls while loading the boat as I tried to get on the water as fast as possible.

The river split into sun-glinted channels between low islands, and I was startled to see dark shapes moving through the water. A small group of caribou—three adults and one calf—was swimming across the river. I stopped paddling and drifted silently toward them. The caribou completed their swim, waded into the shallows, shook themselves off, and trotted away across the tundra toward some unknown destination. Almost immediately, another group appeared on the southern bank, plunged into the current, and swam across. After shaking the water from their pelts on the northern shore, they, too, took off, running, running, running to the North.

The vast but diffuse herd crossed the river all day in groups of five to twenty caribou. I often stopped paddling for a few minutes to watch them, wondering if their urgency was born from fear of pursuing grizzly bears or wolf packs, but I never saw a single predator. Most likely, it was their genetic compass urging them across the landscape.

I had been seeing caribou antlers and droppings since Reindeer Lake, but these were the first living caribou I had seen on the trip. I had hit the jackpot; encountering the caribou herd is a highlight every Arctic traveler dreams of, but it's never guaranteed. These migratory animals roam across an enormous area according to their own rhythms. Sometimes you'll see thousands of animals, but if your timing is wrong or they go a different route, you might not see any.

This part of the river had jogged slightly southward and was brushing up against the top of the tree line, so the tundra here was intermingled with patches of diminutive spruce and tamarack forest. Shallows, riffles, and rapids punctuated the strong current as it wound through the sunlit hills, a mosaic with a thousand shades of green. Occasional truck-sized boulders sat in the river, disconnected from any obvious landscape features. These were glacial erratics, rocks that had been moved hundreds of kilometers by the ice sheets that had blanketed this area just a geological eye blink in the past.

Portage Rapids was ahead, which had a bad reputation. Farley Mowat had described them as ". . . a flume built by colossi down which the bulk of the river thundered over a series of ledges with such cacophony we could hardly make ourselves heard."

Predictably, Mowatt claims to have gotten sucked into these rapids. Predictably, he almost drowned. Also predictably, he and his companion emerged unscathed at the bottom.

More reliable narrators, however, have also found Portage Rapids to be a very serious obstacle. In 1912, Oberholtzer and McGee carried their water-logged eighteen-foot Chestnut canoe on a miserable portage around the whitewater. Oberholtzer noted, "We soon found what a poor welcome awaited us. The walking on the portage was the worst I have ever known—one mile and a quarter across huge boulders with only here and there a slight filling of moss."

I wasn't looking forward to portaging these rapids either, but when I came to the spot marked PORTAGE RAPIDS on the 1:50,000 topographic maps, I was utterly unimpressed.

The fabled rapids were just a short set of big waves in the middle of the river with an easy sneak route on the left-hand side. I didn't even get out of the boat to scout; I just started in the middle and cut hard into an eddy to completely bypass the worst waves.

This was confusing—had I really just bypassed a legendarily tricky obstacle with a single maneuver? I double-checked the maps; yes, the hash marks indicating whitewater were there, and yes, the words PORTAGE RAPIDS were printed on the paper in this location. Something was wrong, but I didn't know what . . .

The mystery was solved ten kilometers later when the broad, slow-moving river abruptly disappeared over a horizon line. The water split around an island and poured over a series of ledges that got bigger and bigger the farther you went. Despite what the map said, this huge rapid fit all descriptions I had read of Portage Rapids.

After scouting, I took the canoe down the left side of the right-hand channel. I floated through the more manageable sections at the top, then switched to lining and wading the boat along the shore as the rapids intensified.

The rapids culminated in exploding waves where the water surged over huge rock shelves on the right side of the river like a watery avalanche rushing down a hill. However, along the left shore, there was much less water, so the same ledges created a series of mini-waterfalls, the water rushing between partially submerged boulders and plunging into pools below. One of these chutes looked wide enough for the boat, so I cinched the spray deck shut and fired the canoe over the brink. It torpedoed into the deeper water below, regained the surface, and returned to shore as I pulled on the stern rope.

It was a huge relief to get past this rapid without portaging! Had the water level been a bit higher, or had a few boulders been in different locations, I would have been carrying everything over the precarious, ankle-breaking, terrain on the shore.

Portage Rapids were actually indicated on the incorrect map sheet, which is a great example of how maps can get important details completely wrong. It's seemingly contradictory, but you have to *both* study your source materials religiously *and* never trust them completely.

To research this route, I had pored over the topographic maps, especially the more detailed 1:50,000-scale maps, looking for hints about the landscape hidden in contour intervals, whitewater hash marks, and esker tracks. I also studied some areas with Google Maps, Bing Maps, and Google Earth, scouting the landscape from the digital heavens.

There weren't any formal guidebooks for the country north of the Churchill. The closest was another book by J. B. Tyrrell called *Report on the Doobaunt, Kazan and Ferguson Rivers and the North-West Coast of Hudson Bay*. Tyrrell dedicated three pages of that 1897 book to the upper Thlewiaza, which was of some use. I also found a few shorter trip reports on the Canadian Canoe Routes Forum online, which I turned into PDFs and exported onto my phone to take with me.

These different sources began to paint a composite picture of the trip ahead. Instead of heading north completely blind, there was now enough information to make plans and backup plans.

Books, maps, magazines, and online forums can be very useful, but my favorite river resources are the historical ones. For example, the account of the upriver exploration of the Fond du Lac River from Lake Athabasca to Wollaston Lake undertaken by Canadian explorer, geologist, and mapmaker J. B. Tyrrell in 1892. On that difficult trip, he took the time to remark about an eagle's nest snugged into an overhang a few kilometers above Brink Rapids.

> The river . . . turns sharply from the south around a sandstone hill on the east side of which is a beautiful cliff seventy feet high, where a pair of golden eagles (*Aquila chrysaetos*) have had a nest for a number of years.
>
> —J. B. Tyrrell, *Report on the Country Between Athabasca Lake and Churchill River*

One hundred and one years later, I ascended the same river as part of a much longer trip from Jasper, Alberta, to Churchill, Manitoba. Tyrrell's account of the route was handy, given that no other descriptions covered going up that river the wrong way. A few kilometers above Brink Rapids, I poled the boat past the same seventy-foot sandstone cliff and there, nestled under a rock overhang, was a gigantic eagle's nest!

The sense of continuity at that moment was incredible. There was no mistaking it—this was the same place where Tyrrell had seen his nest, probably from the same angle. A perfect nest location remains a perfect nest location even a century later. I hope the aerie sheltered the distant descendants of the same eagles that had fished those waters in Tyrrell's day.

The persistence of a nest location tells us there's a lot to be gained by scouring your sources. Not only will you have good information to make plans with, but immersing yourself in the history of an area will enrich your experience of the trip itself.

Relying solely on maps can result in blundering into a very long, cold, and life-threatening experience. Trust but verify. First, triple-check critical pieces of information using multiple sources. Then, corroborate any information with what you see on the ground. You're lost without a map, but following that map too blindly can get you killed.

I paddled on from Portage Rapids, and the day became even better. Occasional white clouds now graced the ethereal blue sky, and the light breeze kept the insects at bay. Small herds of caribou crossed the river all day long. It was heaven.

In the late afternoon, I stopped at the base of an esker and prepared an early dinner. As rice and beans rehydrated in a pot of water, I slung my shotgun over my shoulder and headed for the top of a hill. I ate ripe blue-berries as I climbed and spied on a mother caribou and her calf nibbling on grass, all three of us grazing across the landscape.

I reached the spine of an esker, where a two-foot-wide hole disappeared hori-zontally into the sand under a thick clump of bushes. This was a den excavated by either a wolf or a bear. The sand showed only caribou tracks, so I approached a little closer. The den's ceiling consisted of tangled shrub roots, an ingenious innovation because a hole dug only into pure sand would have collapsed. I was tempted to crawl into the cave on my hands and knees to see how far it went, but I was still chastened after my close encounter with the bear on Nueltin Lake. I had tempted fate enough, and the den remained unexplored.

I ate dinner on the shore as the river rolled by. Then I returned the boat to the river and paddled downstream again. The landscape made it difficult to keep track of time.

The sun was setting when the river fanned out into a maze of islands and sandy shoals. Channels appeared and disappeared; occasionally, I had to drag the boat to deeper waters. The evening was warm, so I didn't mind getting wet one last time today.

I made camp on a narrow crescent beach tucked into a small bay. Caribou tracks were everywhere, and my tent faced calm water that mirrored the sunset. As usual, I set up the tent, hid the food in two places, and strung the bear alarm tripwire around the tent.

A dark array of clouds on the horizon promised rain, but at that moment I didn't care. Endless swifts had carried me seventy kilometers downriver, I had basked in the sun, and had witnessed hundreds of caribou migrate across the tundra. The day had been perfect.

In the tent, I went over every detail, every esker, and every rapid in my mind again. I wanted to burn this day into my memory and make it part of myself to be able to return to every moment of it when I was eighty years old.

LEFT: Heading upstream means more portages around waterfalls and rapids. The Reindeer River is rarely travelled these days, so most of those portages are overgrown with shrubs, bushes, and small trees.

BELOW: After a difficult ascent of the Reindeer River, I finally arrived at Reindeer Lake. This gigantic lake is home to three very small native communities.

ABOVE: I was invited to shelter overnight in a cabin by Hector Morin, a fishing guide and Cree elder from the hamlet of Southend. The rain drummed hard on the roof that night, but I was warm and grateful inside. BELOW: As I headed north on Reindeer Lake it became a much quieter, wilder place. The endless rocky shoreline is largely stripped bare of soil and vegetation by the massive storms that blast the giant lake.

ABOVE: Beaching the canoe after a long day at sea with nighttime thunderstorms coming in. BELOW: Nestling my Hilleberg Keron-3 tent into the scraggly forest and tying it down to logs and rocks in anticipation of the coming rain.

Taking a moment to stretch my legs and figure out how to navigate the next island archipelago on Reindeer Lake.

The sun setting at 10 P.M. on my last night on Reindeer Lake.

ABOVE: Heading upstream on the Cochrane River and supplementing my paddling with some sailing to take advantage of a strong tailwind. This ascent would soon become much more difficult. BELOW: The Cochrane River was high, swollen by the previous week's rains. Consequently, upriver progress was slow and wet.

ABOVE: This campsite had bear signs everywhere, so I kept my shotgun close, both as defensive tool and as a noisemaker. BELOW: Drying clothes at a campsite after a long day of pulling the boat upriver through the willow thickets that lined the shore.

ABOVE: A nearby forest fire blanketed the land in a heavy, choking smoke. I tried to avoid some of the smoke by breathing through a wettened bandana. BELOW: Racing to get to a safe area before the forest fire reached the river.

ABOVE: Having crossed the height of land to the Upper Thlewiaza River, I came to the top of the historic Kasmere Falls Gorge. BELOW: The first of three heavy carries across the long Kasmere portage.

ABOVE: An old trapper's cabin on Kasmere Lake, slowly being reclaimed by the forest. BELOW: Carrying the boat around a waterfall on the Upper Thlewiaza River.

RIGHT: Bear tracks at an old fishing lodge on Nueltin Lake, a large, complex lake that straddles the Manitoba-Nunavut border.
BELOW: Spending some time with poor Yorick the caribou on the shores of Nueltin Lake, where the forest breaks up and turns into open tundra.

LEFT: Eating some energy balls while studying the map, looking for clues to help navigate the Lower Thlewiaza River. This was the last leg of the trip before Hudson Bay. BELOW: The weather had been terrible for days, but one morning, the clouds parted, and caribou started appearing on the shores. It was a giant, diffuse herd journeying north further into the tundra.

ABOVE: Walking the eskers beside the river on a rare bug-free day. Only another week to Hudson Bay now. BELOW: Lining the canoe past impassable rapids on the Lower Thlewiaza River.

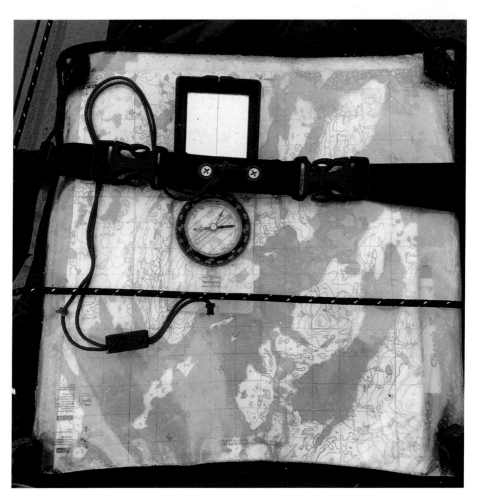

ABOVE: Map and compass skills are necessary when traveling in the incredibly complex terrain found in the Eastern Arctic. RIGHT: Going a little stir-crazy while stormbound, now only a few days from the coast.

Approaching the rendezvous point with the pickup boat, three miles off the Hudson Bay coast.

ABOVE: With Joe Saavikataaq Jr. and Joe Saavikataaq Sr., the two Inuit men who picked me up and brought me to Arviat, Nunavut. BELOW: Jet on the tarmac, waiting to take me south and home.

THE BATTLE OF EDEHON LAKE

August 6, 2019
Start: On a small sandy beach just upstream of Edehon Lake
(60°29'58.3" N 97°24'59.3" W)
Finish: Nestled into the dwarf trees about a sloping sand beach
(60°23'22.1" N 96°54'54.5" W)
Distance covered: 47 kilometers

The mountain doesn't care whether we're here or not. It doesn't compete with us. It isn't burdened by our hopes and dreams. Everything it means to us is only what we bring to it. It's what the mountain reveals about us that has any lasting value.
—David Breashears, *Storm Over Everest*

The first excitement of the day came just a few minutes after midnight. I was lying in my sleeping bag, hovering between sleep and consciousness, when I heard distant hooves: *Clippity clop, clippity clop, clippity clop . . .*

My first sleep-befuddled thought was, *Why is someone riding a horse down the beach in the pitch dark?*

Struggling into wakefulness, I decided this couldn't possibly be a horse: there were no horses for a thousand miles. This had to be a caribou. The hooves got louder; this caribou was running down the beach in the blackness, coming from God knows where and heading toward God knows what.

My tent was squeezed onto a narrow beach between a vertical bank on one side and the water on the other. There were only a few feet of space on either side of the tent, and that's where the tripwire for the bear alarm was strung up.

The caribou hit the tripwire, set off the siren, and shattered the calm of the night. Startled by the alarm and entangled in the tripwire, the animal panicked. It bucked, jumped, and stomped in circles, trying to break the tough nylon line. The thud of its hooves shook the ground close to my head, and I could hear the raggedy huffs of its breath. The prospect of accidentally getting stomped flat by the terrified animal seemed very real.

Then the heavy monofilament line snapped, and the caribou galloped down the dark beach and away into the night. The only sounds remaining were the wailing of the bear alarm and the evil thrum of a million mosquitoes waiting for me to emerge from the tent.

A few minutes later, I was outside, tying torn pieces of tripwire together by headlamp light. The mosquitos feasted on my hands and face. "At least this proves that the bear alarm works," I muttered.

Caribou encounters notwithstanding, the PackAlarm had been a game-changer. Many years previously, I had built a prototype of a similar device using a fishing reel and a small personal alarm that activated with a pull tab. This homebuilt version wasn't reliable, so when I learned there was a better, more reliable version, I couldn't get my credit card out fast enough. Peace of mind in bear country for less than $100? Yes, please!

It was hard to get back to sleep after nearly getting pulverized by a panicked caribou. I dozed fitfully till dawn, then emerged with bleary eyes to survey the sky. Yesterday's magnificent weather had been replaced by cold rain. The temperature was just above freezing, which turned the raindrops into little missiles that sliced into exposed skin. Worse yet, the moaning wind promised slow progress on the water.

It was going to be one hell of a day.

The first challenge was picking a route through the maze of islands, sandbars, and rapids between my campsite and Edehon Lake. Sand from the eskers and other glacial deposits had settled out of the water column here, creating a highly unpredictable environment. One minute the water wouldn't be deep enough to paddle, and the next it all coalesced into a large, bouncy wave train.

In the final rapids before Edehon Lake, a large bull caribou ran alongside me on a low ridge for a few minutes. All the other caribou were bedded down to avoid the frigid rain, so I appreciated the company. Then, as the river swirled into the choppy waters of the lake, he peeled off and disappeared into the hinterland.

Edehon is a relatively large lake, about twenty-five kilometers long, with a varied shoreline that includes boulder fields, low wetlands, bedrock slabs, and cliffs that shoot out of the water. On a warm day, the view from the hilltops around the lake would have been stellar, but the wet, cold, and windy weather shut down any thoughts of sightseeing.

It was my thirty-sixth day in a boat, which greatly sharpened my understanding of how the wind interacted with the landscape. Looking at the map and knowing the wind direction, I could immediately see where the topography would amplify the wind and where it would provide some degree of shelter. I would need to stick close to shore, duck into bays, and hide behind low rocky islands to lessen the winds and the waves. A rhyming couplet from somewhere in my past came to mind: *What though the sea be calm? Trust to the shore: Ships have been drown'd where late they danc'd before.*

I swung the boat parallel to the coast and started to traverse the lake. The howling wind made each meter of progress a battle; anytime I stopped paddling, the boat was immediately blown sideways. And wherever the wind blew across more than a hundred meters of open water, it created steep waves that relentlessly pounded the boat. It rapidly became clear that even the most sheltered route would still involve fistfuls of suffering.

There's a saying in mountaineering, "The mountain doesn't care." A climber's success and the experiences they take away from an expedition are entirely up to them. The mountain isn't invested in what happens to you—it just goes ahead and does the things that mountains do. Similarly, Edehon Lake didn't care. It didn't care that I wanted beams of sunlight to dance on the water. It didn't care that I was cold. It didn't care if I capsized and drowned. The lake wasn't grateful for my presence or bothered by my absence, and the only person who cared about my well-being on that lake was me.

My world shrank to a small list of priorities. I monitored the shape and size of the waves around me, the direction and intensity of the wind, and how close I was to hypothermia.

I hemorrhaged body heat to every icy blast and every cold trickle of rain that ran down the neck of my raincoat. Hypothermia was a genuine concern, and I did everything I could to stay warm. I wore a wool T-shirt, a medium-weight fleece, a heavy Gore-Tex raincoat jacket, and the PFD on my torso. On my head, I pulled the hood of the raincoat over my hat, the brim of which protruded forward to stop the raindrops from slamming directly into my eyeballs. I covered my hands with neoprene paddling gloves, and my legs with nylon pants, Gore-Tex pants, heavy wool socks, and neoprene boots that came to the knees. My legs were still cold, so I wrapped the folded kayak sail around my thighs like a burrito shell.

Every half hour, regardless of whether or not I was hungry, I reached into a Ziplock bag and stuffed my face with another energy ball, chocolate square, jerky, or a handful of gummy bears, salted nuts, or granola bars. This helped fuel the machine, but honestly, 10,000 calories that day wouldn't have kept me warm.

Finally, I continuously monitored my physiology, looking for the nonstop shivering that signaled mild hypothermia and an impending downward body temperature spiral. I resolved that if the shivering became uncontrollable, I'd immediately pull over, pitch my tent, and crawl into my sleeping bag. I continuously checked to see if my thumb and little finger could still touch each other; as long as my hands passed this test, they'd likely still have enough motor control to feed tentpoles into sleeves and set up a tent.

Fine motor control in the fingers is incredibly important in life-and-death situations. One of my wilderness mentors, Ric Driediger, once swamped his canoe and went for a long swim in the cold spring melt waters of the Churchill River. He and his companion eventually rescued their gear and got onto an island. They were now hypothermic and immediately gathered wood for a fire, but their fingers were too numb to light the matches. Things were looking grim, but then they decided to put all their matches in a pile and drop a large rock onto them. The matches burst into flame, allowing them to build a large lifesaving fire.

Conditions on Edehon Lake were truly miserable, but amid the suffering, something extraordinary happened: the rounded head of a harbor seal popped out of the water ahead of the boat. Harbor seals are mostly saltwater animals, common in Hudson Bay, but the tang of the sea was still 200 kilometers away. These seals will sometimes battle strong currents a long way upriver. They lurk in the freshwater, hunting for fish and hoping to get fat before swimming back downstream to winter in the salty ocean.

The seal studied my canoe with big, round dark eyes, trying to identify the giant red fish before him. He circled curiously as I paddled, then whooshed into the depths to search for more fish. He seemed blissfully unaware of the weather, but he was equipped with a waterproof fur coat and a thick layer of fat, adaptations for spending an arctic winter in and around the water. Or maybe he was just more stoic than I was; it's hard to know for sure.

I was thrilled—the seal's presence was an undeniable sign that Hudson Bay was close. It made the successful completion of the journey seem more like a real possibility and less like a fantastical dream.

Five hours of hard paddling brought me to the outflow of Edehon Lake. I dreaded what was coming next because the route bent northeast, directly into the wind. The wind was so strong that I would normally have set up camp to avoid the gale, but this was no ordinary trip.

Gritting my teeth, I rounded the last headland and pointed into the wind. I paddled in a hunched position, looking down at my knees to avoid having the horizontal rain blast my face and run down the inside of my jacket.

I was so tired I didn't know if I could go on. To eat the elephant in small bites, I told myself *Just one hundred strokes,* then counted aloud as I paddled, *One, two, three . . .* A few minutes later, I cursed at how little distance I'd covered. *Just another hundred strokes*, I lied again and continued into the gale. Slowly, so slowly, the boat crept towards the shore.

In the heat of the battle, I didn't spend much time thinking about the entirety of the journey; that would have been much too daunting. My goal was much smaller than that, one hundred strokes. Breaking the task into smaller blocks distracted my mind, made the physical fatigue more bearable, and kept myself from being overwhelmed.

This was the most extreme example of a technique I'd used many times on the trip. Dwelling too long on the entire challenge would have been too daunting, so I mostly tried to focus on the next step in the process. Ascending the next set of rapids . . . Crossing from one island to the next . . . Setting up camp in the wind . . . The next hundred strokes.

This approach came from the sports psychology insight that small successes lead to big successes. You don't want to set yourself giant goals without having smaller intermediate steps; if the increments between steps in your plan are too large, then failure is almost guaranteed. Fail enough times, and it'll erode your confidence. But if you break large, complex tasks down into small, achievable chunks, then, as you succeed again and again, you develop the habit of winning over time. You come to expect success in your endeavors, and this self-confidence then shines through in everything else you do.

In addition to having a series of tiny goals, I also used small rewards as incentives for achieving them. Something, anything, to mark the occasion. I'd tell myself that when I made it to a particular bend in the river, I could have a snack, or when I got to a specific peninsula on a lake, I could get out and stretch my legs. Delaying gratification of a pleasurable activity until I achieved that small, preordained task created a feedback loop that kept me going.

It can be paralyzing to stare at a giant project and lose yourself thinking about the enormous effort required to complete it. The solution is simple: break that project into smaller steps and then attack those small tasks to cross them off the list. Do that for a day, a month, or a year, and you'll be shocked at how far you've come. It's a cliché but it's true, a journey of a thousand miles really does begin with that first single step.

Unbelievably, the wind on my tundra river continued to get worse and worse. The next five hours were brutal. I gave everything, paddling as hard as possible in twenty-minute increments, but I only achieved fifteen kilometers of progress. I don't remember much of the scenery from that afternoon because I could only focus on the next stroke and the next wave.

By 5:00 P.M. I was physically, emotionally, and mentally spent. Exhaustion permeated my entire body. There hadn't been a decent campsite for miles, and I was seriously considering bivouacking in the bushes when I spotted a slanting beach in a bay, slightly sheltered from the wind. I squeezed the tent into a small crowberry-covered clearing among the dwarf spruce just off the beach, moving like an arthritic eighty-year-old. Despite snacking continuously for the whole day, I devoured one-and-a-half full dinners, strung up the bear perimeter alarm, and collapsed into the tent.

The wind howled through the bonsai trees, pruned by wind instead of the gardener's shears. Rain showered the campsite. I had covered forty-seven kilometers today, but my body had taken a terrible beating. Every muscle was in pain, making finding a comfortable position almost impossible. As predicted, it had been a hell of a day.

WINDBOUND IN THE BUSHES

August 7, 2019
Start: Nestled into the dwarf trees about a sloping sand beach,
(60°23'22.1" N 96°54'54.5" W)
Finish: Same place.
Distance covered: Zero kilometers

If the winds rage, doth not the sea wax mad?
—William Shakespeare, *Titus Andronicus*

I awoke feeling thrashed, having slept sorely and not too well. Yesterday's extreme workout had much to do with it, but my air mattress had also deflated during the night and left me lying on the hard, cold ground.

It was drizzling outside. My tent was well protected in its cubbyhole among the dense spruce windbreak, but the wind still moaned across the hills beyond. The tops of the taller spruce trees, heavy with cones, swayed back and forth. Whitecaps danced where the water in the bay met the current of the main river, and there was a complete lack of mosquitoes in the air.

Wishful thinking got the better of me. The river ahead was sufficiently narrow that it wouldn't build up dangerous waves like on a big lake, and besides, maybe the wind wasn't quite as strong as yesterday . . . maybe it was coming from a slightly different direction . . . maybe I could sneak along the shore . . . and maybe yesterday hadn't been so bad . . .

I collapsed the wet tent and stowed all the bags in the boat. The map case, bailer, tracking lines, and spare paddles were all clipped into their prescribed places. The PFD was loaded with survival gear, and I wore even more layers than yesterday. It felt like gearing up for war.

The wind punched me hard in the face the moment I cleared the protection of the cove. The river was frothy as whitecaps fell over themselves and seeded the water with bubbles. No matter how hard I paddled, the boat was instantly blown the wrong way—upriver and against the current. Conditions on the water were actually worse than yesterday, and within two minutes, it became clear that progress was impossible. I turned the boat around and set up camp in the same place I had just left, only now my body and the tent's interior were soaking wet.

One of my favorite sayings is, "No plan of action survives contact with the enemy." This comes from Count Helmuth von Moltke the Elder, the famous German field marshal who had both a fabulous name *and* led the Prussian army to victory against Denmark, Austria, and France in the wars of the 1800s.

Von Moltke's point is that even well-made plans can get scrambled because your enemy gets a vote, too. An unexpected turn of events, changing weather, logistical issues, the fog of war, or random happenstance can scramble your perfect proposition in the blink of an eye.

Trying to make progress in today's wind had been a good plan, but no plan of action in the outdoors survives contact with the weather. Try to seize opportunities where you can, but that doesn't mean they'll always work, which is why you also need backup plans. My backup plan now was to return to the wet tent and try to sleep.

When the showers subsided, I hung my clothing and sleeping bag on a line between two short trees, hoping the wind would flap them dry. I tried fixing the inflatable Therm-a-Rest mattress with every sticky substance in my repair kit: patches, extra silicone goop and lots of heavy-duty repair tape. The sun was hidden most of the day, making the solar panel useless.

The batteries on my phone, camera, GPS, satellite phone, and satellite dish were all running low, and I now had to ration my use of them very carefully.

In the late afternoon, I shouldered the shotgun and headed for the high ground above the campsite.

The beauty of the tundra is found on the small scale and the very large scale. Lie on your belly, and you'll see the charm of small details. Woolly fluffballs bob at the top of slender cottongrass sedges. Inch-high willow catkins emerge from tiny willow plants that have been reduced to only a few shiny green leaves flat on the ground. Tiny plants present delicious blueberries, crowberries, cranberries, and golden cloudberries.

Now, stand up and expand your field of vision to see the large scale. The river shimmers in the valley. Temporary patches of sunlight appear, caress the landscape, and then are gone. A strong gust of wind can be seen on distant slopes by how it bends the grass. The rolling hills, unobscured by trees, march away from you in all directions forever.

I eventually returned to camp, but the wind showed no sign of relenting. The tiny campsite tucked in the deep green bushes would be my home for another night. The delay had been maddening, but my body probably needed it. Still, it was discouraging to be only 170 kilometers from Hudson Bay. There was a strong downstream current, so with good weather, that distance could be covered in three days of paddling. I was so close, and yet so far!

Today had been the first full day of rest in thirty-seven days, and it was nineteen days since I had last seen anyone.

WINDY WHITEWATER

August 8, 2019
Start: Nestled into the dwarf trees about a sloping sand beach
(60°23'22.1" N 96°54'54.5" W)
Finish: On a goose-shit-covered mud bar in an island complex
(60°33'19.3" N 96°30'25.6" W)
Distance covered: 36 kilometers

Two roads diverged in a yellow wood,
And sorry I could not travel both
And be one traveler, long I stood
And looked down one as far as I could
To where it bent in the undergrowth.

—Robert Frost, *The Road Not Taken*

S hortly before sunrise, the alarm went off, urging me to make up for lost time. However, even from the depths of my sleeping bag, I could hear the waves on the beach and the wind in the trees. I didn't need to leave the tent to know that travel was impossible, so I reinflated the leaking air mattress and went back to sleep.

A few hours later I rose again, scanning the landscape to see if travel was possible. In particular, I studied the few spruce and larch trees that had managed to get past the bush stage and grow to more than ten feet tall.

Earlier in the trip, I had come up with a silly little ditty that went . . .

> *If the larch are swaying, down the river I'll be straying,*
> *But if the spruce are swaying, in camp I'll be staying.*

These two tree species were excellent land-based windspeed indicators. Larch trees are particularly spindly and flexible, whereas spruce trees are much stiffer. If you see larch branches dancing, then with some luck, conditions might still be manageable on the water. But if the less flexible spruce tops whip back and forth, the wind is probably too strong to travel.

As the morning went on, the spruce swayed a little less wildly, and the whitecaps on the water became a little smaller. Things were moving in the right direction.

Finally, at noon, I rolled the dice, broke camp again, and headed out onto the river. Conditions were still rough, but the river here was only 200 to 300 meters across, which kept the waves relatively small. However, no matter how the river twisted, the wind somehow realigned itself right back into my face. Once again, I adopted the pattern of paddling as hard as possible for twenty or thirty minutes, then broaching the boat against a boulder until my arms regained function.

The force of the strong current was entirely negated by the wind; in calm conditions, I could easily have gone two or three times faster with much less effort.

The Class I and II rapids on the river were much trickier because of the powerful gusts that frequently blew the boat directly toward boulders and other obstacles. This significantly increased the danger and difficulty of what would otherwise have been relatively easy whitewater.

The wind did serve one good function; by midafternoon, it had forced open the thick gray clouds to reveal small patches of blue. Seals even emerged from the river to sleep on the sunlit rocks.

The increasing abundance of seals was a good reminder of their main predator: the polar bear. Just the previous year, an Arviat local was mauled to death by a polar bear in front of his kids a few miles outside of town.

I resolved to double-check my perimeter alarm and distrust every white boulder for the rest of the trip.

Then my GPS beeped, and a satellite text arrived from my wife with some bad news: the minor improvement in weather had been temporary, and a significant storm was on its way. At best, I had two full days before gale-force winds arrived, which amplified the urgency of completing the remaining 135 kilometers to the coast as quickly as possible.

Driven by the need to use every possible moment on the water, I pushed on and on without a break. At sunset, the river widened into a lake with many sandbars and low mud islands. Still, I kept paddling, focusing on the glorious light orange light bathing the scenery rather than my spasming muscles.

When it got too dark to paddle at 9:30 P.M. I started looking for camp-sites among a jumble of low tundra islands, each ringed with a dense thicket of shrubs. There was nowhere to pitch a tent because all the land was too muddy, hummocky, or bushy.

A flock of Canada geese suddenly launched into the air, honking angrily. My approach had spooked them off a mudbank where they had bedded down for the night. Their vacated area was barely above the river level and consisted of goopy mud with pools of water, sharp rocks, and goose shit everywhere. It was a terrible site, but I was out of options; I had to camp here.

The tent went up on the only patch of mud that didn't have a puddle. The nylon floor would be filthy tomorrow, but at least for now, I had a place to lie down. I carefully tied the boat to a thick willow bush; if night-time rain caused the river to rise, then rescuing the tent and everything in it would be hard enough without worrying about my boat getting washed away as well.

In the tent, I found that the Therm-a-Rest mattress had sprung a new leak and that no amount of glue or tape would fix it. A mattress doesn't just provide comfort, it also keeps you warm because your sleeping bag loses all its insulative value under your body, where it gets compacted. Without a mat, the warmth of your body seeps straight out of you and into the cold ground. I tried to insulate a section of the floor shaped like a chalk outline with a patchwork of every available soft object, including thin padding from the shotgun case, foam from the electronics bag, and all my remaining clothing. This made a very poor mattress, but at least I could lie down for a few hours instead of sitting in a boat.

Despite paddling as hard as possible for 9½ hours, I had only covered thirty-six kilometers. This was a pitiful distance, but at least those were thirty-six kilometers I wouldn't have to do the next day.

On my last patrol of the mudflat before going to bed, I noticed that a gentle breeze had started blowing from the West. This was the tailwind I had long been hoping for. It was too dangerous to paddle this river in the dark, so I set an early alarm instead. With a storm arriving in two days, I needed to maximize the use of every possible weather window, even if it meant driving my body into the ground.

My pace was unsustainable, but sustainability wasn't the goal here. This had become an all-out sprint to cross the finish line in the next forty-eight hours. I was playing on the razor's edge here, cutting deep into my reserves and gambling that I wouldn't physically break down before I got to safety.

Health is like a credit card. Yes, it's possible to buy things on credit and go into debt when you're short on funds, but that's only sustainable for a while. Keep spending and you'll end up in serious trouble, so you do need to pay off your debt at some point. Similarly, you can only borrow against your health for a while; keep pushing hard without a break, and things will eventually go catastrophically wrong.

Pushing past your recovery limits should be done rarely and only for strategic purposes. A medical student studying for the board exams just won't get enough sleep . . . a climber on Everest isn't going to recover much while they're above 8,000 meters . . . and a soldier going through Special Forces selection will be running on empty at times.

Training and testing yourself are two different things. Nobody prepares for the Boston Marathon simply by running a marathon every day; that way lies overtraining and certain injury. As extreme endurance athlete Mike McCastle once said to me, "Train often, test rarely."

Nevertheless, occasionally entering the crucible to test your limits can be a profoundly transformative experience. You might just learn that your limits are quite a bit further out than you thought.

A helicopter is just a flock of spare parts flying in close formation around an oil leak.

—Author unknown

A 95 KILOMETER DAY

August 9, 2019
Start: On a goose-shit-covered mud bar in an island complex
(60°33′19.3″ N 96°30′25.6″ W)
Finish: On a tundra island in the middle of the Thlewiaza
(60°28′28.8″ N 95°23′47.2″ W)
Distance covered: 95 kilometers

On deck, you scabrous dogs! Man the braces! Let down and haul to
run free. Now . . . bring me that horizon.
　　　　　　　　　—Jack Sparrow, *Pirates of the Caribbean*

nother 5:00 A.M. start, and I groaned. It had been a terrible night,
mostly spent rearranging bits of foam under my body, trying and failing
to create a comfortable sleeping arrangement on the cold, cold ground.

Despite the atrocious sleep, I had to push as hard as possible today.
There were only one and a half days left to meet my pickup boat on Hudson
Bay before the predicted storm arrived. If I missed that boat, I'd likely be
pinned down on the coast for several days. Thin nylon tents are no protection against polar bears the size of dining tables.

Blue skies and gentle tailwinds soon followed a calm orange sunrise.
Seals and caribou started appearing, coaxed out of hiding by the fine
weather. Bouncy waves carried me downstream through swifts and easy

rapids. For once, the wind pushed my boat along in the correct direction. This would be the second and final fair-weather day in a week of otherwise miserable conditions.

The riverbanks here were walls of tightly packed boulders. These rocks had been hammered into position by the tremendous power of huge slabs of ice carried downriver by the spring freshet. These rock walls were sometimes more than a hundred feet from the river's edge, formed when ice floes had been driven high onto the land while pushing the boulders before them.

In the early afternoon, the river split into shallow filaments of water running through a confusion of shoals and low, muddy islands at the western edge of Ranger Seal Lake. This delta had formed where the current slowed and could no longer carry the entrained sand grains from upriver.

Eventually, the archipelago opened up into the main body of the lake. The low shores and lack of trees made the far shore seem impossibly distant. I navigated from point to point under blue skies, fluffy white clouds, and the omnipresent tundra breeze. The lake's outflow would have been difficult to find in this treeless land without a compass and a bearing taken from a map.

At three o'clock, I realized I hadn't left the boat for nine hours; eating, drinking, and urinating had all happened afloat. I pulled ashore and wobbled across the rocks to assemble a lunch that consisted of muesli mixed with green protein powder and rehydrated with lake water; food was just fuel now and had nothing to do with taste or aesthetics.

At the lake's outflow, wide rapids twisted northward in a giant S-curve as the river steadily dropped in elevation. This wasn't technical whitewater—mostly just waves and boulders—but it was a fun change of pace compared to the long slog across the lake. The river turned east and continued in a relatively straight line. I was grateful for the current because my upper body was exhausted, my legs were cramping, and my mind was numb.

The rapids had been relatively easy all day, but I came to some serious whitewater in the evening. I clambered atop a large rock to scout the massive rapid. The Thlewiaza was no longer the small, bony river it had been in the headwaters; countless creeks had swelled it and was now more than 500 feet wide, pulsing with thousands of cubic feet of water every second.

Bedrock ridges ran across the green tundra down to the water. At the bank, these ridges slipped under the water to form a series of formidable obstacles. In shallow water, these ledges formed weirs too steep to traverse. In deeper water, they created hydraulics that would send the boat to the bottom of the river and then round and round in the froth, like a washing machine from hell.

The tumult was worse on the right side of the river, where giant standing waves surged and exploded, so I proceeded tight against the left side. There wasn't a proper route here, just continuous ferrying around obstacles and squeezing between boulders in the shallower water. I ensured there was always at least one eddy downstream of me to use as a refuge if I spotted something really ugly ahead. Paddle, ferry, eddy, scout, paddle, ferry, eddy, scout; this pattern took me downriver.

The most worrying maneuver was a long ferry toward the middle of the rapid to avoid some nasty hydraulics close to shore, followed by another ferry back toward shore as soon as those obstacles were behind me. It was hard work with an immutable deadline and very serious consequences if I missed it.

I felt euphoric below the rapid. Navigating the maze of waves had required paddling skill, endurance, and the ability to read rapids on the fly. I was soaked in an exhilarating mixture of dopamine and adrenaline, just as if I had skied a black diamond run, done well in a jiu-jitsu competition, or fought a house fire.

I'm reasonably comfortable in whitewater, but that comfort was built the hard way. To acquire this skill I had taken courses, done clinics, read books, watched videos, sought out people better than me, and practiced in pools. For ten intense years, I navigated waterfalls in specialized kayaks called creek boats and tackled grade 4 whitewater in tricked-out canoes known as play boats. All that paddling built up a vast reservoir of experience that I was now drawing on to navigate the Thlewiaza.

Developing these skills had been a lengthy process. I had often set out for a distant creek early in the morning and returned late at night. By definition, doing this meant not doing other things. There are, after all, only twenty-four hours in a day and 168 hours in a week.

Similarly, every canoe trip I had ever taken to the North also required sacrifice of time and money. Each expedition could have been a wild week at Burning Man instead. Resources spent on canoes and paddles could have been spent on pimped-out cars. Having one thing necessitates giving something else up, and opening one door closes another.

Ultimately, anything worth having probably isn't free, so the question becomes whether or not you're willing to pay for what you want. In the algebra of my life, the sacrifices I had made to spend these six weeks on the Thlewiaza were well worth it.

I camped on an island at the bottom of the rapids as the sun set, having paddled for 14½ hours and covered 95 kilometers. This was the longest distance I had ever canoed in a day, and it had been achieved by simply planting my ass in a boat and refusing to stop paddling.

Sports science is clear that I should have been meticulous about my recovery after such an effort. I should have eaten a large amount of calorie- and nutrient-dense food. I should have stretched. I should have gotten ten hours of good sleep. None of that happened; instead, I stuffed a few energy balls into my mouth while setting up the tent and bear perimeter and then heaped some extra grass under the tent to pad the lumpy ground.

The sunset was a small orange patch amid the blue-gray clouds. The buzz of the rising mosquitos drove me into the tent. Lastly, I used the GPS to confirm a noon pickup at the river mouth tomorrow with my Inuit contact from Arviat.

I wanted that ride to Arviat. Paddling from the mouth of the Thlewiaza to Arviat along the Hudson Bay shore is incredibly dangerous. The tides are huge, the tidal flats are endless, powerful storms come out of nowhere, and you get very little sleep because you're always worried about polar bears. Years ago, I had solo canoed from the mouth of the Seal River to Churchill along the coast, and when I finally reached my destination three days later, I swore I would never paddle that shoreline again.

I collapsed on the inadequate nest of foam scraps, spare clothing, and grass for a short and uncomfortable rest. It was now 11:30 P.M., my thoughts were still racing, and the alarm was set to go off at 5:00 A.M. The river waited just outside the tent.

DAY 41

THE BAY AT LAST

August 10, 2019

Start: On a tundra island in the middle of the Thlewiaza

(60°28'28.8" N 95°23'47.2" W)

Finish: The hamlet of Arviat

(60°22'28" N 95°41'18" W)

Distance covered: 54 kilometers by canoe, 90 kilometers by powerboat

All good things come to an end, and there came a day when we turned our canoes down the Liard and saw Nahanni Butte sink below the horizon—perhaps for the last time? Then it was that I realized we had been allowed to live for a little time in a world apart—a lonely world, of surpassing beauty, that had given us all things from the sombre magnificence of the canyons to the gay sunshine of those wind-swept uplands; from the utter silence of the dry side canyons to the uproar of the broken waters—a land that men pass and the silence falls back into place behind them.

—R. M. Patterson, *The Dangerous River*

I staggered out of the tent, physically crushed. It had taken forever to calm down, and I had slept less than four hours, not nearly enough to recover from the near-continuous exertion and insane headwinds of the last week. The 5:00 A.M. sun climbed into the narrow band of clear sky between the horizon and the clouds overhead, tinging the land with a Tyrian purple glow.

Despite my bone-deep weariness, I was also excited. There were only fifty kilometers left to Hudson Bay, and it was all downriver. This should have been a leisurely morning paddle, but of course, it was not.

A dense bank of clouds moved in as I ate breakfast, removing all color from the world and turning everything monochromatic gray. The light gusts of early morning stiffened into a strong headwind. When I cast off from shore, the boat skittered sideways on the river: the strong downstream current was wholly canceled out by the wind blowing upriver. Instead of the current at my back, there was wind in my face. To make my noon rendezvous, I would have to cover all those fifty kilometers with paddle power alone.

Downriver from the camp was a serious rapid that required a lot of ferrying. Ferrying in smaller rapids is often a short, technical maneuver that relies on precisely calibrating your angle and speed to account for the force of the current. By contrast, ferrying on the large, wide rapids of the Lower Thlewiaza was becoming an endurance exercise where I had to maintain paddle power for extended periods while dodging haystacks, rocks, and curling waves.

The first ledge forced me to ferry out into the middle of the river. Immediately afterward, I had to start working back to the left to avoid a different hydraulic. Then, a final ledge on the left forced me back into the middle of the river again. It reminded me of Frogger, the video game from the early 1980s, where you try to get a frog across a busy highway by moving forward, backward, left, and right without getting squashed by the uncaring traffic.

By the end of the rapids, the wind was howling, but this was just mere foreplay compared to the much stronger storm coming in tomorrow. Missing the pickup boat would have dire consequences, and I knew it.

I struggled for hours against the omnipresent wind, and eventually, the river splintered into many smaller channels, perforating an endless maze of islands. This was the Thlewiaza Delta, the last obstacle before the ocean. Most deltas are languid, lazy affairs where a depleted river drifts down to its final resting place in a lake or ocean. The Thlewiaza was the opposite; the delta churned with rapids for twenty kilometers as the river flung itself off the land and into the sea.

Navigating river deltas is often confusing; the massive number of islands and a changing landscape create an intricate maze where your map doesn't necessarily correspond to what's ahead of you. Today, the ongoing whitewater and eye-blurring rain made tracking my location even trickier.

I also had large, aggressive carnivores on my brain, and glared at every white rock, daring it to become a polar bear. I opened the fasteners holding the waterproof shotgun case shut; there might not be enough room to maneuver around a threat in the narrower channels. *Better the gun get wet from the rain than I die fumbling with buckles*, I thought.

Then I saw a dark brown shape moving side to side on the shore about half a mile ahead. I concluded this must be a skinny tundra grizzly, so I took the shotgun out of the case and laid it on the forward deck of the boat, within easy reach.

A few seconds later, I laughed aloud. This "bear" was only a stone's throw away . . . it had a white head . . . and feathers. It *wasn't* a 500-pound grizzly bear. Instead, it was a ten-pound bald eagle hunting for geese. The rain and lack of trees for reference had completely distorted my sense of distance and scale!

I wish I could say those final few hours on the river produced a cascade of profound revelations from pondering the meaning of forty-one days alone in the wilderness. That would be a lie. The truth was far more prosaic; the mundane, procedural minutiae of travel took up all available mental bandwidth.

> *"Which of these two channels should I go down?"*
> *"The water is deeper to the left of that rock."*
> *"My shoulder hurts."*
> *"I should bail some water out of the boat."*
> *"Did the wind just change direction?"*

Any assignations of meaning would need to come later, during retro-spective analysis.

The current cut through the soil to create tall riverbanks, expose polished bedrock, and produce a dizzying array of diverging and converging river channels. A large river joined the delta from the north; this was the Tha-Anne River, which flows through the remote tundra north of the Thlewiaza and merges with it in the last kilometers before the Bay. The memory of that short glimpse up the Tha-Anne River is singing to me as I write this, urging me to return to the Barren Lands and explore that river. And maybe, someday, I will . . .

Gradually the river slowed, and it became hard to find deep water. The wind faded, and a heavy fog gathered, further decreasing the visibility. The water became gradually saltier, from fresh to brackish to oceanic. I was now in the legendary tidal flats of Hudson Bay. These mud and boulder flats extend out from shore for miles at low tide before you get to deeper waters.

Through the rain and the fog, I saw the remains of a small cabin on a bluff to the north. I was supposed to meet my pickup there, and I rejoiced because, after paddling fifty kilometers without a single break, my body had never felt so tired. My muscles were nearly useless now, and any headwind would have halted all progress. Fortunately, the ocean was calm, and I crawled toward the landmark at a snail's pace.

Just as I reached the cabin, my GPS unit buzzed. The satellite text mes-sage read, "THE TIDE IS OUT. WATER TOO SHALLOW. MEET US AT 60.47 N 94.59 W." Unfortunately, this location was four kilometers away, out in the open water. I should have known better than to fixate so much on one specific goal; the finish line had just shifted, and I felt gutted.

There was nothing to do but glumly swing the boat around and limp into the offshore mist. There was nothing around but shallow water, occasional boulders, and patches of exposed mud. It was a bizarre trust exercise, relying on a compass and GPS to navigate through the fog onto the ocean to a destination I couldn't see.

Those last four kilometers took forever. My physiological gas tank was empty, and I crawled past intertidal boulders and deeper into the fog at a glacial pace. Finally, one of the boulders ahead started changing shape as I got closer . . . it was a boat. A large orange flag had been hoisted into the air to make it more visible, and it had two Inuit men on board.

"Thanks for picking me up!" I said as I paddled my boat alongside theirs.

"No problem."

The men hauled my canoe aboard their open twenty-foot aluminum boat. I was being picked by Joe Saavikataaq Jr., a conservation officer who would soon go on to be mayor of Arviat, and his father, Joe Saavikataaq Sr., the premier of the territory of Nunavut. The premier had been home for a few days and spontaneously decided to accompany his son for the day. I felt honored.

The outboard motor roared us toward deeper water. The cold wind and large chop made me very grateful I didn't have to paddle this section; it would have been a difficult and dangerous journey.

The northern genetics of the two Joes were on full display as they barely needed gloves for the freezing ride. I shivered and stuffed my hands deep into my raincoat; "But it's summertime," the two Inuit men laughed.

During the boat ride, it finally began to sink in that the trip was over. I had traveled the Old Way North, had some amazing experiences, and seen some incredible things. My kidney and I had pushed ourselves to the absolute limit and somehow achieved the goal before everything broke down completely. The doubt, pain, and suffering of the last forty-one days seemed worth it.

Three hours later, low bumps on the shore slowly resolved into the houses of Arviat, a small Inuit town with 2,000 souls. When we landed at the dock, the two Joes loaded my gear onto an ATV and drove me to one of the two hotels in town. Standing in the Padlei Inns in dripping rain gear, I learned exactly one room was left. It was a tiny room, but I didn't care. The decor was drab, but I didn't care. And it was over $300 a night, but I didn't care. It was warm and sheltered—the only two things that were important.

The enclosed space of my room made me realize that I stank the way that only a man wearing the same clothes for weeks could stink. Still wearing my paddling clothes, I walked down to the general store and bought razors, chocolate, and a complete change of clothing. The clothing selection was limited, and the best I could do was grab a ¾ sleeve T-shirt straight out of the early 1990s and fleece pajama bottoms with a green camouflage pattern.

There was no saving my clothes, so they all went directly into the garbage at the hotel. Then I stumbled toward the shower and spent an hour under the hot water, after which I finally felt almost warm.

I ate a simple dinner in the hotel dining room and collapsed onto the tiny bed while the cold arctic rain continued to fall outside.

> I come from the land of the ice and snow
> From the midnight sun where the hot springs flow
> The hammer of the gods I'll drive my ship to new lands
> To fight the horde and sing and cry
> Valhalla, I am coming!
>   —Led Zeppelin, "The Immigrant Song"

ON THE DIFFERENCE BETWEEN HAPPINESS AND SATISFACTION

We are not now that strength which in old days
Moved earth and heaven, that which we are, we are;
One equal temper of heroic hearts,
Made weak by time and fate, but strong in will
To strive, to seek, to find, and not to yield.
　　　　　　　　—Alfred, Lord Tennyson, "Ulysses"

High winds and freezing rain punished passengers crossing the tarmac of the Arviat airport as we boarded a jet bound for the South. The bad weather that had chased me into the small Inuit town of Arviat worsened overnight. The wind had become a gale, the rain had become sleet, and the waves on Hudson Bay had become unsurvivable. If not for pushing myself to the limits of endurance, I would now have been sharing the storm-blasted shores of Hudson Bay with some very wet polar bears.

Once airborne, the endless tundra, lakes, and forests of the Canadian Shield rolled past the plane's window. In minutes, we crossed lakes where I had struggled for days. South, south, south, all that work undone by ninety minutes of air travel.

Nine years prior, I had thought I was financially ruined for life. Five years prior, I had been on the brink of death from kidney failure, and now

I was homeward bound, having completed a goal that had haunted me since my youth. The trip had been a meditation on mortality, fueled by my brushes with life-threatening medical conditions and the loss of my brothers, my mother, and my grandmother. Somehow, a stubborn belief that things would eventually break my way had prevailed, and it turned out that I was still capable of putting it to the touch despite all the mileage on my body and soul.

Despite it being a solo trip, so much of this journey had been enabled by others, and I was very grateful to them. This undertaking would not have been possible without my wife's blessing and had been made much easier by the explorers and native peoples who had shown a path for me in their accounts. I was so lucky that my brother Christoph had been willing and able to give up a kidney and that the medical technology of transplantation existed. Fifty years earlier, I would have been dead. One hundred years earlier, I would have been dead. Anytime other than in the modern era I would have been dead.

In Winnipeg, my checked baggage needed to be X-rayed before it could be loaded into the belly of the plane. "What's that?" gasped the horrified airport security drone, pointing to the image of a sheathed hatchet deep in my backpack.

"That's a very small axe in a sturdy sheath," I replied.

"But what if it cuts through the sheath and out of the bag? Somebody could get seriously hurt!!"

In a calm voice and using small words, I explained that it was impossible for the axe to cut through the hard plastic sheath and all the gear that surrounded it and then magically fly across the hangar into the throat of a baggage worker. After checking with his supervisor, he eventually relented, and I didn't have to trade an axe for the right to board the plane.

It was mind-boggling. Less than twenty-four hours before, I had been making life-and-death decisions multiple times a day. Now I was back in a world where every sharp corner is padded and nincompoops can blurt out, "It's not safe" a hundred times a day without consequence.

I was incredulous and enraged at the time, but it wasn't his fault. The people most fearful of bears are people who have never interacted with them.

This guy, who had never used an axe, was full of trepidation about their imaginary dangers. Since my axe and I made it on the plane, I now think this episode was pretty funny.

My wife was waiting for me in the arrivals area of Vancouver airport, looking impeccable in a sleeveless navy polka-dot sheath. I rushed over in the baggy camouflage fleece pants and the Arviat T-shirt I had bought at the Northern Store, twenty pounds lighter than when I had left, with bloodshot eyes and patchy facial hair from a poor shaving job. I was immediately intercepted by a security guard wanting to see identification; he had quite reasonably concluded that I was a homeless person stealing luggage from the carousels. A few minutes later my wife and I were homeward bound, back to the kids and a new cat. It all felt very strange at first; I had, after all, been gone a long time.

A few days later I grabbed dinner with two old friends. They had questions about the trip, and I was happy to go into details. From being windbound on tiny beaches to paddling fourteen hours a day, I think I told a pretty good story.

Finally, one of them blurted out, "That's a really cool trip, but did you enjoy it?"

The question took me aback, and it took a while to collect my thoughts. When I finally spoke, I explained that this was probably the wrong question.

Yes, this trip had many enjoyable moments, but the trip hadn't been about enjoyment. And yes, I had been happy sometimes, but the trip hadn't been about happiness. Most of the time, I had been worried, cold, wet, scared, or exhausted. The totality of the journey wasn't as simple as seeking enjoyment.

The thrill of enjoyment and happiness fades quickly, leaving you chasing the next hit. Happiness and Type I fun are responses to your current environment, and feelings like that come and go.

Instead of asking about enjoyment the right questions might have been, "Did you find it satisfying?," "What did you learn?," or "How did you change?"

The afterglow of satisfaction is much more durable than the fleeting sugar high of happiness. And yes, the whole thing had been profoundly and immensely satisfying. Experiences that give you satisfaction transform who you are, and you can bring those changes back to the world with you.

You can't get to satisfaction without a lot of hard work and perseverance. Finding meaning in life is largely about the challenges you choose and the person you become when you tackle them. It may not always be easy or fun in the moment, but you can't go wrong with using satisfaction as your North Star.

In the weeks and months that followed, my body slowly healed. My gaunt face filled in and the burning pain that had been my constant companion for so long faded and became a memory. Physically I was back where I had started, but there had been a tectonic shift in my psyche. I had come back stronger, enriched by the journey, excited for what lay ahead, and bursting with a deep admiration for the reservoir of capability that lies in each and every one of us.

> We shall not cease from exploration
> And the end of all our exploring
> Will be to arrive where we started
> And know the place for the first time.
>
> —T. S. Eliot, *Four Quartets*

ENERGY BALL RECIPE

Energy balls were one of the secret weapons I used to complete this trip. Each ball was about 250 calories, and I ate two to four of them each day. They lasted well, and I never got tired of their taste.

This isn't a fine French pastry recipe, where a single extra tablespoon of an ingredient ruins the whole thing. The recipe is very forgiving: you really can add almost anything to the mix, so feel free to experiment, substitute, and add additional ingredients.

- 450 grams fresh, pitted dates
- 900 grams almond butter
- 400 grams rolled oats
- 200 grams almond flour
- 50 grams shredded coconut
- 2 cups chocolate chips
- 1 to 2 cups maple syrup
- Water, as needed
- 1 to 2 cups sesame seeds, for coating the outside of the balls

First, make a paste from the dates and the almond butter using a food processor. Before I had a food processor, I used a clean paint mixing attachment from Home Depot attached to a power drill to mash everything into a paste.

This paste forms the matrix into which you then put everything else. Using a large bowl add all the remaining ingredients except for the sesame seeds.

Next, mold the mixture into golf-ball-sized orbs. If your mixture doesn't stick together very well, you may need to moisten it by sprinkling it with some water in and mixing that in by hand.

Finally, roll the balls in sesame seeds, which adds some extra flavor and prevents the balls from sticking together. You can then freeze or refrigerate the balls in Ziplock bags until you need them for your trip.

ACKNOWLEDGMENTS

Nobody writes a book alone, even a book about a solo journey. There are so many people to thank, but I have to start with Christoph Kesting, who saved my life with his kidney. I have truly enjoyed the extra years your gift gave me, and it seems my children mostly appreciate them, too.

Eva Schubert, where do I even start? You let me run away the day after we got married, were my eyes in the sky during the trip, and then provided invaluable feedback on many manuscript drafts. The term soulmate is often thrown around loosely, but I think it applies here. Thank you.

My sincerest thanks to Murray Weiss, my agent at Catalyst Literary Management. It feels good to have you on my side.

To my editor, Jessica Case at Pegasus Books in NYC, you've been a pleasure to work with and have made the final product much better. Thanks also to Julia Romero and Wesley Wheeler for your contributions—hopefully, we'll work together again!

I am very grateful for my parents: my mother, born Theres Maria Hofer, imbued me with her optimism and unquenchable love of adventure, and my father, Fritz August Kesting, gave me his work ethic and willingness to tackle hard tasks head-on.

Peter and Matthias Kesting, you were lost too soon. Young men do not always live forever, but you are remembered by those who love you.

April Henry, your advice led me through the publishing wilderness, which was almost as arduous a journey as the trip itself. I am very grateful for all your help, including the killer blurb on this book's front cover.

Paul Kindzia, our conversations helped structure the book and moved it away from being yet another travelogue. You also talked me off the ledge when I was ready to burn the manuscript in frustration.

Bjorn Weeks, thank you for your edits and for believing that something of value might be buried in the mess of early notes. Graham Barlow, you did an amazing job going through early drafts and ruthlessly pointing out silly errors, cliches, and repetitions. Regina Ryan, John Will, and Ed Teja, your insights on the publishing process were very valuable.

Thank you to Reid Martin, Ravi Turre, Alex Kask, Zenya, Wolfgang, Uma, and Amber for reading early versions, and to Adrianna Barton for encouraging me that anyone can write a book.

Adam Shoalts, your expeditions and books remain an inspiration. Thank you for the kind words and support. I am also indebted to Bill Mason and Cliff Jacobson, whose books mentored me in the art of wilderness canoeing.

Bill Jeffries, your travels in Northern Saskatchewan have always inspired me. Gino Bergeron, our chance meeting at the Université Laval all those years ago unlocked a monster. Without you, it would have taken much longer to figure out that going solo wilderness canoeing was okay.

I very much doubt that Samuel Hearne, J. B. Tyrrell, P. G. Downes, Ernest Oberholtzer, and Billy Magee will be reading this, but just in case, know that you are giants among men.

This trip would not have been possible without the help of my ex-wife, Ksenia Barton, who took the kids while I was away. Speaking of kids, thanks to Wolfgang, Uma, and Zenya Kesting for putting up with me being physically gone and then being monomaniacally focused on finishing the book when I came back. Amber Little, your help holding down the fort at Grapplearts, my jiu-jitsu business, is still very much appreciated.

I am indebted to my whitewater paddling partners, including Anthony Barker, Mark Paxton, Don Froese, Richard Borek, Pipo Damiano, and Linda Fuerness for teaching me paddling skills and rescuing me when I swam.

Thank you to Dr. Christopher Nguan for cutting me apart and sewing me back together, and to Dr. Steven Sharp for not spitting out his coffee when presented with a very long request list of antibiotics and drugs for my wilderness medical kit.

On the trip, I received help and advice from Ric Driediger of Churchill River Canoe Outfitters, Hector Morin from Southend, Saskatchewan, and Joe Saavikataaq Jr. and Joe Saavikataaq Sr. from Arviat, Nunavut. Every bit of information helped fill in the blank portions of the map.

And to everyone who commented on my social media posts that they wanted a book, I say, "My God, see what we've done!"